2008

Preliminary Overview of the Economies
of Latin America and the Caribbean

DÉPÔT
DEPOSIT

UNITED NATIONS

ECLAC

60
ECLAC

SIXTY YEARS WITH LATIN AMERICA AND THE CARIBBEAN

Alicia Bárcena
Executive Secretary

Laura López
Secretary of the Commission

Osvaldo Kacef
Director of the Economic Development Division

Diane Frishman
Officer-in-Charge
Documents and Publications Division

The *Preliminary Overview of the Economies of Latin America and the Caribbean* is an annual publication prepared by the Economic Development Division in collaboration with the Statistics and Economic Projections Division, the Latin American and Caribbean Institute for Economic and Social Planning (ILPES), the ECLAC subregional headquarters in Mexico and Trinidad and Tobago, and the Commission's country offices in Bogota, Brasilia, Buenos Aires, Montevideo and Washington, D.C.

We are grateful to the central banks and statistical offices of the countries in the region for their valuable cooperation in supplying the statistical information used in the preparation of the *Preliminary Overview*.

The national accounts data presented in this edition of the *Overview* are based on the official figures issued by the countries covered in this report; for purposes of comparison between countries, however, these statistics are expressed in constant 2000 dollars. Thus, in some cases, there may be apparent discrepancies with the information issued by individual countries.

The regional analyses were prepared by the following experts (in the order in which the subjects are presented): Osvaldo Kacef (introduction), Juan Pablo Jiménez (fiscal policy), Rodrigo Cárcamo (exchange-rate policy), Omar Bello (monetary policy), Sandra Manuelito (economic activity and investment and domestic prices), Jürgen Weller (employment and wages), Alejandro Ramos and Luis Felipe Jiménez (external sector).

The country notes are based on studies conducted by the following experts: Olga Lucía Acosta and María Alejandra Botiva (Colombia), Omar Bello (Bolivia), Rodrigo Cárcamo (Ecuador), Stefan Edwards (Suriname), Álvaro Fuentes (Uruguay), Sarah Gammage (Panama), Randolph Gilbert (Haiti), Víctor Godínez (Dominican Republic), Michael Hendrickson (Bahamas and Belize), Daniel Heymann and Adrián Ramos (Argentina), Luis Felipe Jiménez (Chile), Beverly Lugay (Eastern Caribbean Currency Union), Roberto Machado (Trinidad and Tobago), Sandra Manuelito (Bolivarian Republic of Venezuela), Jorge Mattar (Mexico), Armando Mendoza (Barbados, Guyana and Jamaica), Sarah Mueller (Paraguay), Guillermo Mundt (Guatemala and Honduras), Carlos Mussi (Brazil), Ramón Padilla (Costa Rica and Nicaragua), Igor Paunovic (Cuba), Juan Carlos Rivas (El Salvador) and Jürgen Weller (Peru). Claudia Roethlisberger revised the notes on the Caribbean countries. The economic projections were produced by Claudio Aravena, Fernando Cantú and Francisco Villarreal. Alejandra Acevedo, Vianka Aliaga, Jazmín Chiu and Rodrigo Heresi were responsible for the processing and presentation of the statistical data and graphical presentations.

Explanatory notes

The following symbols are used in tables in this edition of the *Preliminary Overview*:
Three dots (…) indicate that data are not available or are not separately reported.
A dash (–) indicates that the amount is nil or negligible.
A point (.) is used to indicate decimals.
Use of a hyphen (-) between years (e.g., 2001-2008) indicates reference to the complete period considered, including the beginning and end years.
The word "tons" means metric tons and the word "dollars" means United States dollars, unless otherwise specified.
References to annual rates of growth or variation signify compound annual rates, unless otherwise specified.
Individual figures and percentages in tables do not necessarily add up to the corresponding totals because of rounding.

United Nations publication
ISBN 978-92-1-121684-4
ISSN printed version: 1014-7802   ISSN online version: 1684-1417
LC/G.2401-P
Sales No.: E.08.II.G.2
Copyright © United Nations, December 2008. All rights reserved
Printed in Santiago, Chile

Contents

Tables

Figures

Regional panorama

South America

Mexico and Central America

The Caribbean

Boxes

Summary

With annual economic growth for Latin America and the Caribbean projected at 4.6%, 2008 will mark the sixth consecutive year of growth and, at the same time, the end of a period which has very few precedents in the economic history of the region. Between 2003 and 2008, regional GDP growth averaged nearly 5% per year, with per capita GDP increasing by over 3% per annum, coupled with improving labour-market indicators and falling poverty in the region. Another noteworthy feature of the period was the fact that policymakers in most of the countries focused on maintaining macroeconomic balances, leading to surpluses in both external and fiscal accounts. The highly favourable external economic environment of the last few years has been another contributing factor.

These results will not be repeated in the coming year, however. Growth projections for 2009 are much lower than for 2008, and the governments of the region will need to make every effort to apply anticyclical policies in order to ward off an even sharper economic decline. The growth rate for Latin America and the Caribbean is projected to be 1.9% in 2009, and that is based on relatively optimistic assumptions regarding the crisis.

Again in contrast to the period 2003-2008, growth projections suggest that the regional unemployment rate will rise from an estimated 7.5% in 2008 to between 7.8% and 8.1% in 2009, depending on the trend in the labour force participation rate, and the informal sector will expand. The behaviour of international food and fuel prices, on the other hand, indicates that inflation will subside from 8.5% in 2008 to around 6% in 2009.

In just over a year, what had begun as a problem in the United States subprime mortgage market in mid-2007 turned into a systemic crisis that crippled credit markets in the developed countries. This will undoubtedly hit the real economy very hard but, as of the end of 2008, it is still too soon to accurately gauge the full impact.

The depth and duration of the recession will depend on the effectiveness of measures to stimulate demand and offset the slump in private spending, as well as on the normalization of credit markets. It is to be hoped that the array of measures implemented by the United States Federal Reserve and other central banks will succeed in containing systemic risk and that, in conjunction with the recovery of their financial systems as well as fiscal policy measures, the developed economies will begin to emerge from the worst of the crisis in the second half of 2009. This is the fairly optimistic scenario on which growth projections for the region for 2009 are based.

Although the region is now better equipped to cope with an economic crisis, there are a number of channels through which its effects are likely to be transmitted to the economies of Latin America and the Caribbean. First, the global slowdown will drive down export volumes and prices, remittances, foreign direct investment and the demand for tourism services. In addition, external financing will be more expensive and will be more difficult to obtain.

Growth in 2009 is projected to stand at 1.9%. This estimate is built on the assumption that the global economy in general, and the economy of the region in particular, will gradually begin to recover during the second half of the year. The projection is based on a comparison of average levels for 2008 and 2009, which points to a sharp slowdown, and the growth forecast largely reflects a statistical effect. Nonetheless, a more pessimistic scenario of continuing and even deepening recession and credit conditions remaining tight cannot be ruled out. In this case, obviously, the aforementioned problems would worsen and the growth rate would be lower than the current projection.

Deteriorating labour-market indicators and falling remittances will have a negative impact on income distribution in the region. Under current circumstances, this means that public policymakers will face the double challenge of implementing anticyclical measures to stabilize economic growth and of developing instruments to shield the most vulnerable sectors of the population from the effects of the crisis. The fiscal resources available to each country for use in financing such policy actions differ considerably, although public finances in general will come under increased pressure owing to the expected decrease in fiscal revenues.

Regional panorama

Chapter I

Introduction

The economic growth rate for Latin America and the Caribbean is projected to be 4.6% for 2008. This will mark the sixth consecutive year of growth, as well as the end of a period which has very few precedents in the economic history of the region. Between 2003 and 2008, the region's economy grew by an average of almost 5% per year, with per capita GDP increasing by over 3% per year. This growth was coupled with improvements in labour-market indicators and a reduction in poverty in the region. One of the most outstanding features of this period has been the fact that, in most of the countries, policymakers have placed priority on maintaining macroeconomic balances, which has helped generate surpluses in both their external and their fiscal accounts. The region has also benefited from the highly favourable external economic environment of the last few years.

These results will not be repeated in 2009, however. Growth projections for next year are significantly lower than for the period that is now coming to a close. In view of this situation, the governments of the region should make every effort to deploy anticyclical policies in order to ward off an even sharper economic decline. The growth rate for Latin America and the Caribbean is projected to be 1.9% in 2009 based on a relatively optimistic scenario in which the existing crisis situation gives way to a gradual improvement in the second half of that year.

Again in contrast to the period 2003-2008, growth projections for the region suggest that the regional unemployment rate will rise from an estimated 7.5% in 2008 to between 7.8% and 8.1% in 2009, depending on the changes that occur in the labour force participation rate in a context of increasing informality. The behaviour of international food and fuel prices, on the other hand, indicates that inflation will subside from 8.5% in 2008 to around 6% in 2009.

What started out as a problem in the subprime mortgage market in mid-2007 became, just over a year later, a systemic crisis that crippled the credit markets of the developed countries. This will undoubtedly have an extremely negative impact on the real economy, although, as of the end of 2008, it is still too soon to accurately gauge the full impact of the crisis.

Table I.1
**LATIN AMERICA AND THE CARIBBEAN:
GROSS DOMESTIC PRODUCT**
(Annual growth rates 2006-2009)

Country	2006	2007	2008 [a]	2009 [b]
Argentina	8.5	8.7	6.8	2.6
Bolivia	4.8	4.6	5.8	3.0
Brazil	4.0	5.7	5.9	2.1
Chile	4.3	5.1	3.8	2.0
Colombia	6.8	7.7	3.0	2.0
Costa Rica	8.8	7.3	3.3	1.0
Cuba	12.1	7.3	4.3	4.0
Ecuador	3.9	2.5	6.5	2.0
El Salvador	4.2	4.7	3.0	1.0
Guatemala	5.3	5.7	3.3	2.0
Haiti	2.3	3.2	1.5	1.5
Honduras	6.3	6.3	3.8	2.0
Mexico	4.8	3.2	1.8	0.5
Nicaragua	3.9	3.8	3.0	2.0
Panama	8.5	11.5	9.2	4.5
Paraguay	4.3	6.8	5.0	2.0
Peru	7.6	8.9	9.4	5.0
Dominican Republic	10.7	8.5	4.5	1.5
Uruguay	7.0	7.4	11.5	4.0
Venezuela (Bol. Rep. of)	10.3	8.4	4.8	3.0
Subtotal Latin America	**5.8**	**5.8**	**4.6**	**1.9**
Bahamas	4.6	2.8	1.5	0.5
Barbados	3.3	3.2	1.5	0.5
Belize	4.7	1.2	6.0	3.0
Guyana	5.1	5.4	4.8	2.5
Jamaica	2.5	1.2	0.0	0.5
Suriname	5.8	5.3	5.0	3.0
Trinidad and Tobago	12.0	5.5	3.5	2.0
ECMU	6.3	5.3	3.1	1.5
The Caribbean	**6.9**	**3.8**	**2.4**	**1.4**
Latin America and the Caribbean	**5.8**	**5.7**	**4.6**	**1.9**

Source: Economic Commission for Latin America and the Caribbean (ECLAC), on the basis of official figures expressed in constant 2000 dollars.
[a] Preliminary figures.
[b] Projections.

In 2008, the world economy underwent a sharp slowdown as growth dropped to 3.7% from 5.0% in 2007.

Measured on the basis of exports, world trade expanded by 4.7% in 2008, which was far less than the 7.1% rate recorded the year before. Global economic activity began to cool as a consequence of the financial crisis, which, with the developed countries as its epicentre, erupted in mid-2007 and continued to deepen throughout 2008 despite the determined efforts made by authorities in numerous countries to contain it. The developed economies as a group grew by 1.4% this year, compared with 2.6% in 2007, and a contraction of 0.5% in the major advanced economies is expected in 2009. Developing countries also experienced a slowdown in 2008, but still managed to post a robust growth rate of 5.9% and are expected to grow by 4.6% next year.

Figure I.1
WORLD GDP GROWTH
(Percentages)

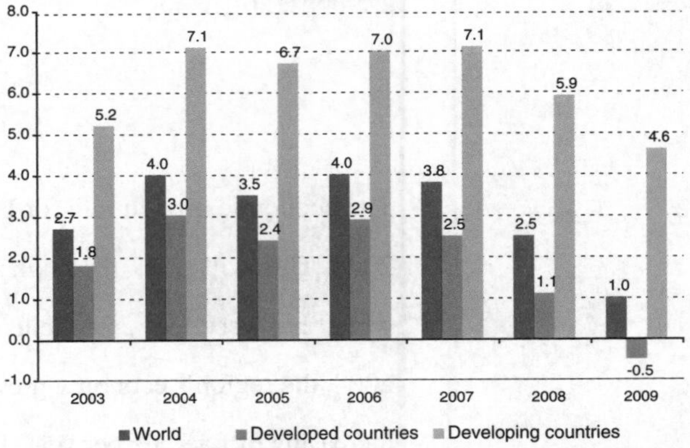

Source: Economic Commission for Latin America and the Caribbean (ECLAC), on the basis of International Monetary Fund, World Economic Outlook [database] April 2008.

A. The financial crisis

Plunging real estate values in the United States were the initial destabilizing factor leading up to the international financial crisis. The upswing in property prices began to slow in 2006 (when monetary policy tightened), and prices actually began to come down in early 2007. By August 2008, one representative housing price index was 17.7% lower than it had been in August 2007. This deflationary process exerted strong pressure on mortgage owners and financial institutions alike. Refinancing schemes were

hampered by rising default rates and the devaluation of the assets backing the loans, which produced a sudden swell in the relative burden of liabilities. The evidence emerging in mid-2007 of a decapitalization of investment vehicles belonging to major international financial institutions made it impossible for them to borrow on the short-term or interbank markets. Potential lenders became extremely reticent to part with liquidity, and this ultimately triggered a severe credit crunch.

The depreciation of stock market assets that began to accompany this process added another deflationary factor to the crisis: the Dow Jones industrial average was 35.4% lower in mid-November 2008 than in (pre-crisis) July 2007. During the first stage, the flows of private capital that were financing the United States current account deficit, though still positive, decreased notably. Between 2003 and the third quarter of 2007, these flows represented, on average, 2.6% of GDP, while from the last quarter of 2007 to the second quarter of 2008, they accounted for barely 0.6% of GDP, leaving the financing of the current external deficit in the United States mainly to official flows, which covered about 90% of the total balance (the equivalent of 5.0% of GDP).

With Japan and the euro zone moving towards a recession and the dollar appreciating from mid-2008 onward, a third deflationary factor emerged in the form of falling commodity prices. This trend was fuelled by the strong downturn in the United States economy in the second half of 2008.

One incident, in particular, marked a turning point in the development of the crisis: the collapse of Lehman Brothers. The repercussions of this event, far from being confined to the shareholders of that financial institution or, as next in line, investment banking in general, brought negative expectations to a head and culminated in widespread panic. Credit markets were virtually paralysed, and demand for liquidity soared. This situation was clearly reflected in interbank markets, which further undermined the already fragile balances of some banks and threatened the very survival of large financial institutions, in addition to fuelling fears of a systemic failure of global financial markets.

From the viewpoint of Latin America and the Caribbean, these events signalled the start of the contagion of financial markets in emerging economies. The effect on corporate financing was also extremely negative, and this hurt the equity position of large corporations, some of which have large subsidiaries in Latin America and the Caribbean while others are headquartered in the region itself.

The response from the world's monetary authorities came in several stages. First, starting in mid-2007, a number of developed countries injected huge doses of liquidity into the system. In the United States, the Federal Reserve lowered the benchmark interest rate, and the government introduced a fiscal stimulus package equivalent to approximately 1.1% of GDP. The next stage was shaped, in March 2008, by a specific bailout operation: the sale of Bear Stearns, which was brokered by the Federal Reserve. The third stage involved the restructuring of key actors in the mortgage market, such as Fannie Mae and Freddie Mac, and the overhaul of the entire investment banking sector in the United States. This required congressional approval in early October for a system-wide plan involving a sum equivalent to about 5% of GDP to bail out the country's decapitalized financial institutions. The inadequacy of this approach, which was made apparent by the stock market crash of October 2008 and the weakness of the credit market, led the government to allow investors to buy shares in financial institutions, a recapitalization measure that had already been introduced in the United Kingdom. In late October, the United States Federal Reserve lowered its interest rates to 1%, and in mid-December it cut them to between 0% and 0.25%.

With the bailout of Citigroup in late November, the approach being taken to financial rescue operations was altered to incorporate guarantees for the toxic assets held by banks. This means that these assets remain in bank portfolios, and the Treasury only needs to deal with any losses that occur in the future. This scheme is designed to generate confidence in the financial system without requiring, at least initially, any large outlays of funds.

B. The transmission of the crisis to Latin America and the Caribbean

Within the framework of this generally bleak outlook, in which the factors driving growth in Latin America and the Caribbean in the past few years have all but disappeared, the international crisis is being transmitted through various channels that are, in turn, having different effects on each one of the countries of the region.

1   The drop in world demand

The looming recession in developed economies and the significant slowdown in the emerging ones will reduce demand for exports from Latin America and the Caribbean. The trend in the region's exports to the United States and China illustrates how the international financial crisis has been affecting the region's economies through trade. The United States' total non-oil imports have grown relatively steadily since mid-2007, when the financial crisis erupted.

This implies that, on average, the effect of rising prices for imported commodities was more or less counterbalanced by the decrease in import volumes. The situation regarding imports by the United States from Latin America and the Caribbean has varied considerably from country to country. Non-oil imports from Mexico began to slow in mid-2007 and continued to fall to the point where they registered a year-on-year contraction of 2.4% in the third quarter of 2008. Imports from the Central American countries have, on the other hand,

behaved similarly to imports worldwide. This is because, although there is evidence of a slowdown and even of a contraction in Central American manufactures destined for the United States market, this decline has been offset by the higher prices obtained for commodity exports. United States imports from the Andean countries and MERCOSUR, a large proportion of which consist of commodities, rose in step with commodity prices from mid-2007 until the third quarter of 2008, when they began to level off. China's imports from Latin America and the Caribbean, which are most significant in the case of the Andean countries and MERCOSUR, followed a similar pattern, but peaked towards the end of 2007 in the case of the Andean countries and in the first quarter of 2008 in the case of MERCOSUR. The data for November 2008, however, show a 2% drop in exports and an 18% drop in imports in the region (compared with November 2007), a decline that has not been seen since 2001.

Figure I.2
UNITED STATES: NON-OIL IMPORTS, JANUARY 2000-SEPTEMBER 2008
(Variation compared with the same month in the previous year) [a]

From Mexico and Central America [b]

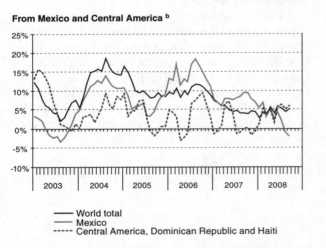

From MERCOSUR and the Andean countries

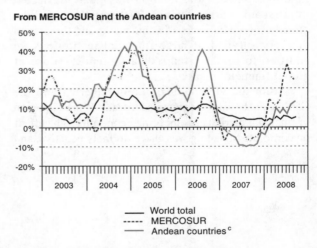

———— World total
———— Mexico
- - - - Central America, Dominican Republic and Haiti

———— World total
- - - - MERCOSUR
———— Andean countries [c]

Source: Economic Commission for Latin America and the Caribbean (ECLAC), on the basis of figures from the United States International Trade Commission.
[a] Based on the three-month moving average of the relevant seasonally adjusted series.
[b] Costa Rica, Dominican Republic, El Salvador, Guatemala, Haiti, Honduras, Nicaragua and Panama.
[c] Bolivarian Republic of Venezuela, Bolivia, Chile, Colombia, Ecuador and Peru.

The decrease in merchandise exports can be expected to have a greater impact on growth in the more open economies, in those that trade more with developed countries and, in particular, in those that sell a larger proportion

of manufactured goods to developed markets, as it will be more difficult to find alternative markets for such goods quickly. As shown in figure, in Mexico, Ecuador, Chile, Costa Rica, Bolivarian Republic of Venezuela and Honduras, trade with developed countries accounts for over 10% of GDP. An examination of manufacturing exports alone, however, reveals that such exports account for over 10% of GDP only in Mexico and Costa Rica, and close to 5% in Honduras.

In some of the region's countries, part of the negative impact on growth will be the result of lower demand for services —particularly tourism, for which demand is extremely income-elastic. Although this issue is explored in greater depth in the accompanying box I.1, the following figure shows that Caribbean countries and some Central American economies may be among the most severely affected. In the Caribbean, exports of tourism-related services represent around 20% of GDP, compared with an average of 5% in Central America (although the figure is just under 10% for the Dominican Republic, Costa Rica and Panama).

Figure I.4
LATIN AMERICA (17 COUNTRIES): MERCHANDISE EXPORTS, BY DESTINATION, 2006
(Percentages of GDP)

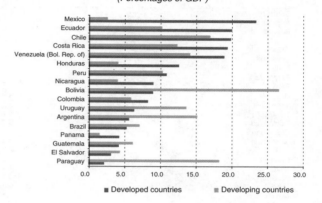

Source: Economic Commission for Latin America and the Caribbean (ECLAC), on the basis of official figures.

Figure I.3
LATIN AMERICA (17 COUNTRIES): MERCHANDISE EXPORTS TO DEVELOPED COUNTRIES, 2006
(Percentages of GDP)

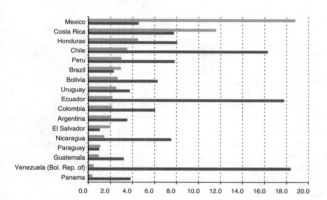

Source: Economic Commission for Latin America and the Caribbean (ECLAC), on the basis of official figures.

Figure I.5
LATIN AMERICA AND THE CARIBBEAN: TOURISM
(Percentages of GDP)

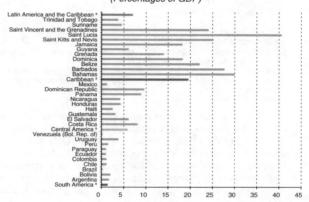

Source: Economic Commission for Latin America and the Caribbean (ECLAC), on the basis of official figures.
[a] Unweighted average.

Box I.1
TRENDS IN THE TOURISM SECTOR AND THE INTERNATIONAL CRISIS

The tourism sector in Latin America and the Caribbean is one of the areas that has enjoyed the most rapid development in recent years, as evidenced by its role in generating greater value added and foreign exchange earnings. Inbound tourism consumption[a] in the English-speaking Caribbean countries —except Guyana, Suriname and Trinidad and Tobago— ranges from 15% to 41% of GDP;[b] as a percentage of exports of goods and services, it is even higher, as tourism is the main foreign-exchange earner and a major engine of growth for the economies.

The World Tourism Organization (UNWTO) estimates total growth in this activity at between 2% and 3% in 2008 (compared with 6.6% in 2007). World tourism activity started to slow significantly between June and August 2008, owing to the continuing deterioration in real incomes and consumer expectations, the volatility of exchange rates and the squeeze on consumer credit resulting from the financial crisis.

In the first eight months of 2008, tourist arrivals in Central America and South America were still buoyant with growth rates of 9.4% and 7.2%, respectively; the Caribbean countries recorded growth of just 3%, with flat growth between June and August,[c] owing to a decline in arrivals in the Bahamas, Barbados, Bermuda and Puerto Rico, four destinations which receive visitors mostly from the United States and Europe.[d] Arrivals in Mexico were up by 4.8% during the same period, but slowdowns and even falls occurred in some segments and destinations towards the end of the period.[e]

Box I.1 (continued)

LATIN AMERICA: INBOUND TOURISM CONSUMPTION

	Inbound tourism consumption as a percentage of GDP [a]	Inbound tourism consumption as a percentage of exports of goods and services [b]
South America [c]	**1.6**	**5.2**
Argentina	1.9	7.5
Bolivia	2.2	5.9
Brazil	0.4	2.9
Chile	1.3	2.8
Colombia	1.3	6.6
Ecuador	1.2	3.5
Paraguay	1.2	2.0
Peru	1.7	6.0
Uruguay	4.0	13.6
Venezuela (Bol. Rep. of)	0.4	1.3
Central America [c]	**6.1**	**17.8**
Costa Rica	8.3	16.9
El Salvador	6.3	23.2
Guatemala	3.3	13.6
Haiti	2.7	19.4
Honduras	4.5	12.9
Nicaragua	4.4	9.7
Panama	9.1	12.6
Dominican Republic	9.8	33.7
Mexico [c]	**1.4**	**5.0**
Caribbean	**19.7**	**41.3**
Bahamas	30.2	62.5
Barbados	27.9	51.7
Belize	22.3	33.8
Dominica	18.5	43.9
Grenada	14.2	47.8
Guyana	6.3	23.2
Jamaica	18.4	44.6
Saint Kitts and Nevis	25.4	53.3
Santa Lucia	40.8	72.2
San Vincent and the Grenadines	24.3	51.9
Suriname	4.7	5.6
Trinidad y Tobago	3.9	5.6
Latin America and the Caribbean [c]	**7.2**	**17.3**

Source: Economic Commission for Latin America and the Caribbean (ECLAC), on the basis of official figures and data from the World Tourism Organization, *Yearbook of Tourism Statistics*.

[a] Corresponds to the income from travel and transport of passengers entered in the balance of payments, as a percentage of GDP in current dollars.
[b] Corresponds to income from travel and transport of passengers as a percentage of exports of goods and services in current dollars, entered in the balance of payments.
[c] Unweighted average.

Tourism in Central America benefited from the relative novelty of this destination, from the projects that were maturing and from the increase in the frequency of flights at a time when high fuel costs were forcing most airlines to cut back on flights. In turn, in this subregion as well as in Mexico, the depreciation of the dollar against the euro early in the year boosted arrivals of European tourists as well as United States tourist who opted for trips to more competitive destinations rather than Europe on account of the high cost of airfares. Mexico also benefited from intraregional flows from countries whose currencies had appreciated against the peso. In South America, intraregional tourism helped to mitigate the impact of the crisis in the developed countries, with most of the inflows coming from countries whose currencies had appreciated.

LATIN AMERICA AND THE CARIBBEAN: INBOUND TOURISM CONSUMPTION AS A PERCENTAGE OF GDP
(In current dollars) [a]

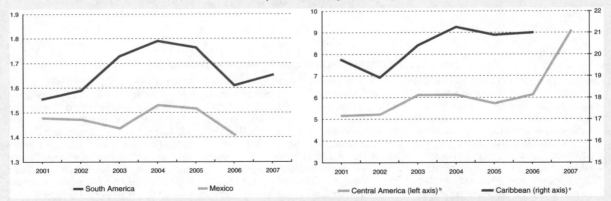

Source: Economic Commission for Latin America and the Caribbean (ECLAC), on the basis of official figures and International Monetary Fund data.
[a] Corresponds to income from travel and transport of passengers entered in the balance of payments, simple average of national figures.
[b] Central America includes the following countries: Costa Rica, Dominican Republic, El Salvador, Guatemala, Haiti, Honduras, Nicaragua, Panama.
[c] The Caribbean includes the following countries: Bahamas, Barbados, Belize, Dominica, Grenada, Guyana, Jamaica, Saint Kitts and Nevis, Saint Lucia, Saint Vincent and the Grenadines, Suriname and Trinidad and Tobago.

Box I.1 (concluded)

The tourism sector has three characteristics that are of especial importance for many countries in the region: (a) it is an activity which has the potential to generate positive externalities on GDP and employment, since it can be structured as a network involving different providers of services and products which offers scope for small and medium-sized enterprises; (b) it is a sector that generates surpluses in the services balance in the smaller economies and compensates for pressures from other balance-of-payments categories thanks to the use of natural resources which, unlike mineral resources, can be exploited —subject to appropriate public policies— without the risk of depletion; and (c) it is an activity that proved to be particularly responsive to stimulation from the sound external context that prevailed during the period 2003-2007. The ratio of inbound tourism consumption to GDP may be used as an indicator to show the growing importance of this activity in Central America and South America during this period, when it increased by 1.5% and 0.2% of GDP, respectively, compared with the period 1997-2001 (see figure). In South America, tourism has acted as one of the engines of post-crisis recovery, particularly in 2003-2004, and maintained a historically high level in subsequent years. In Central America, positive growth in the sector stems from the consolidation of the industry in some countries (Costa Rica and Dominican Republic) and from the emergence of newcomers to the market (El Salvador and Nicaragua). The Caribbean countries also performed well during the growth years.

UNWTO projects that world tourism will expand by between 0% and 2% in 2009. The recession in the developed economies, which are home to approximately 75% of all tourists travelling to the English-speaking Caribbean and over 40% of those travelling to Central America (for Cuba and the Dominican Republic, the percentage is 75%), will have an impact on per capita disposable income and hence on tourism spending. Business travel may be particularly hard hit. Nevertheless, an easing of inflationary pressures and currency depreciation in several countries in the region could compensate in part for these effects and tourist destinations closest to the place of residence could benefit. Price competitiveness and the exchange-rate situation between the different tourist destinations will prove to be much more important for sustaining this activity. Lastly, several countries where significant investments have taken place in recent years will be better placed to compete for the declining demand that seems to be in the offing.

Source: Economic Commission for Latin America and the Caribbean (ECLAC).
ª Income from passenger travel and transport recorded in the balance of payments.
ᵇ Figures relate to 2007.
ᶜ Figures from the World Tourism Organization (UNTWO) *World Tourism Barometer*, Vol. 6, No.3, October 2008.
ᵈ Caribbean Tourism Organization, *Latest statistics* 2008, November 2008.
ᵉ Secretariat of Tourism of Mexico, *Boletín cuatrimestral de turismo*, No. 23, May-August 2008.

2. Expected trend in remittances

The weaker job market in developed economies will have an adverse effect on the remittances that emigrant workers send back to their families in their home country. Remittances have been an extremely important source of external revenues in Latin America and the Caribbean, where they have helped to increase the well-being of low-income families. Any reduction in remittances will therefore have a negative impact on the situation of this socio-economic group, as is discussed in box I.2. Thus, the major challenge facing the region is to prevent poverty indicators from increasing.

Here again, certain Central American and Caribbean countries are the most at risk, as in many such economies remittances represent between 15% and just under 40% of GDP. These countries are, in decreasing order, Haiti, Honduras, Jamaica, El Salvador, Nicaragua and Guatemala. Slightly less at risk are countries where remittances account for between 5% and 10% of GDP. This category includes some South American economies, such as Bolivia and Ecuador (as well as Belize, the Dominican Republic and Grenada).

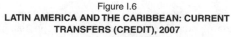

Figure I.6
LATIN AMERICA AND THE CARIBBEAN: CURRENT TRANSFERS (CREDIT), 2007
(Percentages of GDP and millions of dollars)

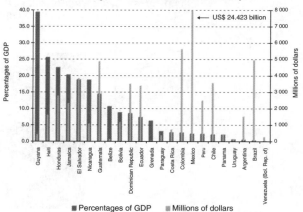

Source: Economic Commission for Latin America and the Caribbean (ECLAC), on the basis of official figures and International Monetary Fund.

Box I.2
CONSIDERATIONS ON THE DISTRIBUTIVE IMPACT OF SLOWER GROWTH

A very significant factor in a region with levels of inequality as high as they are in Latin America and the Caribbean is that not all households are equally affected by slower growth. For the great majority of the region's households, labour market shifts are the main transmitters of this impact. In 2008-2009 the well-being of lower-income households is also being eroded by trends in remittances and domestic prices.

In the current circumstances, therefore, public policies have to deal with the challenges not only of stabilizing economic growth through anticyclical measures but also of developing ways to protect the most vulnerable sectors of the population from those negative distributive effects. Clearly, the scope for action in that direction varies widely among the countries of the region.

Impact on the labour market

It is expected that in 2009, the employment rate will fall and unemployment will rise. The impact of job loss is differentiated by household traits. Figure 1 shows that lower-income households tend to have fewer breadwinners; indeed, that is one of the reasons for their low incomes. Consequently, job loss has a greater effect on low-income households, since it means, at least initially, the loss of a higher proportion of the household's already low income. Urban households in the three highest income quintiles average two breadwinners, so even if one job is lost, one full income is retained. The situation is very different in urban households belonging to the lowest quintile, where, on average, only a third of one wage is retained.

LATIN AMERICA (EIGHT COUNTRIES): NUMBER OF BREADWINNERS BY HOUSEHOLD INCOME QUINTILE AND URBAN OR RURAL AREA, SIMPLE AVERAGE, 2006-2007

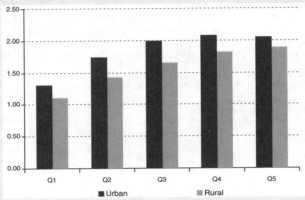

Source: Economic Commission for Latin America and the Caribbean (ECLAC), on the basis of special processing of data from household surveys conducted in the respective countries.

The situation is worse in rural areas, where households in the poorest quintile have, on average, only one breadwinner. In both urban and rural areas, female heads of household are especially vulnerable, since their households average a lower number of breadwinners (see figure below).

Furthermore, the members of the poorest households tend to work in the informal sector, so that when they lose their jobs they enjoy none of the protection mechanisms that, at least in some countries and occupations, are available to workers in the formal sector.

LATIN AMERICA (EIGHT COUNTRIES): NUMBER OF BREADWINNERS PER HOUSEHOLD, BY SEX OF HEAD OF HOUSEHOLD AND URBAN OR RURAL AREA, SIMPLE AVERAGE, 2006-2007

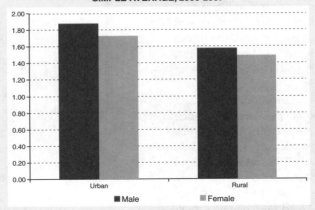

Source: Economic Commission for Latin America and the Caribbean (ECLAC), on the basis of special processing of data from household surveys conducted in the respective countries.

Box I.2 (concluded)

The members of the poorest households tend to work in different job categories and branches of activity from those of wealthier households. For example, in urban areas, employees in the first and second quintiles make up 12.8% and 16.8% of all employed persons, respectively, but 17.2% and 22.2%, respectively, of construction workers. Since in many countries the economic slowdown is impacting heavily on that sector, many households which already have low incomes are likely to suffer major losses in well-being.

In terms of employment category, low-income quintiles tend to be over-represented in domestic work, own-account work (other than professional or technical activities) and unpaid work. Crisis situations often jeopardize domestic employment, since many medium-income households employing domestic workers will dismiss them in the event of income loss or the possibility of a household member losing his or her job. Also, own-account —and unpaid— workers tend to increase in number during low-growth periods because such work is perceived as the only means of generating income or, in the case of unpaid work, of helping to generate it. This often results in a fall in the average incomes of such workers, because the supply of specific goods and services increases while demand stands still or falls.

Impact on remittances

As many studies have emphasized, cross-border migrants do not generally come from the poorest households. Yet the remittances they send home tend to have a positive impact on distribution, since they favour low- and medium-low-income households and stimulate their consumption and investment. Falls in remittances following the cooling of host country economies, together with stricter migration control policies, clearly have a negative impact on the well-being of such households.

Impact on prices

The sharp price rises seen in many countries in 2008 also had a specific distributive impact, since much of the inflationary upsurge was due to spikes in food prices, which have a higher relative weight in consumption baskets at the lowest income levels. Thus, the soaring food prices have had a greater impact on that segment of the population. In those countries in the region which publish such information, the consumer price index (CPI) for the lowest income levels systematically rose more than for the highest levels: in Mexico, in the 12 months to October 2008 the index for the lowest stratum rose by 7.0%, compared with 5.4% for the highest level; in the Dominican Republic the corresponding figures were 18.0% and 10.5%; and in the Bolivarian Republic of Venezuela, 39.5% and 33.9%.

Source: Economic Commission for Latin America and the Caribbean (ECLAC).

3. Commodity prices

Falling commodity prices in the wake of slower world growth will result in a deterioration in the terms of trade for the region as a whole, although the actual effects will vary from country to country.

The rate of increase in commodity prices rose steadily between mid-2007 and mid-2008. Although there was an across-the-board surge in commodity prices, the increase was particularly striking in the cases of petroleum, certain metals such as copper, and foods such as soybeans, maize and wheat (as part of the global "food-price inflation" experienced at that time).

The index for most of the region's exports peaked between June and August 2008; the total aggregate (not including petroleum) skyrocketed in July. From then onward, sharp declines ushered in the new recessionary and deflationary phase of the international crisis. In the case of petroleum, prices at the end of November 2008 were similar to those recorded in late 2004, while metal prices were similar to those observed at the end of 2005. Food prices, which had shown a smaller increase previously, fell less dramatically, with prices in November 2008 being more or less equivalent to those of mid-2007.

Figure I.7
COMMODITY PRICE INDICES
(2000=100)

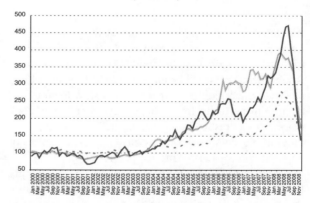

Source: Economic Commission for Latin America and the Caribbean (ECLAC), on the basis of United Nations Conference on Trade and Development (UNCTAD).

For most of the region's countries, commodities make up a considerable proportion of the export basket and, for many countries, they are a significant source of public funds. For all of these countries (including those in South America and Mexico, which had all benefited from improved terms of trade since 2003), commodity price patterns over the next year (or more) are expected to cause one of the region's recent engines of growth to come to a standstill.

For the region as a whole, it is estimated that the terms of trade improved by 4.6% in 2008 and will fall by 15.6% in 2009. For Chile and Peru, which are both metal exporters, the deterioration in the terms of trade is expected to be around 7.5% in 2008 and 24.2% in 2009. Countries that export fuel would have experienced a 20.9% rise in their terms of trade in 2008, and are expected to sustain a fall of approximately 44.4% in 2009. As for MERCOSUR, where food accounts for an extremely significant proportion of exports, the rise in 2008 will be offset by the decline projected for 2009. In Mexico, the terms of trade are estimated to have improved by 2.8% in 2008 and will probably drop by 7.6% in 2009.

In contrast, as Central America and the Caribbean are net importers of commodities, the fall in oil, metal and cereal prices alleviates and partially offsets the consequences of the world economic slowdown and the above-mentioned fall in remittances. In a departure from the figures presented in the previous paragraph, the terms of trade in Central America are expected to deteriorate by 3,4% in 2008, before rising by 5,1% in 2009, which represents around a third of the decline observed in recent years.

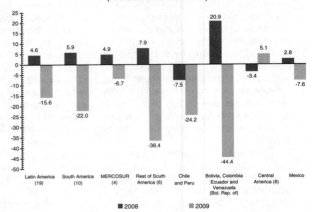

Figure I.8
LATIN AMERICA (19 COUNTRIES): TERMS OF TRADE, 2008-2009
(Annual rate of variation)

Source: Economic Commission for Latin America and the Caribbean (ECLAC), on the basis of official figures.

Recent trends in food and energy prices are easing inflationary pressures. Given the rapid devaluation of many currencies, this has yet to be reflected in price indices. However, inflation rates are expected to be lower as a result in 2009.

4.   Financial contagion

As stated previously, in the wake of the failure of the Lehman Brothers investment bank, the crisis had an increasing impact on the financial markets of Latin America and the Caribbean. In the final four months of the year, the region has experienced a slowdown then a decline in portfolio flows, huge falls in regional stock markets and drastic depreciations, attributable in part to previous speculative positions based on expectations of appreciation for Latin American currencies.

The cost of international borrowing soared, mainly for businesses but also for sovereign debtors, although the region's experience in this regard is merely a reflection of the widespread increase in risk aversion sparked by increasing global uncertainty and what is occurring with the debts of emerging economies in general. As shown in the following figure, the increase in the sovereign risk premiums of the region is actually smaller than in previous crises, although this varies a great deal across countries.

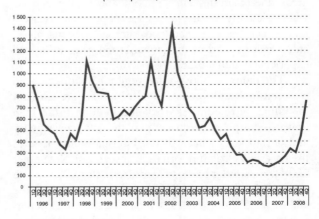

Figure I.9
LATIN AMERICA: INTEREST-RATE SPREADS MEASURED BY EMBI+
(Basis points, end of period)

Source: Economic Commission for Latin America and the Caribbean (ECLAC), on the basis of JP Morgan.

Although the region's financial activity has not been exposed to toxic assets, the problems existing on the interbank market and the impact that the tightening of external credit has had on local credit markets are two ways in which turmoil in the financial markets of developed countries can be transferred to the region. The available information (most of which corresponds to the third quarter) is not sufficient to allow the scale of this impact to be calculated, however.

Of particular concern are the conditions of access to credit for a series of large regional enterprises from various countries that usually find financing on international markets. Given the credit crunch and the higher price of credit in global financial markets, it is expected to become more difficult to meet borrowing requirements. The reduced availability of external financing will force the larger private enterprises to turn to the domestic market. This, along with increased uncertainty, will probably make it more difficult for small and medium-sized enterprises to access financial resources. The backdrop to all this is a liquidity squeeze in local credit markets.

In the final part of the year, companies with debt in foreign currency have seen their balances negatively impacted by the devaluations of several of the region's currencies. This is a striking and somewhat unprecedented feature of this cycle as, unlike the situation in previous crises, it is the private sector that is the most exposed to exchange-rate volatility in many countries.

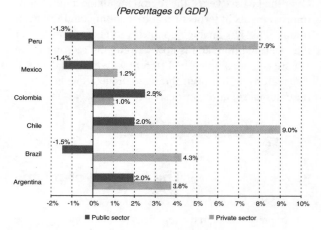

Figure I.10
LATIN AMERICA AND THE CARIBBEAN (SELECTED COUNTRIES): EXTERNAL DEBT, 2006-JUNE 2008
(Percentages of GDP)

Source: Economic Commission for Latin America and the Caribbean (ECLAC), on the basis of official figures.

5.   Impact on foreign direct investment (FDI)

It is also likely that the tightening of international financial conditions will have an adverse effect on inflows of foreign direct investment (FDI), which had been such an important source of resources for some countries in recent years. The figure below shows the high inflows of FDI into countries of the Caribbean (related to tourist activity) where they account for between 15% and 25% of GDP, into the Dominican Republic, Costa Rica and Panama (between 6.5% and 8% of GDP) and into Chile and Peru in South America (with FDI accounting for around 5% of GDP in 2008).

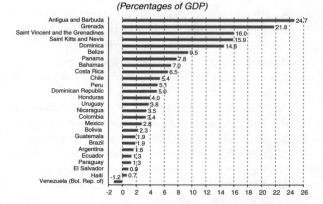

Figure I.11
LATIN AMERICA AND THE CARIBBEAN: NET FOREIGN DIRECT INVESTMENT
(Percentages of GDP)

Source: Economic Commission for Latin America and the Caribbean (ECLAC), on the basis of official figures from the relevant countries and International Monetary Fund.

C. Latin America and the Caribbean is better prepared to face the crisis but is not immune

Over the last six years, the region has made a number of improvements in terms of macroeconomic and financial policy. This has enabled countries to take advantage of the external boom and is now helping the region to face the crisis in a completely different way from in the past. The region has thus been able to continue growing even as the external situation seriously deteriorates. Nevertheless, many of the improvements are beginning to fade and in some cases revert.

Even though the factors described below are clearly different from those observed in past situations, if the crisis deepens and/or its effects become more prolonged, the macroeconomic foundations for the region's recent growth are eventually likely to be weakened. These factors include:

1.   The balance-of-payments current account surplus

It is unprecedented in the region's economic history to see growth coincide with a surplus on the external accounts. Initially, this was due to the combined effect of greater export volumes and higher prices for the exports of most of the region's countries. However, as the volume factor become less important, the increase in export values began to be exclusively dependent on international prices (while economic growth was also accompanied by a rise in imports). Therefore, the recent fall in commodity prices and the expectation that this downward price trend will intensify as a result of slower world growth cast doubt over one of the main strengths of the region in recent years: its independence from external financing. Indeed, in 2008, the above-mentioned factors had already generated a slight current account deficit (0.6%), which is expected to widen in 2009 to a projected deficit of around 2.5% of regional GDP.

2.   The generation of a surplus in the public accounts

Public accounts improved significantly, largely thanks to higher revenues (on the strength of better export prices and increased economic activity) and (up to 2007) to less expansionary spending patterns than in the past. The improvement in public accounts resulted in a substantial reduction in public debt.

More recently, public spending has been on the rise, and this has curbed the expansion of the primary surplus. The surplus has become exclusively dependent on income levels, and the reduction of public debt has also slowed. As with the current account balance, public revenues are expected to come under greater pressure at times when it may become necessary to increase spending to tackle the slowdown in private demand.

Given the predictions for income from exports of non-renewable resources (analysed separately), a small total deficit is forecast for the public accounts in 2008 (0.3% of GDP), although the primary surplus is expected to be maintained. In 2009, there should still be a primary surplus, albeit a smaller one, and the total deficit will expand to 1.5% of GDP.

The region's twin surpluses (on the current account and the fiscal accounts) in the period 2006-2007 are giving way to twin deficits, which will start off small in 2008 and then widen in 2009. The average for the region also reflects individual country trends, as shown in the figure: only three countries will retain their position in the virtuous quadrant with twin surpluses in 2008, while a growing number of countries will find themselves in the quadrant with deficits on the public and external accounts.

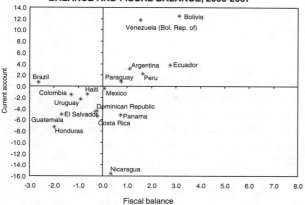

Figure I.12a
LATIN AMERICA (19 COUNTRIES): CURRENT ACCOUNT BALANCE AND FISCAL BALANCE, 2006-2007

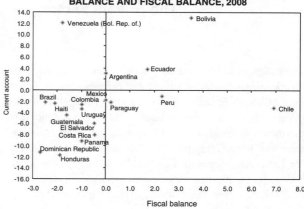

Figure I.12b
LATIN AMERICA (18 COUNTRIES): CURRENT ACCOUNT BALANCE AND FISCAL BALANCE, 2008

Source: Economic Commission for Latin America and the Caribbean (ECLAC), on the basis of official figures.
[a] The data refer to the central government except in the cases of Argentina, Bolivia, Brazil, Colombia, Ecuador and Mexico, where the data refer to the non-financial public sector.

3. The external debt and international reserves

Exceptional liquidity conditions on the financial markets in recent years have meant that the reduction in external debt made possible by the twin surpluses went hand in hand with a tendency to renegotiate debt with better conditions in terms of rates, maturities and even currency in some cases. At the same time, some countries experienced strong capital inflows seeking to take advantage of the significant interest-rate spreads as currencies appreciated.

GDP and was equivalent to almost five times the countries' short-term debt.

The role of financial capital inflows is increasingly significant in terms of the factors that contribute to the growth of international reserves. This is especially true when compared with the share of the increase in foreign exchange reserves that is accounted for by current account surpluses, which showed a markedly downward trend. This makes the stock of reserves somewhat fragile, particularly in some of the countries of the region, in light of the volatile nature of such resources.

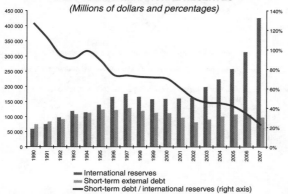

Figure I.13
LATIN AMERICA AND THE CARIBBEAN: SHORT-TERM EXTERNAL DEBT AND INTERNATIONAL RESERVES
(Millions of dollars and percentages)

- International reserves
- Short-term external debt
- Short-term debt / international reserves (right axis)

Source: Economic Commission for Latin America and the Caribbean (ECLAC), on the basis of World Bank, Global Development Finance database [online].

These capital inflows, combined with current account surpluses in many countries and foreign direct investment, led to significant growth in international reserves. As of mid-2008, that growth averaged about 15% of the region's

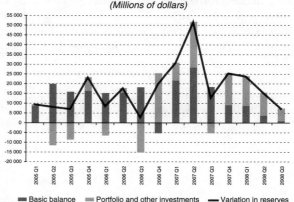

Figure I.14
LATIN AMERICA (SIX COUNTRIES) [a]: BREAKDOWN OF VARIATION IN RESERVES, 2005-2008
(Millions of dollars)

- Basic balance
- Portfolio and other investments
- Variation in reserves

Source: Economic Commission for Latin America and the Caribbean (ECLAC), on the basis of official figures and International Monetary Fund.
[a] Includes Argentina, Brazil, Chile, Colombia, Mexico and Peru.

4.   The private sector

The maintenance of macroeconomic equilibrium requires that the sum of external saving and public saving is equal to the difference between private-sector investment and saving. External saving is equivalent to the balance-of-payments current account balance, but with the sign reversed. From 2003 to 2007 that balance was negative for Latin America and the Caribbean, and this was the counterpart to the aforementioned current account surplus. In 2008, however, the external saving figure is expected to be slightly positive.

When public-sector saving is calculated by means of the overall fiscal balance, the amount by which investment exceeds private saving can be determined; this, in turn, is an approximation of the private surplus (when it is positive) or, inversely, of private-sector overspending (when it is negative). This factor can produce a significant level of external vulnerability, as may be the case in a number of the countries whose private external debts have risen considerably, even if the macroeconomic fundamentals which are followed most closely are solid (as in the case of the twin surpluses seen in the region from 2003 to 2007).

Figure I.15 shows the trends of the current account balance, the surplus on public accounts and the private-sector surplus for the region. The behaviour of these balances in recent years provides a new picture of fundamental economic aggregates in the region. Taking the regional average, the private sector was in surplus from 2003 to 2007, while the public sector cut back its deficit and then achieved a surplus from 2006 onward. Until 2006 the private surplus was very high and easily compensated for the shrinking public-sector deficit, so the region as a whole was in surplus and did not need external saving; the current account balance was positive (i.e., external saving was negative). In 2006 and 2007, negative external saving was mainly a reflection of the public surplus, since the private sector saw its surplus shrink in 2006 and posted a deficit in 2007. From 2008 on, external saving was positive thanks to the combination of a fiscal deficit and excess private spending. In a context of tight international financial markets, this combination of factors is a source of vulnerability.

There are considerable differences across countries in this respect. As shown in figure I.16, the private-sector deficit is larger in Chile and some Central American economies and is somewhat smaller in Peru, Uruguay, Mexico and Colombia. It should be noted, however, that in many cases fiscal data correspond to the central government aggregate, and the figures obtained for the private sector as a residual therefore includes public enterprises.

Figure I.15

LATIN AMERICA (19 COUNTRIES): CURRENT ACCOUNT, FISCAL AND PRIVATE-SECTOR BALANCES
(Percentages of GDP)

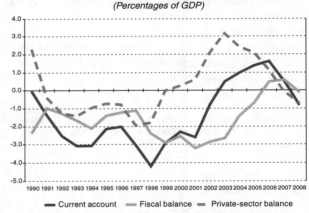

Source: Economic Commission for Latin America and the Caribbean (ECLAC), on the basis of official figures.

Figure I.16
LATIN AMERICA AND THE CARIBBEAN (SELECTED COUNTRIES): PRIVATE-SECTOR OVERSPENDING, 2008
(Percentages of GDP)

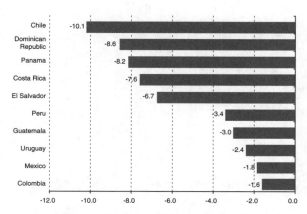

Source: Economic Commission for Latin America and the Caribbean (ECLAC), on the basis of official figures.

D. Measures implemented in the region to cope with the escalating crisis

The Latin American and Caribbean countries have adopted a variety of measures in response to the deepening international financial crisis. They are well aware that, although most of them have macroeconomic foundations that are significantly stronger than in the past, the region will not escape the impact of instability in world financial markets and the expected recession in the developed economies.

The range of measures implemented is quite wide, not only because the effects differ from country to country and the instruments needed for countering them therefore also vary, but also because of differences in the countries' capacities, in terms of the availability of resources, to implement such initiatives.

That availability generally depends, on the one hand, on the fiscal room for manoeuvre available for financing the measures, when their implementation entails the use of public funds; and on the other hand, when they involve foreign-currency transactions, on the availability of external assets (basically, foreign reserves) or of access to foreign-currency credit. In the current circumstances, the latter is limited to dealings with international financial bodies.

Beyond these considerations, taking into account the impact that these measures may have on the rest of the economy, a full analysis of the countries' capacities should encompass, in addition to the aforementioned factors, other elements such as the degree of monetization and the depth of the financial market or the balance-of-payments current account balance. It should be remembered that a demand promotion strategy based on increased public spending, aside from its fiscal impact, may widen the external deficit beyond a country's capacity to finance it. In this case, the availability of foreign-currency resources will be an issue even if there is plenty of fiscal room for manoeuvre.

Table I.2 summarizes the areas of action selected by the governments of the region. In the short term, central banks in several countries have endeavoured to provide liquidity to their financial systems in both domestic and foreign currency in order to enable local credit markets to function normally or to provide funding where those markets cannot do so. Generally, there has been a marked difference between the scope of the policies announced in certain South American countries in comparison with some of the Central American and Caribbean States. This certainly relates to differing capacities to implement anticyclical policies, as referred to above.

Table I.2

SCOPE OF THE MEASURES ANNOUNCED BY COUNTRIES IN RESPONSE TO THE CRISIS [a]

Measure	AR	BO	BR	CL	CO	CR	EC	SV	GT	HT	HN	MX	NI	PA	PY	PE	DO	UY	VE	BS	BB	GY	JM	AG	DM	GD	KN	LC	VC	SR	TT
Monetary and financial policy																															
Reduction of legal reserve requirements or increased flexibility	X			X	X				X		X			X	X	X		X													
Provision of liquidity in national currency	X		X	X	X	X	X		X		X	X			X	X	X	X	X	X			X								
Fiscal policy																															
Tax cuts or increased subsidies	X			X	X		X				X	X	X	X							X			X	X	X	X	X	X		
Spending increased or brought forward (infrastructure)	X		X	X	X	X	X	X	X	X	X	X	X		X	X	X	X	X	X				X	X	X	X	X	X		
Foreign exchange and trade policy																															
Provision of liquidity in foreign currency [b]	X			X	X				X					X	X	X		X													
Increased tariffs or import restrictions	X						X																		X						
Tariff cuts	X			X			X					X	X		X	X				X											
Export financing	X			X	X		X								X	X	X	X		X											
Credit from international financial bodies					X				X	X	X	X	X	X	X	X										X					
Sectoral policies																															
Housing	X			X	X				X		X	X			X	X	X	X													
Small and medium-sized enterprises	X			X	X				X		X	X			X	X		X													
Agriculture			X		X					X	X	X		X				X				X									
Tourism																		X		X			X								
Industry	X																	X							X						
Employment and social policy																															
Promoting job creation	X			X	X				X	X		X			X	X	X														
Social programmes	X			X	X	X	X		X	X	X	X	X		X	X	X	X	X			X		X	X	X					

[a] Updated to 10 December 2008.
[b] Does not include central bank intervention through sale of foreign exchange on currency markets.

Note: AR= Argentina
BO= Bolivia
BR= Brazil
CL= Chile
CO= Colombia
CR= Costa Rica
EC= Ecuador
SV= El Salvador
GT= Guatemala
MX= Mexico
NI= Nicaragua
PA= Panama
PY= Paraguay
PE= Peru
DO= Dominican Republic
UY= Uruguay
VE= Venezuela (Bol. Rep. of)
BS= Bahamas
JM= Jamaica
AG= Antigua and Barbuda
DM= Dominica
GD= Granada
KN= Saint Kitts and Nevis
LC= Saint Lucia
VC= Saint Vicent and the Grenadines
SR= Suriname
TT= Trinidad y Tobago

Box I.3
MEASURES RECENTLY ADOPTED BY EXTERNAL FINANCING AGENCIES

International Monetary Fund

To complement existing balance-of-payment support programmes, the International Monetary Fund (IMF) has announced the creation of a new Short-Term Liquidity Facility (SLF) for countries with access to international capital markets.

- Purpose: Create a facility to provide large upfront disbursements of short-term financing;
- Terms: Disbursements may be up to five times the country's quota in the Fund, and will have a three-month maturity. Eligible countries may draw on these lines of credit up to three times during a 12-month period;
- Eligibility: Countries with a good track record of sound policies (based on the periodic assessments conducted by the Fund) and sustainable debt burdens may qualify. The credits will be disbursed promptly and will not be subject to the procedures and conditionalities that normally apply to the Fund's other programmes.

United States Federal Reserve

The Federal Reserve has established temporary liquidity swap facilities with the central banks of Brazil, Mexico, Republic of Korea and Singapore to provide external liquidity in amounts of up to US$ 30 billion in each case.

Inter-American Development Bank

The Inter-American Development Bank (IDB) announced new quick-disbursing credits to the tune of US$ 6 billion to help countries to maintain economic growth and employment in the midst of the credit crunch.

The Liquidity Program for Growth Sustainability is designed to provide financing through intermediary banks to firms in the region that are facing transitory difficulties in accessing interbank credit lines or credit from world financial centres.

The countries that receive financing out of the Bank's ordinary financial capital can tap into the Liquidity Program. The loan amounts are determined by IDB on a case-by-case basis.

IDB also intends to speed up approval of its loans to finance projects and strengthen social programmes. The objective is to approve a record US$ 12 billion in new loans in 2009, up from about US$ 10 billion in 2008.

If the liquidity facility is fully utilized and the goal for new loan commitments is met, the financing granted in 2009 will amount to about US$ 18 billion. This would represent an 80% increase on the Bank's current financing in the region.

Andean Development Corporation

The Andean Development Corporation (CAF) recently announced the establishment of a contingency line of credit for US$ 1.5 billion.

The Corporation has also pledged to increase the lines of credit set up for the region's financial system from US$ 1.5 billion to US$ 2 billion.

These mechanisms, in conjunction with its traditional loan operations and other financing modalities, will bring total CAF loan commitments to US$ 16 billion for the period 2008-2009.

Latin American Reserve Fund

The Latin American Reserve Fund (LARF) has also offered to make available,

with immediate effect, liquidity credit lines totalling US$ 1.8 billion. The Fund could add another US$ 2.7 billion in the coming months through its contingency lines for balance-of-payments support, depending on how market conditions evolve.

The World Bank and its affiliates

The World Bank is in a position to increase its support to countries with new commitments of up to US$ 100 billion between 2009 and 2011.

The International Development Association (IDA) can provide US$ 42 billion to support countries seeking to enter the capital market and to assist countries experiencing difficulties due to falling commodity prices and weaker remittances.

Between 2009 and 2011, the group will provide support to the private sector, through the International Financial Corporation (IFC), for a total of US$ 30 billion. The initiatives envisaged are as follows:

- Doubling the Global Trade Finance Program (from $ 1.5 billion to $3 billion).
- Investing US$ 1 billion, through IFC, in the global share fund for bank recapitalization. Japan has already pledged US$ 2 billion, and other investors are expected to invest similar amounts.
- Implementing a credit line for privately funded, financially viable infrastructure projects to support them in the renewal of commitments and recapitalization in case of financial constraints.

Source: Economic Commission for Latin America and the Caribbean (ECLAC), on the basis of official information.

E. The current situation and the outlook for the future

1.   The external situation

As of late 2008, it is not yet possible to arrive at an accurate projection of the impact that the financial crisis will have on the real sector of the economy. With uncertainties spreading worldwide, the balance sheets of financial bodies are weakening owing not only to

the loss of value of mortgage guarantees but also, more generally, to the impact of the recession and the severe shortage of liquidity. The uncertainties also extend to the prospects for other major financial-market components such as insurance companies, hedge funds and pension funds, some of which have already been the object of rescue operations.

The recessionary trend is gradually worsening as a result of huge losses of financial and non-financial wealth in the private sector, most of all in the developed countries but also in emerging economies, and the steep fall in credit. The downward trend is also damaging expectations and causing sharp declines in investment and consumption.

As at the fourth quarter of 2008, there are signs that levels of activity and other real variables in the world's principal economies have been weakening considerably, thereby creating a negative feedback loop in financial markets. Macroeconomic aggregates in the United States indicate that, even though levels of economic activity did not worsen initially, growth in the first months of 2008 reflected a combination of a sharp drop in the aggregate formed by consumer durables and residential investment (-6.1%) with a strong upturn in goods and services exports (10.5%), which were stimulated by the real depreciation of the dollar up to mid-2008. This signals a progressive weakening of the domestic market which grew worse towards the end of the year.

The labour market, especially labour demand, has been very sensitive to the effects of the crisis. While in 2006-2007 new jobs created each month averaged about 133,000, between December 2007 and November 2008 nearly 170,000 jobs were lost per month; this trend worsened as the year went by, bringing the unemployment rate to 6.7% in November, its highest level since the early 1990s.

In the other developed economies, not only did the new set of conditions lead to a sharper initial slowdown than in the United States, but the financial problems were passed through to economic activity more rapidly. GDP growth rates in Japan and the euro zone amounted to a meagre 0.7% and 1.4%, respectively, in the first nine months of 2008, compared to 2.0% and 2.6% in 2007. Both recorded a GDP contraction in the second and third quarters of 2008, a clear sign that these economies had moved into recession. This was associated, first, with a downturn in export performance —as a result of real dollar depreciation in the first stage of the crisis, as noted earlier— and weakening capital formation. In a number of countries, such as Japan and Germany, the stretch of export expansion from 2003 onwards had driven a surge of investment in machinery and equipment, which lost momentum in the new conditions. In other countries, such as Ireland and Spain, rising investment in construction was associated with the real estate price boom, which began to be reversed as conditions toughened in the credit market.

The depth and duration of the recession will depend on the effectiveness of steps taken to stimulate demand and offset the slump in private spending, as well as on the normalization of credit markets. It is to be hoped that the array of measures implemented by the United States Federal Reserve and other central banks will be enough to contain systemic risk and that, in conjunction with the recovery of their financial systems and the initiatives launched from fiscal areas, the developed economies will gradually begin to rebound in the second half of 2009. This is the scenario on which the growth projections for the region for 2009 are based.

Figure I.17
UNITED STATES: UNEMPLOYMENT RATE, 1997-2008

Source: Economic Commission for Latin America and the Caribbean (ECLAC), on the basis of figures provided by the United States Bureau of Labor Statistics.

2.   Expected performance of the Latin American and Caribbean economies in 2009

As noted earlier, although the Latin American and Caribbean region is better prepared to face this crisis than previous ones, there are a number of channels through which the economies are likely to be affected.

First, the real channel —the global slowdown— has a number of aspects that do not affect all the countries the same way. Thus, the impact of financial contagion will depend on various factors and the countries of the region are exposed to it in varying degrees.

Growth of 1.9% is projected for the region in 2009. This estimate is built on a scenario in which the worst of the crisis has passed by the second half of 2009 and in which the global economy in general and the region in particular gradually begin to strengthen. This forecast is based on a comparison of average levels for 2008 and 2009 which points to a sharp slowdown and largely reflects a statistical effect.[1] A more pessimistic scenario of continuing and even deepening recession and tight credit conditions cannot be ruled out, however. In this case, obviously, the problems discussed here would worsen and the growth rate could be nil or even negative.

A breakdown by subregion shows smaller differences than those seen in earlier years. Although they all show a strong slowdown, Mexico and Central America continue to post lower growth than South America, and a very sharp downturn is projected in the growth rates of the Caribbean economies.

3.   Global and regional problems call for a concerted solution

Apart from the efforts of the region's countries to deal with the crisis and to do as much as possible to contain its impact on their economies and societies, the situation worldwide calls for coordinated solutions to give maximum leverage to whatever strategies are put in place.

In the last few years the global economy has expanded within the framework of excessive consumption in the developed countries, which has been financed by excess saving in the emerging economies. The surplus saving has largely been a result of the emerging economies' efforts to shield themselves from the impact of a potential financial crisis by building up assets. This form of "self-insurance" was an inefficient yet effective means by which many emerging economies could deal with a situation in which they found the resources and instruments made available by international financial institutions were unsatisfactory. This form of behaviour became more marked in the aftermath of the Asian crisis of 1997.

Clearly, the picture has changed substantially in the last year and half. The combination of wealth loss, credit crunch and rising unemployment will depress consumption in the developed economies and darken their performance expectations, feeding the downward spiral. So, in the near future, it will be up to the emerging economies to produce much of the demand needed to compensate for the negative stimuli in terms of world growth coming from the developed world. In this situation, self-insurance strategies are not only insufficient but are actually counterproductive, since they can do nothing to restart global growth. These strategies originated in real failures, however, which must be borne in mind in the design of a new international financial architecture.

It is therefore essential that the emerging economies are involved in planning that architecture.

It the light of this, it is obvious that the role of the emerging economies in global economic growth has not only grown in importance, but is likely to increase further. They must therefore be included in forums to discuss strategies for coordinating policies to stimulate global growth and be provided, through international bodies, with the resources to finance the implementation of anticyclical policies.

The need to coordinate policies and resources also has a regional dimension. Macroeconomic policy coordination at the regional level and the strengthening of intraregional trade and integration in the broadest sense offer opportunities to leverage the impacts of the strategies being implemented and to counteract the conditions of low GDP and world trade growth that lie ahead.

---

[1]   The reference made here to "the statistical effect" alludes to the fact that GDP figures for any given year are partially a reflection of the growth dynamics of the preceding year. When the economy is growing, as was the case in the Latin American and Caribbean region in 2008, in each quarter the (seasonally adjusted) level of output is higher than it was in the preceding one. As the annual GDP is the sum of the four quarterly GDPs (at constant prices), its growth rate represents, in approximate terms, the change in the level of activity existing midway through the year. However, as the calculations for the next year start from the level "inherited" from the fourth quarter of the previous one, even if there is no growth at all during this second year (i.e., the level of activity stays at the same (seasonally adjusted) level as it was in the fourth quarter of the previous year), the GDP growth rate for that second year will be positive.

Intraregional trade incorporates a higher level of innovation and knowledge, and it can therefore be expected to have a stronger impact on the productive fabric. It is also a form of trade in which small and medium-sized enterprises participate more actively, and it therefore offers greater potential in terms of job creation and, hence, in terms of increased equity. This type of trade is also markedly procyclical, however, and a financial support strategy will therefore be required. This, in turn, means that regional financial institutions will have an important role to play as providers of liquidity to finance these efforts.

Chapter II

Macroeconomic policy

A. Fiscal policy

In 2008, the public accounts and fiscal policies of the countries of the region were subjected to a variety of pressures. In the first half-year, the surge in inflation triggered by escalating food and energy prices tested the ability of existing fiscal instruments to deal with the impact of price rises on income distribution at the macroeconomic level. In the second half, especially from October onwards, the international crisis, its repercussions on the financial sector and the real economy and the decline in commodity prices have been shaping a new climate for the performance of public accounts and new challenges for fiscal policymakers.

At the central government level, the fiscal performance of the region's countries meant that at the end of 2008, the latter were running an average primary surplus for the region equivalent to 1.6% of GDP, compared with 2.4% in 2007; if the overall balance is taken into account (including the payment of interest on public debt) the fiscal balance moves from a surplus of 0.4% of GDP to a deficit equivalent to 0.3% of GDP.

It should be borne in mind that the fiscal data that relate only to the central government is by no means representative of some countries in the region which have more decentralized public sectors. If the figures for the most decentralized countries in the region (Argentina, Bolivia, Brazil, Colombia, Mexico and Peru) cover a wider range of government entities, including public corporations and subnational governments, then the aggregate primary surplus for 2008 in these countries (3.3% of GDP) works out to be slightly higher than in 2007 at the level of the non-financial public sector.

It should be noted that the budgets for 2009 would have been prepared in the countries of the region in the third quarter of the year and presented to the respective legislative councils in about September, the month when the crisis was just brewing; thus, projected revenues were based on higher commodity price estimates than those now being projected for 2009 and the explicit target of the measures included and projected was to mitigate the effects of the surge in inflation that was occurring at that time. In subsequent months, and as discussed in greater detail in this chapter, the governments announced a series of measures defined in order to address the current crisis.

Figure II.1
LATIN AMERICA AND THE CARIBBEAN: CENTRAL GOVERNMENT FISCAL INDICATORS
(Percentages of GDP at current prices)

Source: Economic Commission for Latin America and the Caribbean (ECLAC), on the basis of official figures.

Table II.1
LATIN AMERICA AND THE CARIBBEAN: CENTRAL GOVERNMENT FISCAL INDICATORS [a]
(Percentages of GDP at current prices)

| | Primary balance | | | | | Overall balance | | | | | Public debt [b] | | | | | | | | | |
| | | | | | | | | | | | Central government | | | | | Non-financial public sector | | | | |
	2004	2005	2006	2007	2008[c]	2004	2005	2006	2007	2008[c]	2004	2005	2006	2007	2008	2004	2005	2006	2007	2008
Latin America and the Caribbean[d]	0.6	1.4	2.3	2.4	1.6	-1.9	-1.1	0.1	0.4	-0.3	51.1	43.0	36.0	30.3	26.1	55.3	47.6	39.9	33.0	28.6
Argentina	3.2	2.3	2.7	2.7	3.2	2.0	0.4	1.0	0.6	1.0	126.4	72.8	63.6	55.7	48.0	143.3	87.6	76.3	66.6	58.9
Bolivia[a]	-3.1	0.3	5.2	3.5	4.3	-5.7	-2.3	3.4	2.3	3.0	81.1	75.6	49.8	37.1	30.7	83.9	78.3	52.6	40.0	33.0
Brazil	2.6	2.5	2.1	2.3	2.2	-1.9	-3.6	-2.9	-2.0	-2.6	31.0	30.9	31.7	32.7	30.1	49.3	46.7	46.0	46.1	42.6
Chile	3.1	5.4	8.4	9.4	7.1	2.1	4.6	7.7	8.8	6.9	10.7	7.3	5.3	4.1	3.5	16.8	13.0	10.6	9.1	7.4
Colombia	-1.6	-1.5	-0.1	0.8	0.4	-5.0	-4.5	-3.8	-3.0	-2.7	40.0	39.6	38.1	35.2	33.2	42.4	38.9	36.5	32.6	28.9
Costa Rica	1.4	2.0	2.7	3.7	1.8	-2.7	-2.1	-1.1	0.6	-0.5	41.0	37.6	33.3	27.7	23.5	46.9	43.0	38.4	32.0	27.3
Ecuador	1.5	1.8	2.1	1.9	1.9	-1.0	-0.5	-0.2	-0.1	-0.1	40.8	35.9	29.7	27.5	22.6	43.7	38.6	32.3	30.0	24.7
El Salvador	0.9	1.1	2.0	2.2	1.8	-1.1	-1.0	-0.4	-0.2	-0.6	38.1	37.6	37.5	34.5	31.2	40.8	40.6	39.6	36.5	33.1
Guatemala	0.3	-0.3	-0.6	0.0	0.3	-1.1	-1.7	-1.9	-1.5	-1.2	21.4	20.8	21.7	21.7	19.3	22.4	21.5	21.9	21.9	19.5
Haiti	-2.4	0.4	1.1	-1.2	-1.8	-3.1	-0.6	0.3	-1.6	-2.1	46.7	44.1	35.6	32.2	29.4	51.1	47.5	38.1	34.4	35.0
Honduras	-1.5	-1.1	-0.1	-2.2	-1.2	-2.6	-2.2	-1.1	-2.9	-1.9	59.6	44.7	28.9	17.4	17.4	59.4	44.8	30.2	18.3	17.3
Mexico[f]	1.7	1.9	2.1	1.9	2.0	-0.2	-0.1	0.1	0.0	0.0	20.8	20.3	20.7	21.1	20.4	24.2	23.0	22.7	23.0	22.6
Nicaragua	-0.1	0.1	1.8	2.1	0.3	-2.2	-1.8	0.0	0.6	-0.8	100.6	92.6	68.7	42.2	34.6	100.7	92.8	69.1	43.0	35.4
Panama	-1.2	0.5	4.4	4.7	2.5	-5.4	-3.9	0.2	1.2	-1.0	69.6	65.1	60.3	53.2	46.6	70.4	66.2	61.0	53.7	47.1
Paraguay	2.7	2.0	1.5	1.8	1.2	1.6	0.8	0.5	1.0	0.5	38.0	31.4	23.8	17.3	12.1	41.7	32.8	24.8	20.3	14.2
Peru	0.6	1.1	3.2	3.4	3.9	-1.3	-0.7	1.5	1.8	2.3	41.7	38.2	31.2	27.2	22.8	41.7	38.2	31.2	27.2	22.8
Dominican Republic	-1.6	0.7	0.3	1.8	-2.0	-3.4	-0.6	-1.1	0.6	-3.2	...	22.0	20.4	18.4	16.7	...	...	...	19.0	17.4
Uruguay	2.4	2.8	3.3	2.2	2.8	-2.5	-1.6	-1.0	-1.7	-1.0	74.6	67.1	59.3	50.7	39.9	78.9	70.4	62.7	54.0	42.8
Venezuela (Bol. Rep. of)	1.8	4.6	2.1	4.5	-0.5	-1.9	1.6	0.0	3.0	-1.8	38.1	32.8	23.9	19.3	14.0	38.1	32.8	23.9	19.3	14.0

Source: Economic Commission for Latin America and the Caribbean (ECLAC), on the basis of official figures.
[a] Includes social security.
[b] As at 31 December of each year, applying the average exchange rate for external debt. The 2008 figures relate to balances of June of that year.
[c] Official targets set in the 2009 budget.
[d] Simple average.
[e] General government.
[f] Public sector.

As ECLAC has stressed on several occasions, while the public accounts and fiscal policy of the region's countries currently show definite improvements compared with previous periods, recent evidence suggests that this situation will not last much longer. The improvement in the fiscal situation may be attributed mainly to the sharp increase in commodity prices between 2002 and the first half of 2008; the sudden fall in these prices could therefore have implications for the fiscal space achieved. Certain estimates of the impact of the business cycle (output and commodity prices) on public accounts, which were presented in detail in the *Economic Survey of Latin America and the Caribbean, 2007-2008*, suggest that the structural fiscal balance of the region's countries is not, on average, as positive as the observed fiscal balance.[1] This is true of the region as a whole, but is particularly evident in the case of the raw-material exporting countries, where the gap between the structural fiscal balance and the observed fiscal balance observed widened substantially in 2007 and in the first half of 2008. While it is difficult to make projections, according to the estimate in box II.1, the fiscal position estimated for 2009 suggests that a significant portion of the revenues collected in 2007-2008 would have been non-recurring revenue and therefore, difficult to sustain in the future.[2]

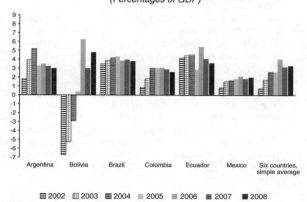

Figure II.2
LATIN AMERICA (6 COUNTRIES): PRIMARY BALANCE OF THE NON-FINANCIAL PUBLIC SECTOR, 2002-2008
(Percentages of GDP)

⊞ 2002 ▦ 2003 ■ 2004 ▨ 2005 ■ 2006 ▤ 2007 ■ 2008

Source: Economic Commission for Latin America and the Caribbean (ECLAC) on the basis of official data.

Figure II.3
LATIN AMERICA AND THE CARIBBEAN: FISCAL PRIMARY BALANCE AND PUBLIC DEBT BALANCE IN TERMS OF GDP, 2002 AND AVERAGE 2007-2008
(Percentage-point variation of GDP)

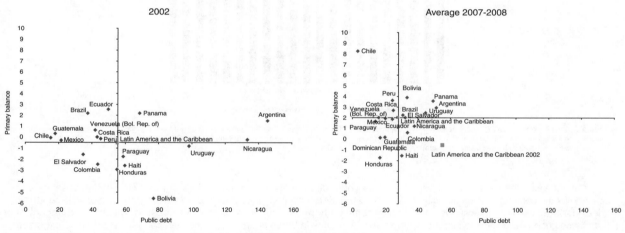

Source: Economic Commission for Latin America and the Caribbean (ECLAC), on the basis of official figures.

The high volatility of economic variables in recent months and the unpredictability of their future movements make it imperative to assess the capacity of the region's governments to respond to these challenges. The two four-quadrant figures shown above present the levels for 2002 and the average for 2007-2008 of the fiscal result and the public debt balance, both in GDP terms.

If the information on the central government primary balance is taken in conjunction with the level of public debt, the public-finance position of the countries may be placed in four categories represented by the four quadrants.

---

[1] For further details on the measurement of cyclically adjusted balances, see Economic Commission for Latin America and the Caribbean (ECLAC), *Economic Survey of Latin America and the Caribbean, 2007-2008* (LC/G.2386-P/E), Santiago, Chile, August 2008. United Nations publication, Sales No. E.08.II.G.2.

[2] See box II.1 for an estimate of the fiscal impact of the fall in revenue derived from natural resources in 2009.

Box II.1

THE IMPACT OF THE FALL IN COMMODITY PRICES ON THE FISCAL RESOURCES OF THE COUNTRIES OF LATIN AMERICA

Several countries of the region earn significant fiscal revenues from their commodity industries. For example, in countries, such as the Bolivarian Republic of Venezuela, Ecuador and Mexico, 30% or more of total revenues comes from oil production, while Bolivia derives the same percentage of revenues from gas exploitation. Argentina, Chile, Colombia and Peru also receive substantial revenues from the exploitation of their natural resources, in these cases to the tune of 18% on average.

In these cases, revenues have become very unreliable since oil, gas, copper and food prices have been extremely volatile in recent months. A look at the pattern of fiscal inflows in the eight countries referred to above shows that income from the exploitation of these types of resources is much more volatile than revenue generated from other sources.

This edition of the Preliminary Overview contains a simulation exercise designed to estimate the impact that the sharp contraction in international commodity prices would have on public finances in the countries of the region.[a]

The simulation carried out for the baseline scenario for 2009 shows that the fall in commodity prices would cause fiscal revenue in the eight countries mentioned above to fall by 2.4 percentage points of GDP on average, compared with the estimated figure for 2008. In this way, total revenue of the group of countries whose economies are specialized in commodities would fall from 24.7% of GDP in 2008 to 22.3% in 2009.

LATIN AMERICA: REVENUES OF COUNTRIES WITH COMMODITY-BASED ECONOMIES
(Percentages of GDP)

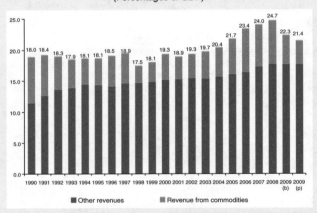

Source: Economic Commission for Latin America and the Caribbean (ECLAC), on the basis of official figures up to 2008 and own projections for 2009.
Note: The figures for 2009 (b) correspond to the baseline scenario and those for 2009 (p) to a more pessimistic scenario (assuming a further 20% drop in commodity prices compared with the baseline scenario).

Nevertheless, the more pessimistic scenario for the contraction in commodity prices in 2009 suggests that fiscal revenue from these goods will decline to just over half the amount collected in 2008. Under this scenario, fiscal revenue from commodities would move from an average of 7.0% of GDP in 2008 to 3.8% in 2009.

This contraction in fiscal revenue is due to the differential impact that falling commodity prices will have on the public accounts in these countries, as observed in the following figure. In terms of GDP, the declines are forecast to be particularly sharp in the Bolivarian Republic of Venezuela, Bolivia and

Ecuador and will vary between 4% and 6% of GDP in the projected scenarios. In the case of Mexico, the impact of the reduction in oil prices is expected to be slightly lower given that the loss of revenue should be between 3% and 4% of GDP.[b]

Box II.1 (continued)

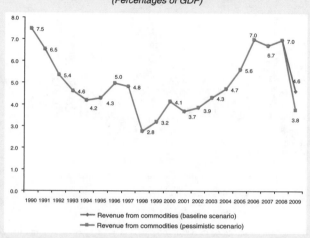

LATIN AMERICA: REVENUE FROM COMMODITY PRODUCTION
(Percentages of GDP)

Source: Economic Commission for Latin America and the Caribbean (ECLAC), on the basis of official figures up to 2008 and own projections for 2009.
Note: The pessimistic scenario takes into account a further 20% fall in commodity prices compared with the baseline scenario.

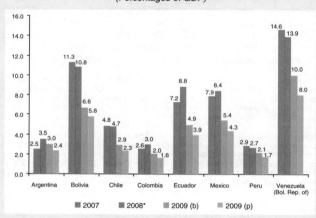

LATIN AMERICA (8 COUNTRIES): FISCAL REVENUE FROM THE PRODUCTION OF COMMODITIES
(Percentages of GDP)

Source: Economic Commission for Latin America and the Caribbean (ECLAC), on the basis of official figures up to 2008 and own projections for 2009.
Note: The figures for 2008 are preliminary estimates; those for 2009 (b) relate to the baseline scenario and those for 2009 (p) to a more pessimistic scenario (a further 20% fall in commodity prices compared with the baseline scenario).

In Chile, the outcome of the simulation exercise is a contraction in the revenue from copper production from 4.7% of GDP to between 2.9% and 2.3% of GDP under the given scenarios. In the case of Colombia, oil revenue will be between 1 percentage point and 1.4 percentage points below the 2008 level.

The downturn in commodity prices in 2009 will have less of an impact in Argentina and Peru than elsewhere in the region, since the revenue generated by commodities in these two countries, both

as a percentage of total fiscal revenue and as a percentage of GDP, is less significant. Under the baseline scenario, the contraction in revenue will be half a percentage point of GDP, while, under the more pessimistic scenario, based on a further 20% decline in prices, the contraction could be equivalent to one percentage point. Nevertheless, one of the measures announced recently by the Argentine authorities contemplates a 5-percentage-point reduction in the rate of tax on exports of wheat and maize,

which could reduce tax revenue from these sources.[c]

Lastly, it is of interest to analyse the fiscal impact of this fall on average public accounts, with countries grouped according to whether their economies are commodity-based or not. This impact on the regional total is very significant, as shown in the figure below, where the region's average primary surplus varies between 0.5% and 0.2% of GDP in 2009, depending on the scenario contemplated.

Box II.1 (concluded)

LATIN AMERICA AND THE CARIBBEAN: PRIMARY BALANCE IN COMMODITY- AND NON-COMMODITY-PRODUCING COUNTRIES
(Percentages of GDP)

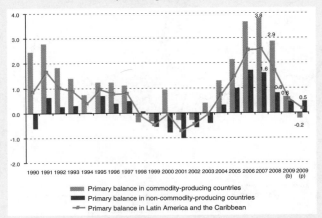

Primary balance in commodity-producing countries
Primary balance in non-commodity-producing countries
Primary balance in Latin America and the Caribbean

Source: Economic Commission for Latin America and the Caribbean (ECLAC), on the basis of official figures to 2008 and own projections for 2009.
Note: The figures for 2009 (b) correspond to the baseline scenario and those for 2009 (p) to a more pessimistic scenario (a further 20% fall in commodity prices compared with the baseline scenario).

The fiscal account situation of commodity-producing countries will undoubtedly be more worrying. Under the baseline scenario, the average primary balance would increase from a surplus equivalent to 2.9% of GDP in 2008 to one equivalent to 0.6% of GDP in 2009, while if there were a further 20% drop in commodity prices, the result would be a primary deficit of the order of 0.2% of GDP. Nevertheless, Argentina, Chile and Peru would continue to record primary surpluses under both scenarios.

This exercise confirms the need to ensure that the sustainability of fiscal accounts in the countries of the region is based on revenues that are more reliable and less exposed to business-cycle variations. In this context, it is fundamental to strengthen taxation systems, and to provide for efforts in terms of both policy and tax administration.

a In estimating fiscal revenues based on the production of commodities, international price forecasts for 2009 have been taken into account as well as nominal exchange rates. The other types of revenue were estimated depending on nominal GDP forecasts prepared by ECLAC for 2009. In terms of projections of levels of expenditure, official information contained in the respective budgets has been used. In general, the government figures refer to the central government, except in the case of Bolivia, where it relates to general government and for Ecuador and Mexico, where the data relate to the non-financial public sector. Two scenarios have been studied: a baseline scenario based on the above hypotheses and another pessimistic scenario, based on the assumption that commodity prices will fall by a further 20% compared with the baseline scenario.
b Nevertheless, the government of this country has obtained forward contracts at US$ 70 per barrel as a hedge against fluctuations in oil prices (the cost of these hedges was US$ 15 billion pesos, which will cater for 90% of its exports); this could help to attenuate the fall in income estimated in this simulation. Furthermore, according to information from the government, it will be possible to draw on the stabilization fund.
c The reduction in the export levy on wheat and maize will bring the rate on wheat down from the current level of 28% to 23% and on maize from 25% to 20%. In addition, the "Trigo Plus" and "Maíz Plus" programmes are expected to start to function, which will mean, in the case of both of these grains, a one-percentage-point decrease in the tax rate on each additional million tons of production over the average for the past few years.

As shown in the figure, practically all the countries of the region recorded a positive variation in their primary balance and the average for the region for 2007-2008 moves from a deficit equivalent to 0.5% of GDP to a surplus equivalent to 2.0% of GDP. Nevertheless, as already mentioned, the revenue derived from taxes on exports accounts for a large proportion of this increase, so that a change in price trends without a corresponding modification in expenditure could seriously erode this primary surplus.

Since the beginning of the price-boom cycle, one of the most controversial issues has been the way in which fiscal authorities have used non-recurring receipts. The reactions have been diverse. Several countries reduced their external public debt, the central banks increased their reserves and set up special funds both at home and abroad to which part of the surplus was credited. The foregoing figure also shows a change in the central government debt/GDP ratio between 2002, the year just before commodity prices started to soar and the average for 2007-2008. As can be seen, the vast majority of countries reduced their debt/GDP ratio between those two years, thanks to liability restructuring, the generation of primary surpluses, debt relief under the Heavily Indebted Poor Countries Initiative and the impact of growth during this period. Some fiscal space was created initially in such cases, to deal with a possible deterioration in the external situation. Nevertheless, in some countries, the procyclical mechanisms applied in administering public revenue and expenditure have at times resulted in significant expansions that would be unsustainable in a context where prices on international markets are less buoyant. Fiscal authorities that were in fact able to create fiscal space will clearly be in a better position to deal with the impact of the external turmoil while maintaining sustainable fiscal accounts in the medium term. Those that were not able to do so will have less margin for manoeuvre and will find it more difficult to face the different fiscal-policy challenges.

This analysis reveals that the countries that did not benefit from the commodity price cycle, which have low tax burdens and high levels of poverty will be those facing the most serious problems in coping with the worsening international situation.

The main feature of the fiscal upturn of recent years was the remarkable increase in fiscal revenues which raised average government funds in the region to record high levels. Tax receipts swelled from approximately 15% of GDP for the 1990-1995 average to approximately 20% of GDP in the past two years.

A large percentage of this increase is attributable to tax revenue deriving from the exploitation of natural resources. In the Bolivarian Republic of Venezuela, Bolivia, Ecuador and Mexico, these revenues account for more than 30% of tax funds while in Argentina, Chile, Colombia and Peru, they account for approximately 18%. Various ECLAC studies demonstrate that revenue from natural resource exploitation is much more volatile than income from other sources, as the past few months have proved. As shown in box II.1, which presents different commodity price forecasts for 2009, revenue from these resources for the eight countries listed is expected to drop by around 2.4 percentage points of GDP, in the moderate scenario and by 3.2 percentage points in a scenario based on steeper price falls.

Some countries did, nevertheless, continue to benefit from strong prices for their export products in 2008. Ecuador received considerably higher oil tax revenue thanks to the efforts undertaken in late 2007 to receive a major percentage of oil earnings. This was partially due to tax reform by virtue of which the proceeds of the former oil funds were apportioned to the central government budget. The Bolivarian Republic of Venezuela also took advantage of this trend to obtain a significant increase in oil royalties and passed a special tax law on exceptionally high prices on the international hydrocarbon market, which enables the government to capture additional resources whenever the oil price exceeds US$ 70.

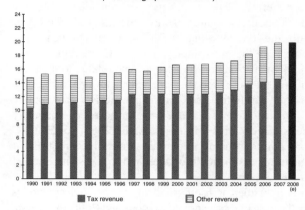

Figure II.4
LATIN AMERICA AND THE CARIBBEAN: TRENDS IN CENTRAL GOVERNMENT FISCAL REVENUE, 1990-2008
(Percentage points of GDP)

■ Tax revenue   ▦ Other revenue

Source: Economic Commission for Latin America and the Caribbean (ECLAC), on the basis of official figures.

Some countries have modified their legislation in order to increase the funds in their coffers. For example, the amendment in Paraguay of the personal income tax, which will take effect in 2009; the income tax reform in Guatemala in 2009; and the single-rate corporate tax of Mexico, which entered into force in 2008. In El Salvador, Honduras and Nicaragua, the application of the Anti-evasion Act averted a sharper decrease in fiscal revenue, while in Costa Rica, tax evasion has been curbed.

Other countries, on the other hand, saw their revenue wane with the decline in commodity export prices. Peru, whose exports were the first to experience a decline, sustained a sharp slowdown in the receipts from some taxes compared with increases in previous years.

The increase in food and energy prices forced the government to adopt fiscal policy instruments to mitigate the impact on the poorest segments of the population. On the income side, these took the form of exemptions, rebates (or the implementation of differential rates) in general value added type taxes (as in the case of the Bolivarian Republic of Venezuela, El Salvador and Peru) or the reduction of import duties (such as those applied to grains, flours and meal by Brazil, El Salvador, Guatemala, Honduras, Nicaragua and Peru). In Panama, one of the measures adopted under the agricultural-sector support plan was tax exemption for low-income households. The Honduras authorities raised the tax-exempt base from 70,000 lempiras to 130,000 lempiras. Nicaragua reduced or temporarily suspended import tariffs for a variety of products including fuel oil, beans, pastas and barley.

On the expenditure side, the region's changing macroeconomic situation has had a marked impact. Transfers and subsidies were the most common response to the effect of price increases on consumption by the population. As regards energy products, the granting of subsidies on fuel consumption was related to the pricing policy; in the most important cases in the region, their implementation does not seem to be related to the price boom that these products experienced towards the middle of the year. In this case, Argentina, Bolivarian Republic of Venezuela, Bolivia and Ecuador have systematically subsidized petrol consumers since 2005. As ECLAC has pointed out on numerous occasions, this type of instrument is difficult to target and to assess in terms of its fiscal cost.[3]

Subsidies on food products are also widespread, as in the case of those applied to foods and flours in Bolivia, Costa Rica (where the fiscal cost has increased to more than 0.5% of GDP since 2006), Dominican Republic, Ecuador and Nicaragua. Nevertheless, some of these subsidies are implicitly targeted, because they apply to products that are consumed primarily by the poorest segments of the population.

The advantage of targeted subsidy programmes is that they reach the relatively low-income population much more efficiently and effectively than tax rebates and general subsidies. To be implemented, however, they require careful planning and a considerable administrative and institutional capability, which is not always available in the countries where this type of measure is most needed. Putting such programmes into practice may call for a lengthy preparation and design, and relief in the emergency situation may thus be delayed.

Increase in expenditure may also take the form of higher public investment, especially in infrastructure. Mexico, Costa Rica and Ecuador doubled their gross fixed capital investment in 2008. Nicaragua invested heavily in infrastructure rehabilitation in the wake of Hurricane Felix and the rains that battered the north-east of the country, while Peru has continued a policy of reviving public investment.

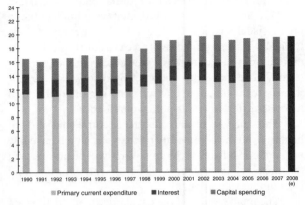

Figure II.5
LATIN AMERICA AND THE CARIBBEAN: COMPOSITION OF CENTRAL GOVERNMENT FISCAL SPENDING, 1990-2008
(Percentage points of GDP)

Source: Economic Commission for Latin America and the Caribbean (ECLAC), on the basis of official figures.

As shown in figure II.6, the balance of public debt in terms of GDP diminished slightly with respect to the previous year. While some countries, such as Ecuador and Peru reduced their debt (through prepayments to the Andean Development Corporation (CAF) and Brady bond redemptions), others such as Honduras and Guatemala saw their position undermined by the global economic situation, and, more than ever, are actively seeking sources of financing to be able to cope in 2009. The Government of Honduras signed a stand-by agreement with IMF and is applying for various soft credit lines from the Bolivarian Republic of Venezuela, the Central American Bank for Economic Integration (CABEI) and the Inter-American Development Bank (IDB).

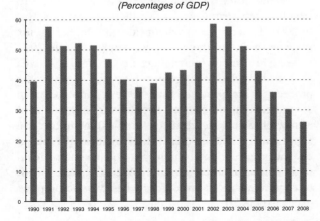

Figure II.6
LATIN AMERICA AND THE CARIBBEAN: CENTRAL GOVERNMENT PUBLIC DEBT
(Percentages of GDP)

Source: Economic Commission for Latin America and the Caribbean (ECLAC), on the basis of official figures.

---

[3]   For further information, see Luis Felipe Jiménez, Juan Pablo Jiménez and Osvaldo Kacef, "Efectos macroeconómicos y respuestas de política ante la volatilidad de los precios de bienes energéticos y alimentarios en América Latina y el Caribe", *Macroeconomía del desarrollo series*, No. 68 (LC/L.2965-P), Santiago, Chile, Economic Commission for Latin America and the Caribbean (ECLAC), at press.

As stated in previous editions, the countries of the region, improved their fiscal accounts in recent years. This, together with strong growth in GDP, has enabled most of them to reduce their debt/GDP ratios and, in some cases, to build up assets in the form of sovereign funds. In such cases the public sector's borrowing requirements will be lower once there is a certain degree of fiscal space for a possible countercyclical policy.

In other cases, the fiscal space created in recent years is less, so that now with external financing tighter, there may be constraints that point to the need to keep a lid on spending. The reduction in external debt during the previous years suggests that the effects of this state of international financial markets will not be as serious for government budgets and fiscal and social policies as they have been in past crises.

Each country's capacity to exercise a countercyclical public action is linked, among other factors, to the fiscal spaces attained. These different capacities depend on how periods of high public revenue, due, in many cases, to the export price boom of recent years, is dealt with. The reversal in prices in recent months proves that over the long term public revenue cannot be reliant just on the improvement in these inflows. Public finance must be sustainable over time; if not, it will be impossible to create sufficient fiscal space to support a countercyclical fiscal policy.

The purely accounting dimension of public finances, which is expressed in terms of the fiscal position or of the public debt balance, is not sufficient to guarantee the sustainability of public finances unless the contributions made by the various groups are in keeping with the notion of equity and the results of the public action are able to meet the growing demand for security, social protection, education, health care and the environment and social capital formation and infrastructure in general that is characteristic of the process of economic development.

The fiscal covenant advocated by ECLAC refers, precisely, to the need to harmonize the growing demand for public goods and services, normally associated with growth and development, and the contributions or sacrifices in terms of income that the different groups participating in a social agreement must be prepared to make. The current situation has once again brought to the fore the need to secure a sustainable covenant. In some cases, this is because, despite the sound fiscal position achieved in recent years, it is feared that public finances may not be sustainable in the long term, insofar as the social demands for public goods or socially provided goods have mounted along with the rise in income levels, but tax burdens have not evolved accordingly and their structure is not perceived to be equitable.

In other cases, in particular in those countries that have faced a deterioration in their terms of trade and displayed a high poverty incidence, the debate has resurfaced inasmuch as the consequences of the tense global economic situation have proven that the public sector in these countries is not robust enough to provide for the needs of the people, not only because of institutional deficiencies, but also on account of the very low tax burdens.

B. Exchange-rate policy

As the international financial crisis emerged in mid-2008, there was a change in the regional trend of real effective exchange-rate appreciation observed during 2006 and 2007. Although the extraregional real effective exchange rate of Latin America and the Caribbean (which excludes trade between the countries in the region) continued to appreciate in the first eight months of 2008, in September and October several South American countries and Mexico experienced a significant effective depreciation that caused the regional aggregate to depreciate. Compared with the same period in 2007, the average appreciation in the first 10 months of 2008 was 6.2%, with effective appreciations in 19 countries. Although both South America and the aggregate for Central America, Mexico and the Caribbean recorded effective appreciations in relation to the rest of the world, appreciation was 8.7% for the former and 3.8% for the latter. However, what these 2008 averages do not reveal is that, from August 2008, the extraregional real effective exchange rate of several South American countries and Mexico depreciated rapidly in line with the international financial crisis (see figure II.7).

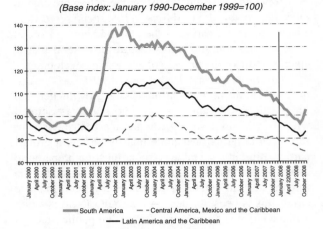

Figure II.7

LATIN AMERICA AND THE CARIBBEAN: EXTRAREGIONAL REAL EFFECTIVE EXCHANGE RATE

(Base index: January 1990-December 1999=100)

——— South America   – – Central America, Mexico and the Caribbean
——— Latin America and the Caribbean

Source: Economic Commission for Latin America and the Caribbean (ECLAC), on the basis of official figures.

The first period lasted until mid-2007. In this time, the context was extremely favourable for the region in terms of the prices of commodities exported by South America and good external financing conditions (as indicated by improved country risk ratings in the region) that facilitated inflows of capital and foreign direct investment (FDI) to some South American countries. Both factors contributed to nominal currency appreciation in several South American countries, in a context of relatively low inflation (except in the Bolivarian Republic of Venezuela). In Central America, countries received a high and growing level of income from emigrant remittances during this time. Generally speaking the real effective exchange rate in the region tended to appreciate throughout the period.

Exchange-rate trends in Latin America and the Caribbean between 2007 and 2008 can be roughly divided into three periods.

The second period runs from the end of the second quarter of 2007 to the second quarter of 2008. During this time, international food and energy prices soared, which in turn resulted in an inflationary shock in all of the region's economies. The rise in inflation was more keenly felt in countries with a high energy and food component in their price indices (such as in Central America), and led to a rapid real currency appreciation in those same countries. At the same time as the inflationary shock, the central banks of many of the region's countries raised interest rates during the period in question (as described in the section on monetary policy).

During the period, international capital markets were also increasingly concerned about the slowdown in the United States, which was partly the result of problems in that country's financial sector. The problems, which

originally occurred as part of the crisis in the subprime mortgage market, were transmitted to other parts of the financial sector, resulting in huge losses. Amidst the slowdown in the United States and the constant growth of emerging economies, as well as rising prices for the products exported by South America, some countries of this subregion continued to receive external resources through the financial account surplus of the balance of payments, in the form of both FDI and portfolio investment. This resulted in nominal currency appreciation in those South American countries. The countries that received significant resources and experienced nominal currency appreciation during the period include Brazil, Colombia and Peru. In some Central American countries (such as El Salvador, Guatemala and Honduras), the cooling of the United States economy heralded a slowdown in emigrant remittances.

Also during the second period, the central banks of several South American countries responded to currency pressure by attempting to build up international reserves. Regardless of why central banks ultimately increased reserves —whether it was as a precaution against possible future reverses in the prices of the country's commodity exports, to moderate exchange-rate volatility in order to stabilize the rate around the trend rate, or to communicate to the markets what they perceived as a currency misalignment— volumes of international reserves certainly did increase in Brazil, Colombia and Peru. In Brazil and Colombia, however, the central banks intervened less in the foreign exchange market during this period than in the first half of 2007. In early 2008, the Peruvian monetary authorities adopted a series of measures aimed at moderating domestic demand without causing exchange-rate appreciation. The measures included increasing the legal reserve requirement on accounts in dollars, introducing new sterilization instruments (certificates of deposit with restricted negotiation issued by the Central Reserve Bank of Peru (BCRP)), charging a commission on the transfer of ownership of BCRP certificates, raising the minimum reserve and increasing the non-yield-bearing reserve on bonds in soles held by non-resident financial institutions. In this period, Chile then Peru increased the percentage of pension funds run by pension fund management companies that can be invested abroad.

The third period can be identified as beginning in the third quarter of 2008, when international financial turmoil was triggered by problems that had begun in 2007 with the subprime mortgage crisis in the United States. The crisis of confidence really took hold from early September 2008. Since then, exchange-rate patterns in the region have varied considerably. On the one hand, several South American countries and Mexico saw a rapid nominal depreciation of their currencies in relation to the United States dollar between September and November 2008. From August 2008, depreciations were particularly significant in countries with a higher level of integration in international capital markets, such as Brazil (40.5%), Mexico (29.6%), Colombia (25.7%) and Chile (25.5%). Central American and Caribbean countries, on the other hand, posted extremely slight depreciations (in contrast to what happened in South America).

These exchange-rate movements coincided with a change in the approach adopted by several central banks in South America compared with the previous period, in terms of their interventions on the foreign-exchange market. Countries that had previously accumulated high levels of reserves, intervened in foreign-exchange markets by selling off reserves in September and October 2008. Examples include Argentina, Brazil, Paraguay, Peru and Uruguay (as shown in figures II.8, II.9 and II.10). In addition to foreign-exchange interventions (spot, repo and using derivatives), several countries also introduced measures to reduce the demand for foreign exchange and increase the supply thereof on the local market. For instance, the central banks of Brazil and Mexico set up a currency swap line of US$ 30 billion with the United States Federal Reserve. The central bank of Chile reintroduced currency swap auctions to increase liquidity in foreign currency. The Ministry of Finance of Brazil eliminated the 1.5% rate on exchange operations for incoming foreign capital and the 0.38% rate on foreign-currency loans. In Argentina, measures adopted by the authorities included a limit on the amount of United States dollars sold to individuals to US$ 2 million and a reduction by the central bank of the maximum time allowed to exporters before they have to deposit dollars obtained in the financial sector. In Peru, the Government removed the reserve requirement for long-term loans from abroad.

Figure II.8
ARGENTINA AND BRAZIL: PURCHASES AND SALES OF FOREIGN EXCHANGE BY THE CENTRAL BANK
(Percentages of annual GDP)

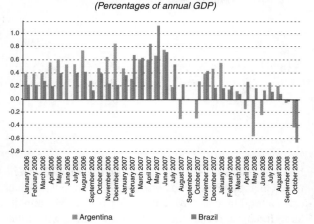

Source: Economic Commission for Latin America and the Caribbean (ECLAC), on the basis of figures provided by the central banks of Argentina and Brazil.

Figure II.9
COLOMBIA AND PERU: PURCHASES AND SALES OF FOREIGN EXCHANGE BY THE CENTRAL BANK
(Percentages of annual GDP)

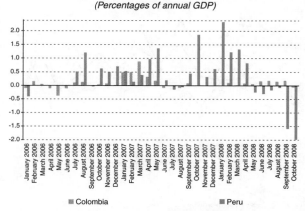

Source: Economic Commission for Latin America and the Caribbean (ECLAC), on the basis of figures provided by the central banks of Colombia and Peru.

Figure II.10
PARAGUAY AND URUGUAY: PURCHASES AND SALES OF FOREIGN EXCHANGE BY THE CENTRAL BANK
(Percentages of annual GDP)

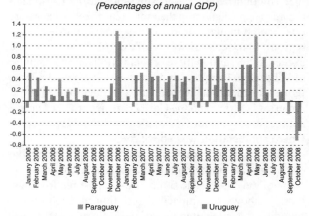

Source: Economic Commission for Latin America and the Caribbean (ECLAC), on the basis of figures provided by the central banks of Paraguay and Uruguay.

In the third period, the slowdown in emigrant remittances that had begun in late 2007 continued in Central American countries and in some South American countries such as Ecuador. Slower growth in the United States and the financial crisis have affected remittances to Mexico as well as to Central American countries. This is because many of the emigrants from the region were employed in sectors that have been seriously affected by the financial crisis, such as construction. For South American countries with high numbers of emigrants, the effect that the slowdown in the United States had on growth in remittances was compounded by increased unemployment in Spain and slower growth in other European economies. Figure II.11 shows the growth rates of emigrant remittances in the period 2007-2008.

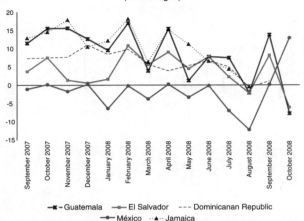

Figure II.11
EMIGRANT REMITTANCES: 12-MONTH RATE OF VARIATION
(Percentages)

━■━ Guatemala ━●━ El Salvador - - - Dominicanan Republic
━●━ México ···▲··· Jamaica

Source: Economic Commission for Latin America and the Caribbean (ECLAC), on the basis of figures provided by the central banks of the respective countries.

A comparison of averages from 2008 and 2007 shows that 16 countries of Latin America and the Caribbean recorded appreciations in their total real effective exchange rate (which includes trade between the countries in the region). In the case of six out of the 16, the appreciation exceeded 5%, and in three of them (Bolivarian Republic of Venezuela, Paraguay and Uruguay), it reached double figures. In addition, eight countries of the group "Central America, Mexico and the Caribbean" recorded effective appreciations, although Jamaica was the only country where appreciation was above 5%.

Figure II.12 compares the total real effective exchange rate in the region's countries compared with those of the 1990s. The figure illustrates three findings. First, it shows the impact of inflation in 2008 on the real effective exchange rate of the Bolivarian Republic of Venezuela, Guatemala and Honduras. All three

countries had below-average effective exchange rates in the 1990s. The Bolivarian Republic of Venezuela and Honduras had *de facto* fixed regimes in relation the United States dollar during that time. Second, in Bolivia, inflation in 2008 and depreciation in its trading partners from September 2008 caused a strong appreciation in the effective exchange rate, although the rate remains 10% lower than the level observed in the 1990s. The situation was similar in Ecuador, which adopted the United States dollar as its currency in 2000. Third, Brazil, Chile and Mexico went from having exchange rates below the reference period in July 2008 to exchange rates above those levels in October 2008. Colombia also experienced a significant depreciation of its total real effective exchange rate in relation to July as a result of the rapid nominal depreciation of its currency, as did Brazil, Chile and Mexico.

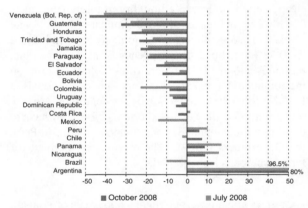

Figure II.12
**LATIN AMERICA AND THE CARIBBEAN (20 COUNTRIES):
TOTAL REAL EFFECTIVE EXCHANGE RATE**
(Levels in July 2008 and October 2008 compared with the 1990-1999 average)

■ October 2008 ■ July 2008

Source: Economic Commission for Latin America and the Caribbean (ECLAC), on the basis of official figures.

C. Monetary policy

Between January 2007 and October 2008, the central banks of most of the countries of the region raised their monetary-policy interest rates to attenuate the second-round effects of rising food and fuel prices on world markets. In Colombia, for example, it was raised from 9.5% to 10% in two steps, and in Chile it was increased five times,

bringing it up from 6% to 8.25%. In Peru the authorities raised their monetary policy rate on six occasions, adding up to a total increase from 5% to 6.5%; both Guatemala and Honduras raised their rates four times, with total increases from 6.25% to 7.25% and from 7.5% to 9%, respectively. Costa Rica posted the largest increase in the course of 2008, from 6% to 10.87%, while in Brazil the nominal SELIC rate was raised for the first time in three years, from 11.18% to 12.92%.[4]

In the second half of 2008 the situation facing the central banks of Latin America and the Caribbean was characterized by increasing uncertainty and liquidity problems in world markets and by considerable falls in commodity prices. The growing lack of confidence worldwide as a result of the financial crisis has affected the region's economies, resulting in stronger preference for foreign-exchange assets which in turn led to nominal exchange-rate depreciations from September onwards. Faced with this new situation, central banks are awaiting further developments while providing liquidity to financial systems in order to keep credit markets afloat. The measures taken include cuts in reserve requirements, shortening of payment periods or the suspension of operations to reduce liquidity, and creation or expansion of special lines of credit for discount and repurchase operations.

Measures taken by the region's central banks include the following:

- In early October, the Central Bank of Paraguay reduced the legal reserve requirement for domestic- and foreign-currency deposits, made a one-point cut in the curve of the base lending rate for monetary regulation instruments and set up a liquidity facility for local financial entities, known as the Short-term Liquidity Facility with Repurchase of Monetary Regulation Instruments (FLIR). In mid-November, the base-rate curve was cut again and the special liquidity facility was expanded.

- Beginning in the third quarter of 2008, the Central Bank of Bolivia cut back its open-market operations to reduce liquidity, in contrast with what it had been doing since early 2007.

- In October, the Bank of the Republic in Colombia decided to reduce the reserve requirement on current and savings accounts and on fixed-term certificates of deposit.

- In September, the Central Bank of Brazil cut its real reserve requirement, streamlined discount operations and was authorized to acquire portfolios of small and medium-sized banks and to provide loans in foreign currency.

- The Argentine monetary authorities reduced the dollar reserve requirement and made a series of changes which led to a fall in the real reserve requirement in national currency. It also launched an automatic repurchase programme for paper issued by the Central Bank of Argentina that was due to mature within six months and tripled the line of credit for local banks.

- In November, the Central Bank of Uruguay began a two-stage advance repurchase process for bonds issued by the central bank, so that it could provide liquidity to the financial system in national currency or dollars.

- The Central Reserve Bank of Peru lowered the reserve requirement twice (October and November), in both national and foreign currency.

- The Central Bank of Chile implemented swap arrangements and repurchase operations to increase liquidity in pesos and dollars. In the case of the repurchase operations, bank deposits are accepted as collateral.

- The Mexican central bank announced a cut in long-term debt instruments and offered additional short-term lines of credit for the banking sector. Banks were also temporarily authorized to provide liquidity to their own investment funds.

- Also in October, the monetary authorities in Honduras cut the reserve requirement for 2008 from 12% to 10%. In November, it offered the financial system a temporary line of credit of about US$ 106 million for mortgage loans on new housing, and in December it reduced the reserve requirement in both dollars and lempiras for banks directing over 60% of their loan portfolios in those currencies to productive sectors.

- In November, the Bank of Guatemala temporarily and moderately increased the flexibility of the computation of the bank reserve,[5] created a discount window to inject dollar liquidity at agreed rates, temporarily suspended the issue of fixed-term certificates of deposit with maturities of over seven days, and created a window for early redemption of such instruments.

- Lastly, exercising caution in response to the international situation, most of the region's banks have kept their monetary-policy interest rates unchanged. Faced with a possible fall in inflation in the first half of 2009, some countries' central banks may cut their interest rates, and this became more likely after the United States Federal Reserve lowered its monetary-

---

[4] The nominal SELIC rate had declined over the past two years. Brazil remains the economy with the region's highest monetary-policy rate.

[5] It was provided that the calculation of the reserve requirement should include in this order: certificates of deposit issued by the central bank, treasury bonds issued by the Guatemalan Treasury and mortgage loans provided by the Mortgage Insurance Institute, for a combined total of 25 million quetzales for each banking institution. In addition, the proportion of cash funds to be added in the calculation was increased from 25% to 100%. With this measure, banking entities were provided with fresh resources amounting to some 720 million quetzales.

policy rate in mid-December. Against the background of the crisis, the effectiveness of kick-starting the economies of the region through monetary-policy rate cuts needs to be re-examined; it appears that such an approach has failed to produce the desired results in the case of the developed countries.

1. Bank lending

In 2008, the credit boom observed since 2003 continued. This is related to the fact that the region's economies continued to grow, since there is a positive correlation between the growth of economic activity and that of credit in real terms. Table II.2 shows that all the countries for which information was available recorded growth in their lending. Unlike previous years, however, in some countries the growth of consumer credit and of mortgage lending has slowed. The percentage variation of consumer credit in Colombia, Chile and Mexico went from 32.9%, 9.1% and 25.3% in 2007 to 7.3%, 1.7% and 3.3% in 2008, respectively. Mortgage lending is not the most significant area in the total lending of the banking sector in the Latin American countries. To take the region's seven largest economies as examples, in 2008, it averaged 15% of total lending in Argentina, 11% in the Bolivarian Republic of Venezuela, 5% in Brazil, 18% in Chile, 8% in Colombia, 15% in Mexico and 12% in Peru.

A likely consequence of the worldwide slowdown caused by the financial crisis is that there may be liquidity problems in some Latin American countries which could lead to reductions in the various types of credit, especially consumer credit, mortgage lending and industrial credit. As a result, many central banks in the region are on the alert and have begun taking measures such as those described above. This is all the more significant since capital markets in the Latin America and the Caribbean economies have little depth, so businesses seek financing from both domestic and external financial sectors. External financing had in fact been very attractive for many businesses in the previous three years, when there were large nominal exchange-rate appreciations against the dollar, price rises for many of the region's commodities and increasingly positive interest-rate differentials in relation to the United States. The private external debt of Argentina, Brazil, Chile, Colombia, Mexico and Peru rose by 19.1%, 70.6%, 47.6%, 22.4%, 17% and 148.5%, respectively, over the last two years.[6] In those countries, the rate of increase of private external debt during that period was greater than that of public external debt. Unless the borrowers are generators of foreign exchange, this recent development in private external debt will leave them more vulnerable to the recent exchange-rate variations. The Bolivarian Republic of Venezuela was the only one of the region's seven major economies where that type of debt fell during the same period, by about 19.3%.[7]

As for the relationship between deposits and external debt in the banking sector, the individual cases of countries are of interest. In the case of Peru, from October 2006 and October 2008, financial obligations and indebtedness as percentages of total liabilities rose by 7.5 percentage points and the ratio of deposits to total liabilities fell by 9.9 points. In October 2006, 50.3% of financial liabilities were with foreign entities; in October 2008 the figure was up to 69.3%. Lastly, banking-sector external debt rose from 3.9% to 10.5% of liabilities over the same two-year period. In the case of Brazil, however, that same ratio remained almost constant, rising by only 0.3 of a percentage point between September 2007 and September 2008.

---

[6]   This increase was basically observed in short-term private external debt at the close of the second quarter or the third quarter, depending on the case; short-term internal debt as a percentage of total private external debt stood at 65%, 33.3%, 25.2%, 31.3%, 32.3% and 48.4% for Argentina, Brazil, Chile, Colombia, Mexico and Peru, respectively.

[7]   The Bolivarian Republic of Venezuela had the highest growth in all types of credit over the previous two years.

Table II.2
LATIN AMERICA (SELECTED COUNTRIES): BANK LENDING
(Real annual percentage increase)

Country	Period	Industrial credit		Commercial credit		Mortage lending		Consumer credit		Total credit	
		2007	2008	2007	2008	2007	2008	2007	2008	2007	2008
Argentina	October to October	...	...	...	...	26.9	19.2	47.7	29.2	28.6	32.7
Brazil	October to October	23.5	33.2	16.1	26.8	20.3	29.2	27.3	20.4	21.4	26.5
Chile	October to October	...	...	14.3	19.4	15.2	12.7	9.1	1.7	12.6	4.6
Colombia	September to September	13.6	17.1	20.3	11.8	1.3	3.7	32.9	7.3	21.8	9.9
Mexico	September to September	...	...	32.7	...	14.8	-1.2	25.3	3.3	20.1	8.8
Peru	October to October	28.1	23.6	25.5	35.0	13.5	18.5	43.5	36.7	27.3	30.7
Venezuela (Bol. Rep. of)	September to September	65.3	11.7	56.5	9.1	90.1	45.0	92.8	38.0	67.8	22.1

Source: Economic Commission for Latin America and the Caribbean (ECLAC), on the basis of official figures.

Box II.2
INFLATION IN FOOD PRICES AND OVERALL FOOD PRICES

The rise in food prices (food inflation) did, undeniably, have an impact on inflation in the countries of Latin America and the Caribbean starting in the second semester of 2007. Is there a statistically significant relationship between the two variables, however? In order to answer this question, the following equation, in which the inflation rate is a dependent variable and the rate's first 12 lags and the food inflation rate lagged 12 times are independent variables, was estimated for 17 of the region's countries [a]:

$$\pi_t = \alpha + \sum_{j=1}^{12} \beta_j \pi_{t-j} + \sum_{i=1}^{12} \phi_j \pi_{t-j}^{food} + \varepsilon_t \quad (1)$$

The equations were estimated using the ordinary least squares (OLS) method on the basis of monthly data from 2001:1 to 2008:6. The null hypothesis contrasted to 5% was $\sum_{j=1}^{12} \phi_j \pi_{t-j}^{food} = 0$. A rejection of this hypothesis suggests that there is a statistical relationship between the inflation rate for food and the inflation rate. For eight of the 17 countries, the null hypothesis was rejected, which means that the food inflation rate is statistically

relevant for predicting the inflation rate in those countries.

The next question is whether this statistical relationship existed prior to 2002. If so, the relationship can not be attributed to the increase in food prices in international markets. To answer this question, equation (1) was applied again to all the countries but using data for the period 1995:1-2001:12. This time, the null hypothesis was rejected only in the case of two countries. In other words, for most of the countries, there was no statistical relationship between these variables prior to 2002.

The following modification of equation (1) was then applied for each country and for the same samples:

$$\pi_t^{without\ food} = \alpha + \sum_{j=1}^{12} \beta_j \pi_{t-j}^{without\ food} + \sum_{j=1}^{12} \phi_j \pi_{t-j}^{food} + \varepsilon_t \quad (2)$$

The dependent variable of equation (2) is the inflation rate excluding food, $\pi_t^{without\ food}$, instead of the inflation rate. It should be noted that in 2005-2008, the food inflation rate was higher than the inflation rate without food.[b] In this case, the goal was to study whether the external shock

that affected the food component of the CPI spread to other components of the CPI. The null hypothesis was the same as before. In the estimates made for the period 2002:1-2008:6, the null hypothesis was rejected in the case of four countries,[c] which means that food inflation cannot be said to have spread in general to the other components of the CPI.

Lastly, the hypothesis of convergence between the inflation rate and the inflation rate excluding food was contrasted.[d] To do this, the following equation was estimated:[e]

$$\pi_t - \pi_{t-12} = \alpha + \theta * (\pi_{t-12} - \pi_{t-12}^{without\ food}) + \varepsilon_t \quad (3)$$

The inflation rate reverts to the inflation rate without food if $\theta=-1$. This is precisely the null hypothesis. This hypothesis was rejected for the estimates of seven countries, which means that for 10 countries, the inflation rate reverts to the inflation rate without food. Is this good news? That depends, because the inflation rate is reverting to a rate that was higher before commodity prices began to soar.[f]

Source: Economic Commission for Latin America and the Caribbean (ECLAC), on the basis of O. Bello, R. Heresi and O. Zambrano, "The present decade boom of commodity prices in historical perspective and its macroeconomic effects in Latin America", Santiago, Chile, ECLAC, 2008, unpublished.
[a] The countries analysed are: Argentina, Bolivarian Republic of Venezuela, Bolivia, Brazil, Chile, Colombia, Costa Rica, Dominican Republic, Ecuador, El Salvador, Guatemala, Honduras, Mexico, Nicaragua, Paraguay, Peru and Uruguay.
[b] Even though the inflation rate without food includes fuel-related expenses.
[c] As in the case of equation (1), estimates were made for the period 1995:1-2002:12. In this case, the null hypothesis was rejected for two countries.
[d] The ideal variable for contrasting this hypothesis is core inflation rather than inflation without food. Core inflation was not used because only five countries in our database publish this variable.
[e] This equation is based on S. Cecchetti, "Commodity prices, inflation and monetary policy", 2008, unpublished. This author used core inflation instead of inflation without food.
[f] Prior to the soar in commodity prices this decade, food inflation and inflation without food were not statistically significant.

Table II.3
LATIN AMERICA (SELECTED COUNTRIES): EXTERNAL DEBT, 2007-2008
(Millions of dollars)

		2007				2008			
		I	II	III	IV	I	II	III	IV
Argentina	Total external debt	112 018	118 736	120 967	123 989	127 377	128 685	...	...
	Private external debt	48 352	50 827	53 127	53 172	56 011	58 171	...	...
	Long- and medium-term	15 975	18 413	18 997	18 996	19 341	20 038	...	...
	Short-term	32 378	32 414	34 130	34 176	36 669	38 132	...	...
Brazil	Total external debt	182 081	191 358	195 331	193 219	201 637	205 536	212 374	214 279 [a]
	Private external debt	105 279	118 061	123 579	122 947	132 112	136 547	144 523	147 401 [a]
	Long- and medium-term	71 172	72 156	80 811	84 068	93 143	95 290	97 504	98 363 [a]
	Short-term	34 108	45 905	42 768	38 878	38 970	41 256	47 018	49 038 [a]
Chile	Total external debt	46 808	49 458	52 144	55 822	57 995	63 314	68 459	...
	Private external debt	36 299	38 529	40 480	43 428	46 409	50 416	54 475	...
	Long- and medium-term	29 601	31 028	32 737	34 672	36 619	37 744	40 719	...
	Short-term	6 698	7 501	7 743	8 756	9 790	12 672	13 756	...
Colombia	Total external debt	42 299	43 233	43 523	44 721	45 364	45 613	45 847	... [b]
	Private external debt	15 026	15 395	15 385	15 902	16 011	16 343	16 914	... [b]
	Long- and medium-term	9 903	10 635	10 853	11 269	11 579	11 467	11 613	... [b]
	Short-term	5 123	4 760	4 532	4 634	4 432	4 876	5 301	... [b]
Mexico	Total external debt	121 425	123 395	124 493	124 583	127 950	126 196	...	...
	Private external debt	62 750	65 556	67 365	69 228	68 371	68 565	...	...
	Long- and medium-term	43 062	44 186	46 626	47 570	45 538	46 470	...	...
	Short-term	19 688	21 371	20 739	21 658	22 834	22 095	...	...
Peru	Total external debt	28 097	30 127	30 921	32 566	35 467	35 961	...	...
	Private external debt	6 497	8 478	9 003	11 564	13 660	15 140	...	...
	Long- and medium-term	3 459	4 572	4 634	6 679	6 996	7 810	...	...
	Short-term	3 038	3 906	4 369	4 886	6 664	7 330	...	...
Venezuela (Bol. Rep. of)	Total external debt	48 021	48 672	50 999	52 949	53 269	56 198	50 378	...
	Private external debt	15 666	14 967	15 245	15 770	12 291	13 719	12 303	...
	Long- and medium-term	...	...	...	...	...	...	...	...
	Short-term	...	...	...	...	...	...	...	...

Source: Economic Commission for Latin America and the Caribbean (ECLAC), on the basis of official figures.
[a] Data to October.
[b] Data to August.

Box II.3
INFLATION TARGETING

In 2008, the countries in the region with an inflation targeting regime (Brazil, Chile, Colombia, Mexico, Paraguay and Peru) or an inflation target range (such as Costa Rica, Guatemala and Honduras) saw prices increase by more than the inflation target set by their central banks. In most cases, this was in strong contrast to the inflation patterns of the three preceding years.

The figure below shows that in 2008 both core and actual inflation were above target in Chile, Colombia, Mexico and Peru.

In Chile, measured inflation has been more than twice as high as the 4% upper limit of the target range since February 2008. The same situation has arisen in Peru since August 2008, when 12-month inflation exceeded 6%. In Colombia, actual inflation has been above target range since January 2007 and has exceeded the upper limit of the range by more than 50% since June. In Mexico, inflation began to move off target in March 2008, exceeding it at first by almost one third

and then almost doubling it in September that year. Brazil was the only country in which price rises remained within the target range established by the central bank, although inflation rose steadily throughout the year. In Paraguay, which has the highest upper limit for targeted inflation in the region (7.5%), 12-month inflation has been falling since June and was within target range by October.

This behaviour is associated with the external shock that rocked international

Box II.3 (concluded)

markets and drove up prices for agricultural products and hydrocarbons, particularly in the third quarter of 2007 and the second quarter of 2008. At the domestic level, this translated into major hikes in prices for food and the goods and services affected by the rise in fuel prices. As this was a supply shock, central banks held back at first before increasing the monetary policy rate. Later, between the fourth quarter of 2007 and the third quarter of 2008, they raised the monetary policy rate several times to try to minimize the effects of the second round of international commodity price rises. The shock lasted longer and was more far-reaching than expected. Although the prices for many agricultural raw materials, food items, metals and petroleum products came down during the second semester of 2008, average prices at the end of the year will be higher than in 2007 and not low in historical terms. Twelve-month inflation has begun to decline, and, as the monetary policy reports of various central banks show, inflation is expected to be within target range once more in the medium term.

INFLATION TARGETS, ACTUAL INFLATION AND CORE INFLATION
(Indices)

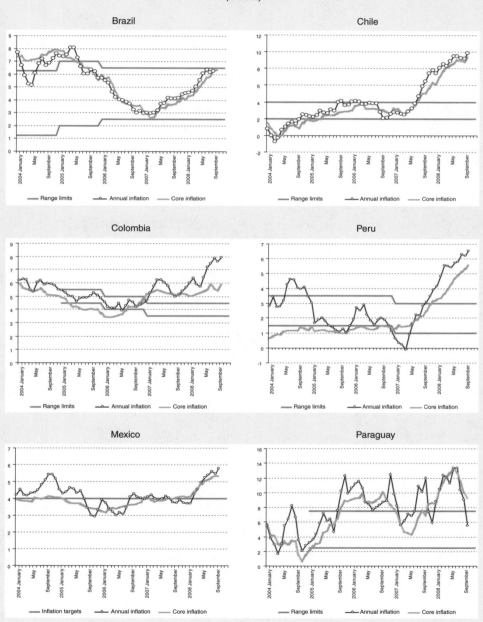

Source: Economic Commission for Latin America and the Caribbean (ECLAC), on the basis of official figures.

Chapter III

Domestic performance

A. Economic activity and investment

The growth rate of economic activity in Latin America and the Caribbean for 2008 was 4.6%, with per capita GDP growth of 3.3%. Thus, the region has achieved five consecutive years of per capita GDP growth in excess of 3%. The cumulative figure for the region's per capita GDP growth for 2004-2008 will be 22.2%, equivalent to an annual average of 4.1%. At the subregional level, economic growth in 2008 is estimated at 5.9% for South America and 4.3% for Central America. The figure for the English-speaking Caribbean countries will be 2.4%. The growth rate for the region will be 5.2% expressed as a simple average, while the median growth rate will stand at 4.7%.

If the 2008 result is compared with those of the early 1990s, the region's per capita GDP in 2008 is 38.8% higher than that in 1990, with the strongest increases in South America (54.3%) and the English-speaking Caribbean (54.9%).

The whole region enjoyed positive growth in 2008, but most of the countries saw a decline in external activity in the second half of the year, especially with the sharp slowdown in internal demand which hit the developed economies in the fourth quarter. As a result, GDP growth in most of the economies was lower than in 2007, with the exceptions of Bolivia (5.8%), Brazil (5.9%), Ecuador (6.5%), Paraguay (7%), Peru (9.4%) and Uruguay (11.5%). GDP growth in Mexico was 1.8% (3.8% in 2007), one of the region's lowest growth rates, together with Haiti (1.5%). The highest growth figures were recorded in Uruguay, Peru and Panama (9.2%).

Figure III.1
LATIN AMERICA AND THE CARIBBEAN, ANNUAL RATES OF GDP AND PER CAPITA GDP GROWTH
(In constant dollars at 2000 prices and percentages)

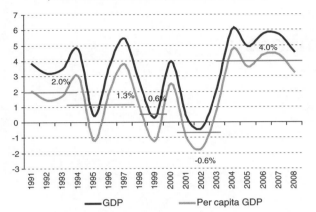

Source: Economic Commission for Latin America and the Caribbean (ECLAC), on the basis of official figures.
Note: the rates of variation shown correspond to the average rate for each subperiod.

Figure III.2
LATIN AMERICA AND THE CARIBBEAN, PER CAPITA GDP
(In constant dollars at 2000 prices)
Indices 2000=100

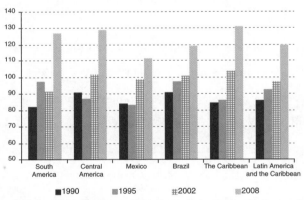

Source: Economic Commission for Latin America and the Caribbean (ECLAC), on the basis of official figures.

The performance of the region's economy in the course of 2008 was characterized by two opposing trends. In the first half of the year, and up to the third quarter in some countries, growth followed the trends which had been seen in the world economy since 2003, with widespread strong year-on-year growth, high levels of liquidity in financial markets, and easy access to capital markets for emerging economies. External demand for the region's export commodities remained strong, as did their prices, producing significant increases in export earnings, and in most of the countries this also meant an increase in fiscal revenues. This also took place against a background of high growth in internal demand on both the consumption

and the investment sides. Private consumption was boosted by continuing availability of credit and improvements in employment indicators, while investment benefited from continuing growth in the construction sector, as well as exchange-rate appreciations for many of the region's national currencies, which favoured imports of machinery and equipment.

The situation changed in the final months of 2008. In the fourth quarter, the countries of Latin America and the Caribbean found access to international financial markets increasingly difficult in terms of both the availability of credit and its rising cost. There were sharp drops in the international prices of their export commodities and internal demand slowed in both the developed and the emerging economies. Furthermore, in a number of countries the authorities had introduced interest rate hikes, raising the cost of credit. They also made significant cuts in the growth of monetary aggregates in the first half of 2008, in response to inflationary surges; this in turn affected the growth of internal economic activity.[1] Some economies were also slowed by the impact of natural disasters (Cuba, the Dominican Republic and Haiti). Lastly, in the fourth quarter of the year, a number of countries saw their industrial activity held back by slowing external demand and worsening expectations for internal demand.

The slowing of the world economy is expected to continue throughout 2009. The countries of Latin America and the Caribbean will be hit by the crisis through financial channels (it will remain difficult to obtain financing owing to reduced availability of financial resources but also to rising risk premiums and higher world interest rates) and real ones (lower world market prices for their main exports and reduced export volumes, as well as weaker internal demand). Thus, economic growth is forecast to slow considerably in 2009, to about 1.9%.

In annual terms, the region performed well in 2008 despite the sharp turnaround in the world situation in the last few months of the year and its negative impact on the region's economies. The growth of internal demand remained high (6.6%), exceeding GDP growth. Private consumption was up 5.2% and the growth of public consumption accelerated to 4.6% from its 2007 figure of 4%. Gross fixed capital formation increased by 10.0% in 2008, somewhat below its 2007 performance (12.3%). This added up to a cumulative figure of 74% for 2003-2008, which to a great extent was due to strong investment growth in machinery and equipment (its growth over the same period exceeded 100%), mostly

---

[1]   Furthermore, the region's financial systems in general raised their requirements for providing credit, cutting back severely on the growth of debt in the region.

imported;[2] the growth of the construction sector, on the other hand, has been declining slowly since 2006.

Given these results, the region's gross fixed capital formation, as a percentage of GDP and in constant dollars, continued its upward trend in 2008 to stand at 21.9% (20.8% in 2007). Its growth was strongest in Panama, Peru and Uruguay, with increases of over 20%, while the Bolivarian Republic of Venezuela, Haiti and Nicaragua showed the lowest growth rates. Indeed, as a percentage of GDP, gross fixed capital formation in the Bolivarian Republic of Venezuela actually fell in 2008.[3]

In subregional terms, the strongest growth of gross fixed capital formation was recorded in the South American countries; as a group, they achieved 13.1% growth in 2008 (15.8% in 2007). In the Central American group of countries, despite the sustained growth of the past three years (8.3%, 12.3% and 17.4% in 2008, 2007 and 2006, respectively), gross fixed capital formation as a percentage of GDP was less in 2008 (17.9%) than in 2000 (18.4%), and 1.5 percentage points below the 1998 figure (19.4%).

In 2008, the rapid growth of internal demand in the region was reflected in the increase in the volume of goods and services imports (10.7%), which has been at two-digit levels since 2004. The growth of export volumes in goods and services continued the slowing trend that began in 2004 as a result of changes in the real exchange rate and the supply constraints caused by falling agricultural and mining activity in a number of countries. As a result, the volume of goods and services exports rose by 2.6% in 2008. This meant that the contribution of net exports continued its negative growth in 2008.

In current dollars, domestic gross investment as a percentage of GDP continued the upward trend seen since 2004, reaching 22.2% (22% in 2007). Unlike previous years, it was financed by both domestic and external savings. The region's level of national savings as a percentage of GDP fell to 21.6% (22.5% in 2007), after rising gradually since 2001, when it had stood at 17.2%. In contrast with the period from 2003 to 2007, external saving was positive in 2008, equivalent to 0.6% of GDP.

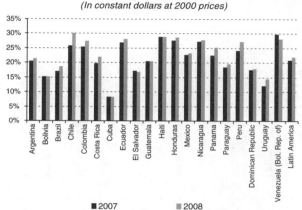

Figure III.3
LATIN AMERICA: GROSS FIXED CAPITAL FORMATION AS PERCENTAGES OF GDP
(In constant dollars at 2000 prices)

■ 2007   ■ 2008

Source: Economic Commission for Latin America and the Caribbean (ECLAC), on the basis of official figures.

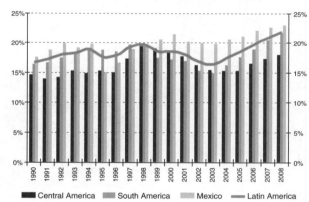

Figure III.4
LATIN AMERICA: GROSS FIXED CAPITAL FORMATION AS PERCENTAGES OF GDP, BY SUBREGIONS
(In constant dollars at 2000 prices)

■ Central America   ■ South America   ■ Mexico   ━ Latin America

Source: Economic Commission for Latin America and the Caribbean (ECLAC), on the basis of official figures.

The sustained rise in national saving, combined with rising prices for capital goods on international markets, has been among the causes of the sharp increase in gross fixed capital formation in machinery and equipment in the region since 2003, since it has made possible a considerable climb in the purchasing power of national saving in terms of capital goods.[4]

---

[2] In the period from January to September 2008, compared with the same period in 2007, the value of capital goods imports rose by more than 30% in Argentina, Bolivia, Brazil, Chile, Ecuador, Peru and Paraguay, between 20% and 30% in Colombia and Costa Rica, and by less than 20% in Mexico and Panama. The Bolivarian Republic of Venezuela and Guatemala were the exceptions, with falls in that aggregate over the same period.

[3] From 2003 to 2007, the Bolivarian Republic of Venezuela enjoyed the region's strongest growth in gross fixed capital formation.

[4] The unit value index of United States capital goods imports was used as a proxy for an international index for such goods, because the United States imports a wide range of goods from various regions of the world. Measured by that index, international capital goods prices fell steadily until 2006; between 1990 and 2006 they showed a cumulative fall of 47.7%, but in 2007-2008 there was a cumulative rise of 1.8%.

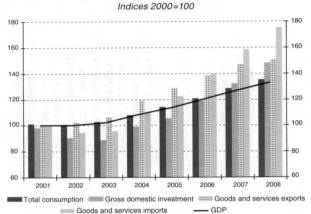

Figure III.5
LATIN AMERICA: COMPONENTS OF AGGREGATE DEMAND
(In constant dollars at 2000 prices)
Indices 2000=100

■ Total consumption ■ Gross domestic investment ▓ Goods and services exports
▓ Goods and services imports ── GDP

Source: Economic Commission for Latin America and the Caribbean (ECLAC), on
the basis of official figures.

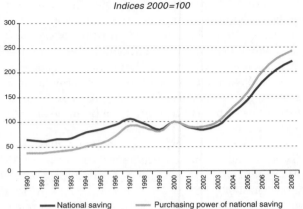

Figure III.6
**LATIN AMERICA: NATIONAL SAVING AND PURCHASING
POWER OF NATIONAL SAVING IN TERMS OF CAPITAL GOODS**
(In constant dollars at 2000 prices)
Indices 2000=100

── National saving ── Purchasing power of national saving

Source: Economic Commission for Latin America and the Caribbean (ECLAC), on
the basis of official figures and Bureau of Economic Analysis, Department
of Commerce of the United States.

Figure III.7
LATIN AMERICA: FINANCING OF GROSS DOMESTIC INVESTMENT, CURRENT VALUES, AS A PERCENTAGE OF GDP
(In current values)

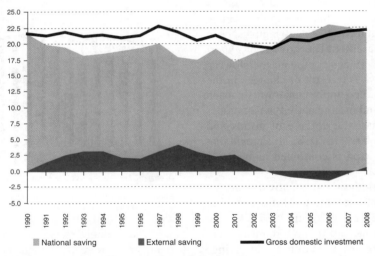

■ National saving ■ External saving ── Gross domestic investment

Source: Economic Commission for Latin America and the Caribbean (ECLAC), on the basis of official figures.

The performance of global demand was reflected in the performance of the different areas of activity. Regionally, the most dynamic were service-related sectors, particularly transport and communications and commerce. The transport and communications sector was mostly boosted by the strong growth of communications (Bolivarian Republic of Venezuela, Dominican Republic, Uruguay), while the performance of commerce reflected the growth of private consumption (Argentina, Bolivarian Republic of Venezuela, Brazil, Peru and Uruguay). The strength of the tourism sector in the first half of the year contributed to growth in transport and in restaurants and

hotels. In the period from January to August 2008, tourist arrivals were up 3% in the Caribbean, 9.4% in Central America and 7.2% in South America in comparison with the same period in 2007.

Greatly improved cereal harvests (Paraguay, Uruguay) and the output of crops both for export and for domestic consumption (El Salvador) led to substantial expansion in the agricultural sector; in other countries, however, natural disasters such as hurricanes or heavy flooding had negative impacts on the sector's performance (Barbados, Bolivia, Cuba, Dominican Republic, Haiti, Jamaica, Saint Kitts and Nevis and Saint Vincent and the Grenadines).

Figure III.8
LATIN AMERICA: VARIATION OF GROSS DOMESTIC PRODUCT AND DISPOSABLE GROSS NATIONAL INCOME, 2007 AND 2008
(In constant dollars at 2000 prices, and annual rates of variation)

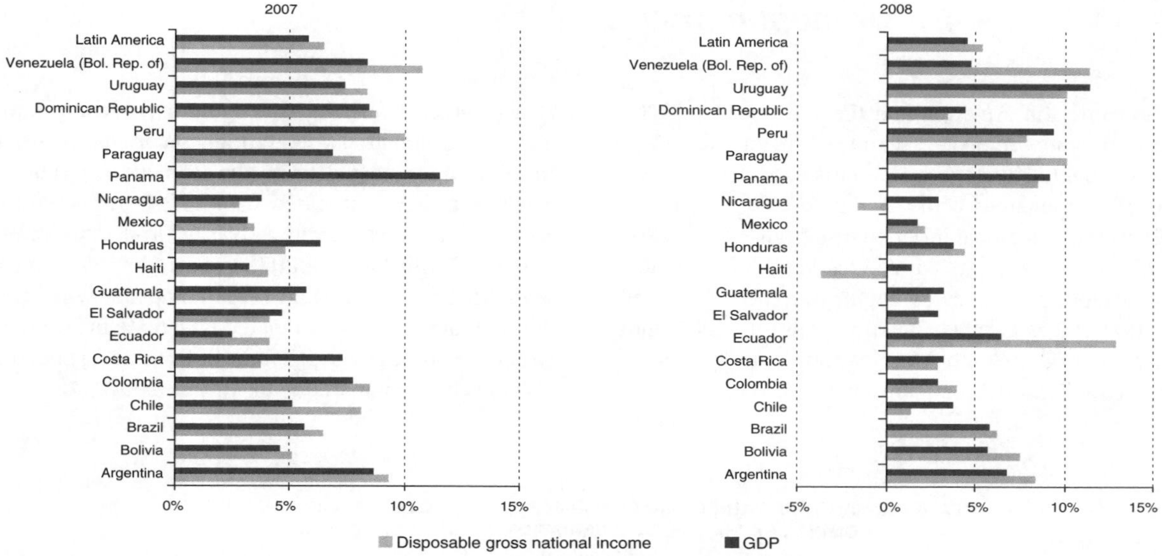

Disposable gross national income   GDP

Source: Economic Commission for Latin America and the Caribbean (ECLAC), on the basis of official figures.

Mining activity declined at the regional level but performances were uneven at the country level; there were heavy falls in Argentina, Chile, the Dominican Republic and Mexico, but in the Bolivarian Republic of Venezuela, Bolivia, Brazil and Peru, the sector's expansion was greater than in 2007. The industrial sector grew less than in 2007 because of falling internal and external demand growth. The exceptions were Brazil, because of rising growth in production of capital goods and consumer durables; Paraguay, owing to an upturn in agroindustry; and Uruguay, thanks to the launch of a major wood-pulp company.

The growth of construction in the region was lower than in 2007, although its performance was varied at the national level. While it expanded at greatly reduced rates in some countries (Argentina, the Bolivarian Republic of Venezuela, Bolivia, Colombia and Guatemala), it was stronger in others (Brazil, Chile, Ecuador and Paraguay). Panama and Peru continued to report two-digit growth rates. In the Bolivarian Republic of Venezuela and Guatemala, the slower growth of construction was mainly due to falling public investment in the sector. The expansion of domestic credit, financial transactions and domestic activity was reflected in the growth of financial and business services. The latter, however, saw negative growth in some countries owing to significant contractions in financial intermediation (sharp declines in the expansion of credit).

At the regional level, as in 2007, sharply rising commodity prices, especially for oil and food, meant that the terms of trade remained favourable in 2008.

For the region as a whole, as a percentage of GDP, the terms-of-trade effect increased from 3.5% in 2007 to 4.6% in 2008. As in 2007, this mostly benefited the South American countries and Mexico, although some of the former (Chile and Peru) saw a fall in that aggregate.[5] For the Central American countries, the terms-of-trade effect has been increasingly negative since 2002, and in 2008 it stood at 4.8% of GDP. Factor income payments were close to their 2007 levels, equivalent to 2.7% of GDP, and current transfers expressed in constant dollars continued the downward trend begun in 2006; in 2008, in regional terms, they were equivalent to 1.7% of GDP (1.9% in 2007). Thanks to a strong swell in the terms-of-trade effect, expressed in dollars at 2000 prices, the region's gross national disposable income once again rose faster than GDP; in 2008 it was up 5.4% (6.4% in 2007). The largest increases in gross national disposable income were concentrated in a few oil exporting countries (Bolivarian Republic of Venezuela and Ecuador) and grain exporting countries (Argentina and Paraguay), while the mining-sector export earnings of some countries (Chile and Peru) were hit by sharp falls in the prices of metals and minerals in the last few months of 2008.

---

5   In 2008, measured against 2007 prices, the disposable gross national income of Chile and Peru fell by 3.7% and 1.5%, respectively. In the case of Chile, the fall was due to lower export prices and volumes for metals and minerals. For Peru, the fall was caused by falling export prices. Both countries were hit by soaring import prices, mostly for food.

B. Domestic prices

Inflation in Latin America and the Caribbean in 2008 rose significantly compared with the previous year. The region's weighted average inflation is expected to reach almost 9% (compared with 6.5% in 2007). In terms of simple averages, regional inflation rose from 8.3% in 2007 to 11.6% in twelve months up to October 2008 (see table III.1). Inflation rose in every country in 2008 compared with 2007. Prices climbed steadily from mid-2007 until September 2008 in South America and Central America, although the Central American countries experienced the

sharpest rises in inflation (see figure III.9). In the region as a whole, the countries with the highest cumulative inflation in 2008 are expected to be the Bolivarian Republic of Venezuela (31% compared with 22.7% in 2007), Costa Rica (15.7% compared with 10.8% in 2007), Ecuador (9.0% compared with 3.3% in 2007), El Salvador (6% compared with 4.5% in 2007), Haiti (19% compared with 10% in 2006), Panama (8.5% compared with 6.4% in 2007), Peru (6.5% compared with 3.9% in 2007) and Trinidad and Tobago (10% compared with 7.6% in 2007).

Table III.1
**LATIN AMERICA AND THE CARIBBEAN: CONSUMER AND WHOLESALE PRICE INDICES AND
NOMINAL EXCHANGE RATE VARIATION, 2006, 2007 AND 2008**
(Percentages)

	Consumer prices			Wholesale prices			Exchange rate		
	Dec. 2006-Dec. 2005	Dec. 2007-Dec. 2006	Oct. 2008-Oct. 2007	Dec. 2006-Dec. 2005	Dec. 2007-Dec. 2006	Oct. 2008-Oct. 2007	Dec. 2006-Dec. 2005	Dec. 2007-Dec. 2006	Oct. 2008-Oct. 2007
Argentina	9.8	8.5	8.4	7.1	14.6	11.2	1.0	3.0	8.5
Bahamas	2.3	2.8	5.1 [a]	...	...	...	0.0	0.0	0.0
Barbados	5.6	4.7	8.9 [a]	...	...	...	0.0	0.0	0.0
Bolivia	4.9	11.7	13.3	...	...	...	-0.7	-4.5	-9.2
Brazil	3.0	4.5	6.4	4.3	9.4	14.7	-8.5	-17.3	24.2
Chile	2.6	7.8	9.9	7.9	14.0	25.5	3.9	-7.2	35.5
Colombia	4.5	5.7	7.9	5.5	1.3	11.8	-2.6	-10.7	19.3
Costa Rica	9.4	10.8	16.3	13.5	17.9	32.1	4.3	-3.8	7.1
Cuba	5.7	2.9	0.4	...	...	...	...	...	...
Dominica	1.8	5.7	5.8 [b]	...	...	...	0.0	0.0	0.0
Dominican Republic	5.0	8.9	12.8	...	...	...	-3.1	1.6	3.9
Ecuador	2.9	3.3	9.8	7.2	18.2	-2.2	0.0	0.0	0.0
El Salvador	4.9	4.9	7.4	6.9	0.6	11.3	0.0	0.0	0.0
Grenada	3.3	7.8	8.5 [b]	...	...	...	0.0	0.0	0.0
Guatemala	5.8	8.7	12.9	...	...	...	0.1	0.1	-1.5
Guyana	4.5	14.6	8.2 [b]	...	...	...	0.4	1.2	1.1 [a]
Haiti	10.2	10.0	18.0	...	...	...	-12.6	-2.2	11.6 [e]
Honduras	5.3	8.9	13.1	...	...	...	0.0	0.0	0.0
Jamaica	5.8	16.8	24.0	...	...	...	4.1	5.4	4.5 [e]
Mexico	4.1	3.8	5.8	7.3	5.4	9.4	0.9	-0.1	19.7
Nicaragua	10.2	16.2	23.0	...	...	...	5.0	5.0	5.0
Panama	2.4	6.4	9.5	...	...	...	0.0	0.0	0.0
Paraguay	12.5	6.0	5.5	6.6	8.0	11.2 [c]	-15.2	-6.1	-20.8
Peru	1.1	3.9	6.5	1.3	5.2	10.9	-6.7	-6.3	2.9
Saint Kitts and Nevis	6.6	2.1	3.9 [b]	...	...	...	0.0	0.0	0.0
Saint Vincent and the Grenadines	4.2	8.3	11.6 [b]	...	...	...	0.0	0.0	0.0
Saint Lucia	-0.6	8.2	10.1 [b]	...	...	...	0.0	0.0	0.0
Suriname	4.7	9.4	18.1 [c]	...	...	...	0.2	0.0	0.0
Trinidad and Tobago	9.1	7.6	15.4	...	...	...	0.0	0.5	-1.9
Uruguay	6.4	8.5	8.1	8.2	16.1	15.4	1.2	-11.9	5.3

Table III.1 (concluded)

	Consumer prices			Wholesale prices			Exchange rate		
	Dec. 2006-Dec. 2005	Dec. 2007-Dec. 2006	Oct. 2008-Oct. 2007	Dec. 2006-Dec. 2005	Dec. 2007-Dec. 2006	Oct. 2008-Oct. 2007	Dec. 2006-Dec. 2005	Dec. 2007-Dec. 2006	Oct. 2008-Oct. 2007
Latin America and the Caribbean (weighted average)	5.0	6.4	9.3	...	...	...	...	...	...
Latin America and the Caribbean (unweighted average)	5.6	8.3	11.3	7.6	10.7	15.0	...	...	...

Source: Economic Commission for Latin America and the Caribbean (ECLAC), on the basis of official figures.
a As of June 2008 relative to June 2007 levels.
b As of March 2008 relative to March 2007 levels.
c As of September 2008 relative to September 2007 levels.
d As of April 2008 relative to April 2007 levels.
e As of July 2008 relative to July 2007 levels.

Figure III.9
LATIN AMERICA AND THE CARIBBEAN: ANNUALIZED MONTHLY VARIATION OF THE CONSUMER PRICE INDEX, 2007 AND 2008
(Unweighted three-month moving averages, percentages)

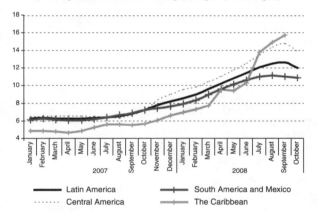

Source: Economic Commission for Latin America and the Caribbean (ECLAC), on the basis of official figures.

The figures for 2008 reflect the sharp increase in the prices for certain goods and services, particularly the sustained rise in prices for foodstuffs (cereals, oilseed and oils) and fuels (gasoline and other oil derivatives and natural gas), which began to be felt in international markets in the second half of 2007 and intensified during the first eight months of 2008. The impact of the rise in food prices on the consumer price index (CPI) was particularly strong because of the relative weight of food in the CPI basket in the region's countries.[6] The increase in oil prices throughout the year also translated into higher domestic prices for fuel, transport and basic services.[7] Supply constraints affected some countries, in the case of both food (Bolivia and the Bolivarian Republic of Venezuela) and energy (Chile).

An overview of the evolution of the wholesale price index in the countries that publish information on this variable shows that, with the exception of Ecuador and the Bolivarian Republic of Venezuela, the wholesale price index increased more than the CPI in each case. On average, accumulated 12-month wholesale inflation rose from 10.7% in December 2007 to 15% in October 2008 driven by the rise in prices for raw materials (including food), metals and minerals and energy products. The relative impact of import prices and domestic prices on the wholesale index varied from country to country. In some (Paraguay, the Bolivarian Republic of Venezuela), the rise in wholesale inflation was triggered by the increases in prices for national products, in other countries (Argentina, Chile), the prices of imported goods rose more than the prices for domestic ones.

Towards the second semester of 2008, regional core inflation began to climb steadily, reflecting the pass-through effect of the increase in food prices to other components of the CPI, mainly services, whose price formation mechanisms are one way or another indexed to the evolution of aggregate inflation in the preceding months. This was most noticeable in the case of basic services, health care and education (see figures III.10, III.11 and III.12).

---

6   The relative weight of the food and beverages component in the CPI basket is 23% in Brazil; between 25% and 30% in the Bolivarian Republic of Venezuela, Chile, Colombia, Costa Rica, Ecuador, Mexico and Uruguay; between 30% and 35% in Argentina, Dominican Republic, Honduras and Panama; and between 35% and 40% in Bolivia, El Salvador, Guatemala and Paraguay. The countries in which food and beverages represent the highest proportion of the general CPI are Peru (47.5% of the CPI for the metropolitan area of Lima) and Haiti (50%).

7   In order to mitigate the negative impact of rising international prices on domestic food and fuel prices, some governments in the region implemented grant programmes for the poorest families and transport and fuel subsidies. In some countries, despite the rises in international fuel prices, domestic fuel prices have been fixed since 2005 (Bolivia, Ecuador and the Bolivarian Republic of Venezuela).

Food prices increased more than the general CPI in every country in the region (see figure III.13). From September 2008 onwards, there was a dramatic change in some of the circumstances that had accounted for the rise in regional inflation since mid-2007. The upward trend of food and energy prices reversed, and the dollar prices for these products dropped sharply in the last few months of the year. The impact of this reversal has not been the same in each country, however. In some, the appreciation of national currencies in the first half of 2008 (and in several countries right up to September 2008) was followed by strong depreciations in the last months of the year, which mitigated the pass-through effect of the drop in international prices to domestic ones.[8] Meanwhile some of the countries that had introduced subsidies or tax reductions for fuel and transport announced the gradual elimination of those subsidies and the return of tax rates to previous levels. Nevertheless, regional inflation has slowed slightly in the last few months of 2008 and is projected to be lower in 2009.

Figure III.10
LATIN AMERICA AND THE CARIBBEAN: TWELVE-MONTH VARIATION [a] OF THE CONSUMER PRICE INDEX AND THE FOOD AND BEVERAGE COMPONENT OF THE CONSUMER PRICE INDEX, AS OF OCTOBER 2008
(Percentages)

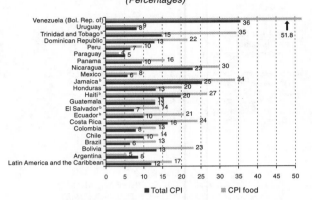

Source: Economic Commission for Latin America and the Caribbean (ECLAC), on the basis of official figures.
[a] Variation of the CPI for the month compared with the same month the previous year.
[b] Data for Ecuador, El Salvador, Haiti, Jamaica and Trinidad and Tobago correspond to September 2008.

Figure III.11
LATIN AMERICA AND THE CARIBBEAN: 12-MONTH VARIATION[a] OF CONSUMER PRICE INDICES FOR FOOD AND BEVERAGES AND THE OTHER COMPONENTS OF THE CPI BASKET, 2006-OCTOBER 2008
(Percentages)

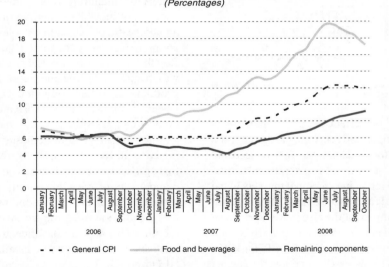

Source: Economic Commission for Latin America and the Caribbean (ECLAC), on the basis of official figures.
[a] Variation of the consumer price index for the month compared with the same month the previous year.

---

8   These currency appreciations mitigated the impact of rising domestic prices, which were being driven up by the increased prices of imports. As foreign goods became relatively cheaper, imports swelled.

Figure III.12
**LATIN AMERICA AND THE CARIBBEAN: 12-MONTH VARIATION OF THE CONSUMER PRICE INDEX,
CORE INFLATION AND PRICE INDICES FOR SELECTED COMPONENTS**
(Unweighted averages, percentages)

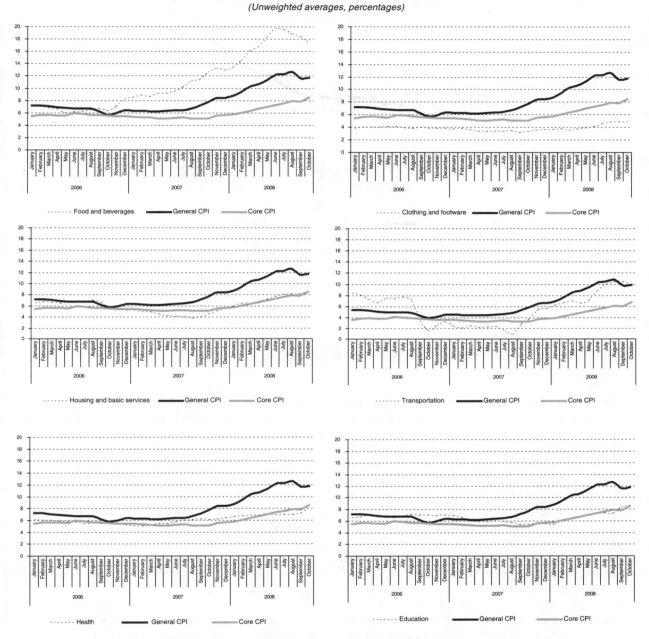

Source: Economic Commission for Latin America and the Caribbean (ECLAC), on the basis of official figures.

Figure III.13
LATIN AMERICA AND THE CARIBBEAN: 12-MONTH VARIATION[a] OF THE CONSUMER PRICE INDEX AND CORE INFLATION
(Unweighted averages, percentages)

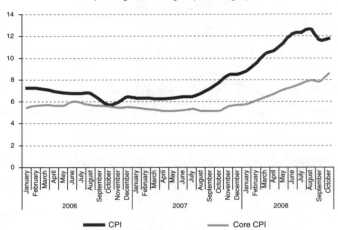

Source: Economic Commission for Latin America and the Caribbean (ECLAC), on the basis of official figures.
[a] Variation of the consumer price index for the month compared with the same month the previous year.

C. Employment and wages

At the regional level, the rising employment levels and falling unemployment seen in preceding years continued for much of 2008. As an annual average, therefore, the regional employment rate will end the year 0.3 percentage points up on 2007, while the unemployment rate will have dropped by 0.4 percentage points to 7.5%. Although unemployment fell in most of the countries, the cooling of the economy in the second semester slowed job creation.

As in the three preceding years, falling unemployment was combined with moderate growth in the labour force, which increased at the same rate as the working-age population, since the labour force participation rate stood still at the regional level. Although the trends in the countries have varied in this regard (see annex table A-16), the relatively favourable economic and working conditions do not appear to have prompted a flood of new entrants to the labour market, since there was a four-year period with no rise in the regional participation rate. It may thus be inferred that opposing long-term trends counteracted each other during these years, with young people staying longer in the education system —which leads to a drop in labour force participation, especially among young men— and increased participation rates for women. In fact, in 2008 the gender gap in labour market participation narrowed again: the unweighted average for the nine countries for

which information was available for the first three quarters of the year shows that the rate for men decreased by 0.2 percentage points while the rate for women held steady.

In keeping with the small drop in yearly economic growth, job creation fell off slightly; thus employment rate projections for the year overall are up by just 0.3 percentage points. This performance has been fairly even across the countries, although the rate appears to have dropped or stood still in Argentina, Costa Rica, Ecuador, Jamaica, Mexico and Peru (see annex table A-18).

Most of the countries will also record a drop in urban unemployment, although more will post a deterioration or standstill in this indicator than in 2007 (see annex table A-17). In Chile and Colombia the rise in unemployment coincided with a rise in the employment rate, indicating that the higher unemployment figure reflected a rapid rise in the labour supply. Conversely, weak job creation was the main culprit for rising unemployment in Jamaica and, to a lesser extent, in Mexico. As an average for the year, the fall in the unemployment rate represented a reduction of than 800,000 in the numbers of urban jobless. Thus the five years of economic growth in 2004-2008 helped achieve a reduction of over 5 million in the number of people facing this form of social exclusion. An average of 16 million were jobless in 2008.

In most of the countries for which information is available, visible underemployment also decreased, as usually occurs when open unemployment comes down. In 2008, both indicators improved in Argentina, Brazil and Ecuador, but some countries managed to reduce visible underemployment without any change in unemployment (Colombia, Costa Rica, Mexico and Peru). Only Chile and Uruguay recorded increases in underemployment.

Job creation by occupational category also suggests that the quality of employment has continued to improve for most of the year. Wage employment increased as a proportion of total employment in the region overall, since it rose at faster rates than own-account work in Brazil, Chile, Mexico, Panama and Peru. These trends were not common to all the countries, however. For example, the Bolivarian Republic of Venezuela, Costa Rica and the Dominican Republic recorded higher growth in own-account work.

In addition, many countries again witnessed rapid creation of formal wage employment covered by social security systems. This category of employment increased at rates of around 5% or more in Argentina, Brazil, Chile, Colombia, Costa Rica, Nicaragua, Panama and Peru. Formal job creation slowed as the year wore on, however.

From a sectoral point of view, employment in manufacturing, which expanded at high rates in 2004 and 2005, but more slowly in the following years, decreased again as a proportion of total employment in 2008. The data available show that this occurred in 8 out of 10 countries. At the opposite extreme, employment in financial services, real estate and business services rose rapidly in seven of nine countries for which information was available and held steady in another two. This branch of activity thus continued the expansion seen in previous years at the regional level. Employment in commerce was also up in most of the countries (quite steeply in some of them), which in a number of cases reflected dynamic domestic demand, particularly in the form of rapidly rising household consumption.

The picture was more uneven in other areas of activity. Up to September, construction employment rose quite strongly on average in Chile, Panama and Peru, but fell as a proportion of total employment in other countries (Dominican Republic, Colombia, Costa Rica and Mexico). Employment in community, social and personal services increased as a proportion of total employment in some cases but decreased in others.

Data available for the year overall show that the main employment indicators have continued to post major gains on previous years, but a quarterly review shows signs of cooling from the third quarter on. As shown in figure III.14, the employment rate failed to rise between the second and third quarters of 2008, for the first time since

the growth period began in 2003, while the unemployment rate edged up. Also, some of the countries that registered a year-on-year drop in the unemployment rate in the first semester saw that rate begin to rise in the third quarter. This was the case in Colombia, Mexico and Peru.

Figure III.14
LATIN AMERICA (9 COUNTRIES): QUARTERLY EMPLOYMENT AND UNEMPLOYMENT RATES
(Weighted averages)

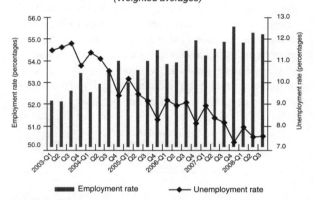

■ Employment rate — ◆ Unemployment rate

Source: Economic Commission for Latin America and the Caribbean (ECLAC), on the basis of official figures.

Although employment is projected to rise and unemployment to fall in the fourth quarter for seasonal reasons, with the region's economies now cooling, these upturns are expected to be more moderate than in previous years. As a result, a slight year-on-year drop in the employment rate is expected in the last quarter of 2008, while the unemployment rate is likely to be similar to last year's.

Another sign that labour markets are losing momentum is the growing unevenness between the countries' performances. As noted earlier, although many countries have registered significant improvements (see annex tables A-17 and A-18), more have seen their employment rates decrease or their unemployment rates increase than in previous years. The overall regional performance has been heavily skewed by the positive labour indictors of Brazil, which had one of the best years of its recent history. In the first 10 months of the year, the employment rate rose in Brazil by a full percentage point and its unemployment rate dropped by 1.6 percentage points, while the proportion of wage earners was up by 0.6 percentage points and formal wage earners by 1.6 points. Visible underemployment came down by 0.7 points and the proportion of employed earning less than the minimum hourly wage decreased by 0.2 points, while the real minimum wage itself increased by 4.2%.[9] If Brazil were excluded from the regional calculations, the region's

---

[9]   Data from six metropolitan areas.

projected employment rate for the year would stand still and the unemployment rate would drop by only a tenth of a percentage point with respect to the 2007.

Real wages in the formal sector have risen only slightly over the last few years, despite the relatively robust economic growth. To make matters worse, inflation spiked in most of the countries in 2008. As shown in figure III.15, the countries with the highest rises in inflation (Bolivarian Republic of Venezuela and Nicaragua) experienced larger losses in real wages. Other countries, including Paraguay, also recorded double-digit inflation in 2008, but the hike was not so severe with respect to 2007 and the government's wage policy and indexing mechanisms prevented larger losses in workers' purchasing power. Formal sector real wages increased slightly in the region's two largest economies, Brazil and Mexico.

Figure III.15
LATIN AMERICA (11 COUNTRIES): REAL WAGES AND VARIATION IN INFLATION

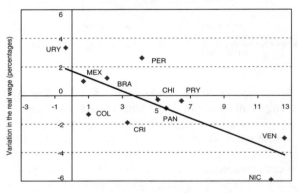

Change in the inflation rate (percentage points)

Source: Economic Commission for Latin America and the Caribbean (ECLAC), on the basis of official figures.
Note: The same reference period is used for both variation in real wages and inflation in each country, but this period varies from one country to another by data availability.

As a weighted average for the countries of the region, the real wage is projected to have risen by a modest 1.2%.[10] Since real wage trends have been less favourable in many smaller countries, however, the median shows a drop of 0.6%.

The labour-market outlook for 2009 obviously depends on developments in the wider economy. As noted earlier, in several countries indicators such as quarterly employment and formal wage employment were already showing the effects of the cooling of the economy in the third quarter of 2008. Those effects will continue to be felt in 2009. To measure by recent trends, economic growth of 1.9% will result in a drop of 0.2 of a percentage point in the employment rate, because of a sharp fall-off in wage employment creation. Since, in addition, the downtrend in the unemployment rate is projected to slow up, the number of jobless will rise for the first time since 2003. Moreover, the rate of unemployment is expected to rise in the wake of an increase in the labour force participation rate due partly to a break in emigration trends, which functioned as an escape valve for the labour supply in previous years, and to job losses in lower-income households, which tend to propel the secondary workforce into the labour market. This would imply that, with economic growth of 1.9%, the region's average unemployment rate would come in at between 7.8% and 8.1% in 2009, depending on the behaviour of labour force participation. Labour-market informality is likely to increase.

The unemployment rate will also be affected by whatever countercyclical policies the region's government can put in place in 2009, depending on the fiscal and monetary instruments they have at their disposal. A number of countries have announced a public investment drive which should offset job losses, especially in construction. Temporary employment programmes should also help to slow the rise in open unemployment. Not all the countries are in a position to implement such programmes on a large scale, however.

Two factors will be at work as regards real wages. In a number of countries these could rise nominally above the rate of inflation, which is projected to come down in 2009, as workers strive to recoup the losses sustained in the 2008 inflationary spike. On the other hand, workers may find their bargaining power decline as demand for labour slackens. In general terms, therefore, real wages are projected to remain largely unchanged.

[10] Excluding Argentina, the rise would be 0.6%.

Chapter IV

The external sector

A. Trade in goods and services

Trade in goods in the region went through two clearly distinct stages in 2008 (see figure IV.1). Exports mushroomed in the first semester owing to the exceptional upward trends in the markets for several of the commodities exported by Latin America and the Caribbean (petroleum, minerals, foodstuffs and agricultural commodities). Rising prices, together with buoyant domestic activity and currency appreciations in several countries, extended the surge in imports that had started in 2007. The situation changed dramatically, however towards the middle of the year. During the second semester of 2008, and in the fourth quarter in particular, exports were hit by the sudden collapse of international commodity prices and the heightened uncertainty in world financial markets. Imports also slowed as external inflationary pressure eased, activity levels waned and, in some countries, signs of exchange rate instability began to appear. Despite this, in 2008, the values of average annual goods imports and exports are expected to be up 23.0% and 18.3%, respectively (see figure IV.2). Total trade in goods (imports plus exports) is projected to reach a record high of US$ 1.8 trillion, approximately 45% of regional GDP. This represents a 20% increase over the 2007 level. It has only been surpassed once in recent years: in 2004, when the region was embarking upon an economic recovery process. Average trade levels were exceptionally high in 2008, although they followed a clearly cyclical pattern. The positive balance for trade in goods is estimated to close the year at about US$ 48.3 billion, (1.2% of GDP), continuing the downward trend in the surplus that started in 2007 and was generated by the accelerated growth of imports in 2008.

Figure IV.1

LATIN AMERICA AND THE CARIBBEAN: MONTHLY VARIATION IN FOREIGN TRADE, JANUARY 2002-OCTOBER 2008 [a]

(Three-month moving averages of year-on-year variations, in percentages)

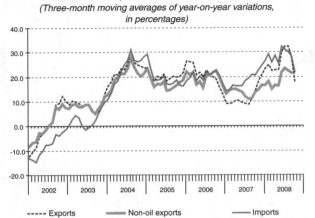

----- Exports   Non-oil exports   Imports

Source: Economic Commission for Latin America and the Caribbean (ECLAC), on the basis of official figures.

[a] Estimates. The data for October correspond to six countries that account for 74% of exports and 77% of imports between January and September 2008; non-oil exports up to September.

Figure IV.2

LATIN AMERICA AND THE CARIBBEAN: ANNUAL VARIATION IN FOREIGN TRADE IN GOODS, 2001-2008

(Imports and exports: annual rates of variation in percentages; trade balance: billions of dollars)

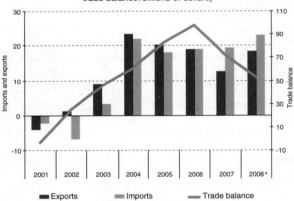

■ Exports   Imports   Trade balance

Source: Economic Commission for Latin America and the Caribbean (ECLAC), on the basis of official figures.

[a] Preliminary figures.

Measuring imports and exports at constant prices reveals the factors underpinning the behaviour of the foreign trade variables in 2008: in constant prices, exports

are projected to grow by only 1.8%, while imports are projected to grow by 10.6% (see figures IV.3 and IV.4). Much of the overall increase in trade can therefore be attributed to price increases, especially in the case of exports. Durable consumer goods and capital goods account for most of the growth in import volumes, in line with the buoyant domestic demand witnessed for much of 2008. The sharp increase in commodity prices in the first part of the year is linked to measures (such as lowering of interest rates and injections of capital) which the major developed countries started to implement at the end of 2007 to mitigate the effects of the international financial crisis. With the depreciation of the dollar (initially sparked by the financial crisis) at a time when demand was still high, these policies pushed up the prices for many commodities, which became refuges for investors fleeing the instability of the world's money and capital markets. The appearance of undeniable signs of recession in the world's main economies in the second half of 2008 reduced the inflationary pressure that characterized the first stage of the crisis.

Figure IV.3

LATIN AMERICA AND THE CARIBBEAN: VARIATION IN GOODS EXPORTS, f.o.b., BY UNIT PRICE AND VOLUME, 2008 [a]

(Percentages)

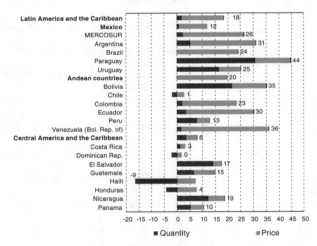

■ Quantity   ■ Price

Source: Economic Commission for Latin America and the Caribbean (ECLAC), on the basis of official figures.

[a] Preliminary figures relating to annual rates of variation in the value of exports; the subregional aggregates are averages weighted by nominal levels of exports from the respective countries; logarithmic rates are used to break down the price and volume effects.

Figure IV.4

LATIN AMERICA AND THE CARIBBEAN: VARIATION IN GOODS IMPORTS, f.o.b., BY UNIT PRICE AND QUANTITY, 2008 [a]

(Percentages)

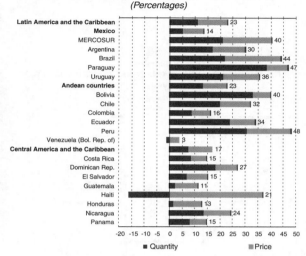

■ Quantity   ■ Price

Source: Economic Commission for Latin America and the Caribbean (ECLAC), on the basis of official figures.

[a] Preliminary figures relating to annual rates of variation in the value of imports; the subregional aggregates are averages weighted by nominal levels of imports into the respective countries; logarithmic rates are used to break down the price and volume effects.

Trade at the subregional level reflected these vicissitudes. Export growth was most intense in the countries of MERCOSUR (26.2%) and in the Andean Community and Chile (19.7%). In Chile, export growth was almost entirely accounted for by price increases, as was largely the case in Mexico and MERCOSUR. In Central America and the Caribbean (where price was a far less relevant factor) and in Mexico, external sales expanded less: 7.9% and 12%, respectively. Price and volume were equally important factors in import growth in the region as a whole, although rising prices played a more predominant role in Mexico and in Central America and the Caribbean. The price factor was clearly predominant in the Central American and Caribbean countries that are highly dependent on food and energy imports. Buoyant activity in South America led to robust import growth: 40.4% in the countries of MERCOSUR and 22% in the

Andean Community and Chile. Although all members of MERCOSUR posted a sharp rise in imports, Brazil accounted for 75% of the increase recorded by the trading block as a whole. Larger import volumes largely explained this increase in imports, although the countries of MERCOSUR were not immune to the inflationary pressure of the world economy during the first half of 2008, which was passed through to their imports. In Brazil, for example, half the rise in imports was due to price increases. In Mexico, six tenths of the 13.5% increase in imports was generated by price rises.

Trade in services in the region (exports plus imports) is estimated to have expanded by 19.9% in 2008 compared with 17.5% in 2007. Import growth (20.9%) outpaced export growth (18.5%), widening the deficit in services trade to 0.9% of GDP from 0.7% in 2007. Rising transportation costs strongly influenced this result. Tourism receipts remained steady for much of the year in most of the countries in which income from tourism is highly important, but began to fall in the last quarter of 2008 (see box I.1).

Intraregional trade, as measured by exports, is expected to reach close to US$ 185 billion, approximately 20.6% of total goods exports. The Andean Community, MERCOSUR and the Central American Common Market account for 8.5%, 14.6% and 21.3% of intraregional trade, respectively. The countries of CARICOM account for slightly over 16%. Subregional export flows swelled in all the trading blocks. A worsening of the world economy in 2009 will negatively affect the region's external trade because demand will decline, commodity prices will come down further, and tourism flows to Latin America and the Caribbean will subside, bringing both the region's imports and exports of goods and services to below the levels recorded in 2008. Sustained levels of domestic demand and a more rapid expansion of intraregional trade could, at least in part, offset the loss of the stimulus generated by the import activity of the United States, the European Union and the Asian countries that might occur during the course of the year.

1. Terms of trade

In 2008, the relative behaviour of the prices of exports and imports resulted in a 4.6% improvement in the terms of trade for the region as a whole, twice the improvement recorded the previous year (see figure IV.5). This is the seventh year of improvement in the terms of trade of Latin America and the Caribbean, which have increased 28.1% since 2001. In 2008, export prices rose by 16.2% and import prices by 11.2%. These variations are estimated to have generated US$ 43.6 billion and represented 82% of the merchandise trade surplus recorded for the region as a whole. This figure conceals a highly heterogeneous situation across the region, however: the countries of Central America and the Caribbean are suffering a 3.4% loss in their terms of trade (compared with a deterioration of 0.5% in 2007), while the Andean countries and Chile have seen their terms of trade improve by 9.4%, MERCOSUR by 5.3%, and Mexico by 2.8% in 2008, mostly thanks to their petroleum exports.

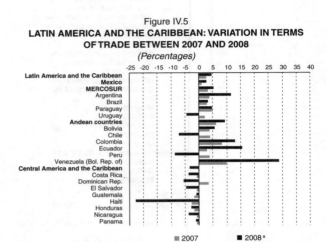

Figure IV.5
LATIN AMERICA AND THE CARIBBEAN: VARIATION IN TERMS OF TRADE BETWEEN 2007 AND 2008
(Percentages)

■ 2007   ■ 2008[a]

Source: Economic Commission for Latin America and the Caribbean (ECLAC), on the basis of official figures.
[a] Preliminary figures: the subregional aggregates correspond to weighted averages based on the nominal values of the imports and exports of the respective countries.

2. The balance-of-payments current account

In 2008, for the first time in five years, Latin America and the Caribbean posted a deficit on the balance-of-payments current account. This deficit reached US$ 27 billion, equivalent to 0.6% of GDP, and represented a deterioration of about US$ 46 billion since 2007 (see figure IV.6). With the exception of Argentina, Bolivia, Ecuador and the Bolivarian Republic of Venezuela, the other countries of Latin America recorded a deficit on this account, while Suriname and Trinidad and Tobago were the only countries in the Caribbean to record a surplus. Surpluses were attained in the countries that specialize heavily in exporting cereals, fuel and certain minerals, in other words, the products that benefited from the sharp rise in international commodity prices. The change from surplus to deficit on Latin America's current account was due largely to the turnaround of the situation in Brazil from a US$ 1.7 billion surplus in 2007 to a deficit of about US$ 27.8 billion at the end of 2008. The Andean countries (excluding the Bolivarian Republic of Venezuela) and Chile together recorded a deficit of 2.5% of GDP (compared with a 1.2% surplus in 2007). Mexico meanwhile is expected to turn in a deficit equivalent to 1.4% of its GDP, in other words, one that is 0.9 percentage points larger than the deficit in 2007. The unfavourable trend in the trade in goods in the countries of Central America, whose trade deficit is estimated at 21.5% of GDP, lies behind the record deficit (equivalent to 9.9% of GDP) posted on the subregion's balance-of-payments current account. In the case of the Caribbean countries, the current account deficit for the subregion as a whole (as a simple average) is expected to widen from 8.2% to 9% of GDP, and from 17.1% to 17.9% when the countries projected to turn in a surplus in 2008 are excluded.

Figure IV.6
LATIN AMERICA AND THE CARIBBEAN: CURRENT ACCOUNT BALANCE
(Percentages of GDP at current prices)

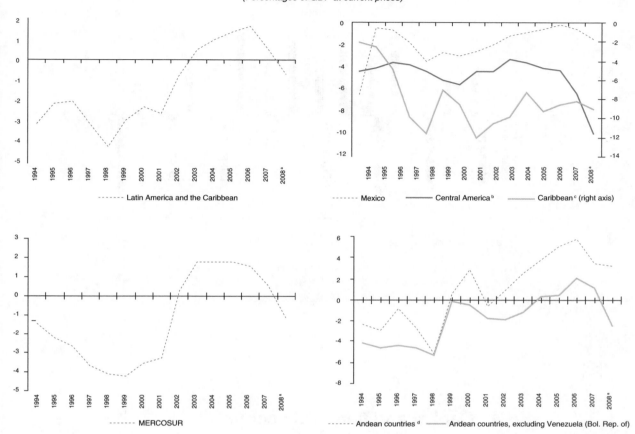

Source: Economic Commission for Latin America and the Caribbean (ECLAC), on the basis of official figures.
[a] Preliminary figures.
[b] Costa Rica, Dominican Republic, El Salvador, Guatemala, Haiti, Honduras, Nicaragua and Panama.
[c] Bahamas, Barbados, Belize, Guyana, Jamaica, Organization of Eastern Caribbean States, Suriname and Trinidad and Tobago; simple average.
[d] Bolivarian Republic of Venezuela, Bolivia, Chile, Colombia, Ecuador and Peru.

The structure of the current account for the region as a whole reveals a deterioration of all the balances, particularly the trade balance, whose surplus shrank from 2% to 1.4% of GDP, and the income balance, whose deficit expanded from 2.5% to 3% of GDP (see figure IV.7). The worsening of the trade balance was produced by the surge in imports, and the worsening of the income balance was associated with the drastic increase in net income payments (repatriation of profits and dividends). In 2008, these outlays reached about US$ 110 billion (21.5% more than in 2007) and were concentrated almost entirely in the Bolivarian Republic of Venezuela, Brazil and Colombia. In Brazil and Colombia, a significant proportion of the notable improvements in the terms of trade (83% and 69%, respectively) was offset by the increase in net income payments. The positive influence of the increase in commodity prices underpinning the improvement in the terms of trade was largely cancelled out by the increase in income payments. The expansion of the current transfers surplus (which is hugely important in some countries) has slowed again this year, from 3.2% in 2007 to 2.4% in 2008. This contrasts strongly with the average year-on-year growth rate of 19% observed between 2002 and 2006 and reflects the gradual decline of the remittances sent by migrant workers, which started when the economies of the developed countries began to show signs of recession. In Central America and the Caribbean, the increase in the surplus of transfer payments (US$ 1.5 billion) made up for only one third of the loss that can be attributed to the worsening of the terms of trade.

Figure IV.7
LATIN AMERICA AND THE CARIBBEAN: STRUCTURE OF THE CURRENT ACCOUNT, 2001-2008 [a]
(Percentages of GDP at current prices)

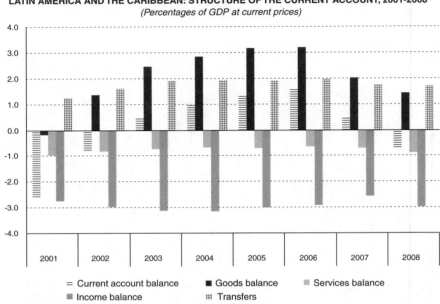

= Current account balance   ■ Goods balance   ▨ Services balance
■ Income balance   ▦ Transfers

Source: Economic Commission for Latin America and the Caribbean (ECLAC), on the basis of official figures.
[a] Preliminary figures.

B. Capital and financial account

In the first half of 2008, the external environment remained favourable, although less so than in 2007. This was reflected in indicators of terms of trade, access to external resources and financial flows to the region. The second half of the year was witness to major global external risks that, along with the downward trend in the current account balance, altered the performance of components of the regional capital and financial account. Despite the fact that international reserves expanded during the year (by almost 11%), this was significantly lower than the 43.2% growth rate observed in the previous year.

The first increases in the various risk ratings for emerging countries were recorded in mid-2007, triggered by the subprime mortgage crisis in the United States. However, it was not until the second half of 2008 that the trend intensified, as the cost of credit soared and financial flows to the region dropped considerably.

First, estimates of the foreign direct investment (FDI) of Latin America and the Caribbean show a slight reduction in inflows: from US$ 110 billion in 2007 to US$ 105 billion in 2008. Outward FDI, for its part, expanded to US$ 23.4 billion in 2008 (compared with US$ 21.5 billion in 2007). As a result, net FDI remained significant but was lower, representing US$ 81.6 billion in 2008.

Flows that are more sensitive to short-term conditions reacted to variations in market conditions throughout the year.

As shown in figure IV.8, the Emerging Market Bond Index Global (EMBIG) (which represents the country risk premium for a group of emerging countries) climbed sharply in 2008. The ratio between the global index and the index for Latin America and the Caribbean shows a premium that reflects the region's lower level of risk compared with other regions (thanks to its better economic situation and lower external vulnerability). Nevertheless, from September onwards the extreme uncertainty on international financial markets caused the risk ratings of all emerging regions to deteriorate without exception.

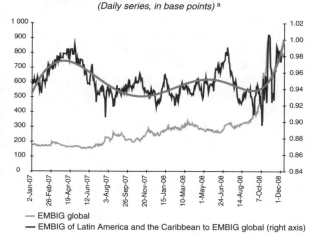

Figure IV.8
EMBIG OF LATIN AMERICA AND THE CARIBBEAN AND ITS RATIO TO EMBIG GLOBAL, 2007-2008
(Daily series, in base points) [a]

— EMBIG global
— EMBIG of Latin America and the Caribbean to EMBIG global (right axis)

Source: Economic Commission for Latin America and the Caribbean (ECLAC), on the basis of figures from JP Morgan.
[a] EMBIG – Emerging Market Bond Index Global.

The increase in risk was first observed in Ecuador, the Bolivarian Republic of Venezuela and Argentina, which along with the Dominican Republic form the group of countries with the region's highest risk premiums (significantly higher than the other countries, although these also posted major rises) (see figure IV.9).

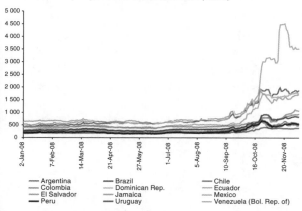

Figure IV.9
LATIN AMERICA AND THE CARIBBEAN: COUNTRY RISK, 2007-2008
(Daily series of EMBIG, in base points) [a]

— Argentina — Brazil — Chile
— Colombia — Dominican Rep. — Ecuador
— El Salvador — Jamaica — Mexico
— Peru — Uruguay — Venezuela (Bol. Rep. of)

Source: Economic Commission for Latin America and the Caribbean (ECLAC), on the basis of figures from JP Morgan.
[a] EMBIG – Emerging Market Bond Index Global.

Higher risk premiums have meant considerable rises in the cost of financial resources. This has had a greater impact on the corporate sector. The reason for this is that external public debt has fallen both as a percentage of GDP and in many cases in absolute terms thanks to

fiscal surpluses, increased access to domestic markets and the results of debt-reduction programmes in heavily indebted countries.

In this context, the issue of new sovereign and corporate debt on the global markets declined dramatically in 2008, particularly following the turmoil of September, to stand at US$ 17.0 billion (which is 60% lower than in 2007).[1]

As for flows of short-term financial investment, there are few indicators. Partial evidence, based on market performance, suggests that the first part of the year saw a continuation of share flows, especially those towards enterprises based on natural resources, for which prices remained high. As expected, the worsening of the global financial crisis and plummeting commodity prices made that investment less attractive, thereby triggering net outflows of capital and falls in local stock markets. From May, the value of the region's main stock exchange indices went into freefall, particularly in Brazil and Peru (see figure IV.10).

Figure IV.10
LATIN AMERICA: MORGAN STANLEY CAPITAL INTERNATIONAL INDICES (MSCI)
(Daily series, index at 1 January 2007=100)

▓ Argentina - - Brazil ∙∙ Chile — Colombia — Mexico — Peru

Source: Economic Commission for Latin America and the Caribbean (ECLAC), on the basis of figures from Bloomberg.

Also affected were financial investments based on carry trade operations that would use interest-rate differentials in a context of relative exchange-rate stability. This was the case of interest-rate spreads between Chile and Brazil (along with a relatively stable relationship between the currencies of the two countries), and between Brazil and the United States (with the Brazilian real tending to appreciate). Indeed, the increased cost of funds and

---

[1] See ECLAC, "Capital flows to Latin America. Recent developments" (LC/WAS/L.97), Washington, D.C., ECLAC Office in Washington, D.C., May 2008. See also the section on monetary policy, which details the buoyancy of external private debt issues in previous years.

severe liquidity restrictions in the countries of origin, combined with the higher risk of devaluation in destination countries, seriously reduced the profitability of this type of operation. This resulted in capital outflows in the second half of the year.

In contrast to this negative trend, the Standard and Poor's risk rating for Brazil, Panama, Peru, Trinidad and Tobago and Uruguay improved during 2008.

In regional terms, net financial flows to the region were negative (to the tune of an estimated US$ 4.1 billion), despite the fact that several countries recorded positive net inflows.[2] In the first half of the year, capital inflows remained buoyant. However, in the second six months of the year, there were net outflows of resources as a result of reduced access to the resources of the international financial system, private capital outflows in the wake of uncertainty triggered

by the crisis on the financial markets of some developed countries, and the continued build-up of sovereign external assets on the part of commodity exporter countries. This translated into sharp hikes in exchange rates.

The combined effect of these factors included major changes to international reserves during the year. As shown in table IV.1, reserves continued to build up in several countries for the first part of the year. In the second half of 2008, growth was slower and even negative in come cases. Overall, thanks to the performance from the first half of the year, and in spite of the current account deficit and sudden changes in the availability of external liquidity, international reserves were US$ 49.5 billion higher at the end of the year than in December 2007. This demonstrates that the region is in a better position to face external variability than in previous periods.

Table IV.1
LATIN AMERICA (19 COUNTRIES): INTERNATIONAL RESERVES
(US$ millions)

	Reserves		Variation in reserves in 2008		
	December 2007	December 2008	1st half year	2nd half year	Twelve months
Latin America	447 884	497 461	48 874	702	49 576
Argentina	46 176	46 072	1 340	-1 444	-104
Bolivia	5 319	7 615	1 800	497	2 297
Brazil	180 334	207 346	20 493	6 519	27 012
Chile	16 910	22 028	3 340	1 778	5 118
Colombia	20 955	23 169	1 900	314	2 214
Costa Rica	4 114	3 744	221	-590	-369
Ecuador	3 521	5 267	2 582	-836	1 746
El Salvador	2 198	2 413	106	108	214
Guatemala	4 320	4 726	451	-46	405
Haiti	329	643	-25	339	314 [a]
Honduras	2 733	2 505	-228	0	-228 [a]
Mexico	87 211	89 666	6 834	-4 379	2 455
Nicaragua	1 103	1 115	20	-8	12
Panama	1 935	1 757	-178	0	-178 [a]
Paraguay	2 462	2 657	734	-539	195 [a]
Peru	27 720	31 282	7 830	-4 268	3 562
Dominican Republic	2 946	2 533	-363	-51	-413 [a]
Uruguay	4 121	5 952	1 979	-149	1 831
Venezuela (Bol. Rep. of)	33 477	36 971	37	3 457	3 494

Source: Economic Commission for Latin America and the Caribbean (ECLAC), on the basis of data published by the central banks in the respective countries.
[a] Estimate based on the latest figure available as at 10 December 2008.

---

2   These net outflows include the inflows resulting from the recent reserve swap agreements between the United States Federal Reserve and central banks from Brazil and Mexico for US$ 30 billion each.

For 2009, projections point to a possible reduction in flows of foreign direct investment (FDI), owing to expectations of lower profitability in sectors that export raw materials, as well as to smaller capital inflows in the form of portfolio investment (as foreign investors seek to play it safe with the assets of developed countries). Governments and business will probably find it more difficult to access the resources of the international financial market amidst the squeeze on credit made available by financial institutions of developed countries. Demand for credit is therefore expected to turn to domestic markets. International reserves may drop or remain unchanged in 2009 as a result of the projected current account deficit and the complex external financial situation. Not all trends are negative however: the possible reduction in international reserves should be offset by access to the resources of multilateral financial agencies, and funds accumulated abroad during the recent boom in export prices.

The main factor of uncertainty is how long and intense the current financial crisis will be. Most predictions expect credit for emerging countries to begin to normalize in mid-2009, once measures are under way to resolve the main problems afflicting domestic credit in developed economies.

South America

Argentina

The Argentine economy once more expanded noticeably during 2008 as a whole, although there was a slowdown especially in the last few months of the year. In a context of historically low unemployment rates, towards the end of the year there were signs of falling labour demand, which became a focus of public attention. Despite the surge in import volumes, the average rise in international export prices recorded during the year helped to maintain a significant trade surplus, which in turn generated a current account surplus. At the same time, however, there were massive outflows of private capital, which at times caused tension on the foreign-exchange market and prompted the central bank to use reserves to support the exchange rate. The price of the United States dollar fluctuated, with a moderate cumulative increase for the year as a whole. Variation in the consumer price index in Greater Buenos Aires was less than 10%, but measurements in some provinces showed much more rapid movement. Price hikes appear to have been particularly rapid in the middle of the year, before slowing subsequently. Tax receipts swelled considerably, thanks to domestic activities but especially exports. This sustained the Government's primary surplus, in spite of soaring expenditure in the form of transfers made to the private sector in an attempt to curb energy, transport and food prices.

Macroeconomic performance was affected by strong external forces and various economic policy measures. At the beginning of the year, amidst rapid increases in activity and domestic spending and inflationary patterns, international prices for agricultural export products shot up. The Government responded by applying a sliding scale of export duties, so as to channel resources into the public sector and prevent the increases from being transferred to domestic prices. The measure caused a strong reaction in the agricultural and urban sectors of society, which in turn not only generated political tensions but also had a negative impact on supply (owing to road blocks) and demand. In this context of increased uncertainty, there was a rise in purchases of foreign exchange and bank deposit withdrawals. This forced the central bank to intervene decisively. Lastly, the bill on withholdings was not approved by parliament.

The impact of the international macroeconomic crisis on Argentina manifested itself in falling export prices (thereby reversing the price rises observed between mid-2007 and the recent highs for main export products such as soya) and sharp drops in share and bond prices, whose levels had already been affected by domestic uncertainty. The prospects for exports suffered as a result, particularly given the smaller grain harvest predicted for the forthcoming growing season. The reduced supply of credit slowed down the demand for goods in an economy that still has relatively low levels of credit. Meanwhile, there are growing doubts about the public sector's ability to face principal and interest payments due on the public debt in 2009. The international financial turmoil has also been hampering the Government's attempts to regain access to external credit by negotiating debt forgiveness with the Paris Club and reopen the bond swap introduced in 2005 to include parts of the debt that had remained in dispute (holdouts). Another source of debate is the reform of the retirement system proposed by the Government at the end of October, which includes plans to eliminate the capitalization system and transfer to the public sector the account balances of pension system contributors who opted into the State pay-as-you-go segment. In addition, in late November the Government set up the Ministry of Production and proposed schemes to standardize tax and social security obligations and promote outsourcing and the entry into the country of funds held abroad by residents. The Government also announced measures to cut labour costs, as well as plans for large investments in public works to support the demand for labour and goods.

In the first nine months of the year, fiscal management resulted in an improved primary result (which had dropped as a proportion of GDP in 2007), with a nominal increase of almost 100%, representing a level of 3% of GDP. The financial surplus also widened. Current revenues and primary expenditure both climbed considerably (by around 35% each). With international prices and taxable quotas higher than in the previous year, export duties were the fastest growing tax category, as receipts more than doubled. Other taxes grew in line with aggregate growth. The moderate slowdown in the growth rate of expenditure (which had been 46% in 2007) represented a departure from the pattern seen in previous years when outlays had exceeded income. Within expenditure, current transfers to the private sector (driven by higher transport and energy subsides) showed the largest percentage increase (54%), despite the marked slowdown observed in the third quarter.

Monetary and financial conditions varied throughout the year, with moments of tension in the second quarter and in October, related to drains on international reserves and private-sector bank deposits. Despite this, in the first 10 months of the year private deposits grew by almost 9% and banking credit to the private sector rose even more, by around 22%. In the second part of the period, there were restricted movements on the credit markets, as seen in rising interest rates and tumbling prices for financial assets, shares and bonds. In particular, implicit yields on public bond prices shot up to levels comparable to those recorded at the beginning of the decade.

The year-on-year increase in GDP (7.8 % in the first half of the year) was driven by hikes in various components of internal demand. Private consumption continued to grow impressively, in line with GDP. The growth rate of public consumption also quickened its pace, although this remained below the rate of increase in GDP. In aggregate terms, national saving easily covered investment requirements. Construction spending remained buoyant, although it was far from regaining levels seen in years gone by. Investment

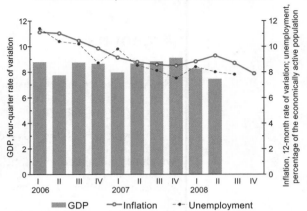

ARGENTINA: GDP, INFLATION AND UNEMPLOYMENT

Source: Economic Commission for Latin America and the Caribbean (ECLAC), on the basis of official figures.

in durable equipment showed increases that were more moderate, but nonetheless considerable on average for the year. In the final part of the period, however, there were signs of a visible slowdown in aggregate expenditure, with investment being especially affected.

The average increase in economic activity throughout the year was spearheaded by services, while merchandise production sectors also grew significantly but to a lesser degree. Grain production in the 2007-2008 growing season maintained the high levels of the previous year (95 million tons). The forthcoming harvest had been expected to suffer from the lower international prices and the repercussions of the dispute on export retentions. In the first 10 months of the year, industrial activity posted a year-on-year increase of 5.8%, mainly thanks to basic metal industries (primary aluminium production) and automotive production for the domestic market and the export market. Within services, transport and communications continued to grow rapidly.

The consumer price index in Greater Buenos Aires registered a 6.5% variation in the first 10 months of 2008, whereas some calculations for provinces and private entities showed a greater variation. The wholesale price index rose by 9.4% in 10 months (12.7% in the year-earlier period). The cumulative growth rate of commodities fell from 14.1% in 2007 to 1.9% in 2008, owing to lower domestic prices for crude petroleum and gas, and a slowdown in wholesale agricultural prices. Industrial prices climbed by 11.4% in the period concerned, while growth for prices of import products rose to 14.3%. In the first 11 months of the year, the nominal exchange rate posted a moderate nominal depreciation (of around 8%) against the United States dollar. This resulted in a 7% appreciation against the euro and an appreciation of around 20% in relation to the Brazilian real.

The ratio of urban employment to urban population was 42.1% in the third quarter of 2008, which is 0.3 percentage points lower than in the same period of 2007. However, the open unemployment rate dropped by 0.3 percentage points to stand at 7.8%, as economic activity declined by around half a point. On average, the first nine months of the year saw wages in the formal private sector grow by almost 15% year on year, while wages rose by almost 30% in the informal sector. Public sector wages posted an intermediate growth rate of approximately 20%.

In the first six months of 2008, the current account surplus was almost US$ 1 billion smaller than in the previous year. Although the merchandise trade surplus was considerable (US$ 6.5 billion) and similar to 2007, the income account deficit (profits, dividends and interest) swelled by over US$ 800 million, while the real services deficit expanded by around US$ 350 million. Capital movements in in the non-financial private sector chalked up a deficit of just under US$ 3.3 billion, partly owing to net outflows of almost US$ 5 billion in the second quarter. From this second quarter, foreign-exchange market performance was characterized by hefty outflows associated with the private sector, which offset the surplus resulting from trade operations.

In the first 10 months of 2008, the value of merchandise exports grew by 37% compared with the year-earlier period. This impressive increase is attributable to higher international prices. In the case of industrial manufactures, there was a considerable increase in volumes. In terms of value, a striking performance was turned in by commodities, while sales of fuels and energy displayed the lowest growth (as volumes plummeted). International conditions

ARGENTINA: MAIN ECONOMIC INDICATORS

	2006	2007	2008 [a]
	Annual growth rates		
Gross domestic product	8.5	8.7	6.8
Per capita gross domestic product	7.4	7.6	5.8
Consumer prices	9.8	8.5	7.9 [b]
Average real wage [c]	8.9	9.1	8.7 [d]
Money (M1)	20.0	26.8	15.0 [e]
Real effective exchange rate [f]	2.3	2.1	5.1 [g]
Terms of trade	5.7	3.7	11.6
	Annual average percentages		
Urban unemployment rate	10.2	8.5	8.0 [d]
National public administration overall balance / GDP	1.0	0.6	1.0
Nominal deposit rate	6.5	7.9	10.1 [h]
Nominal lending rate	8.6	11.1	17.3 [h]
	Millions of dollars		
Exports of goods and services	54 547	66 100	85 455
Imports of goods and services	41 120	53 371	68 839
Current account	7 712	7 113	10 406
Capital and financial account	6 800	4 660	-10 766
Overall balance	14 513	11 772	-360

Source: Economic Commission for Latin America and the Caribbean (ECLAC), on the basis of official figures.
[a] Preliminary estimates.
[b] Twelve-month variation to November 2008.
[c] Manufacturing sector. Registered workers in the private sector.
[d] Estimate based on data from January to September.
[e] Twelve-month variation to September 2008.
[f] A negative rate indicates an appreciation of the currency in real terms.
[g] Year-on-year average variation, January to October.
[h] Average from January to October, annualized.

strongly altered the outlook for exports throughout the year, as buoyancy faltered.

Merchandise imports grew by 37% year on year for the first 10 months of 2008, on the strength of larger quantities and, to a lesser extent, higher prices. Imports of capital goods posted above-average expansion, with even higher increases for imports of fuel (owing to higher prices) and consumer goods (mainly motor vehicles).

Bolivarian Republic of Venezuela

In 2008 there was a change in the trend of a number of variables that had been driving economic performance in the Bolivarian Republic of Venezuela since 2003. Aggregates such as gross fixed capital formation, monetary liquidity and bank lending fell in real terms, while public spending also posted a considerable real decline. This was in addition to the sharp fall in oil prices in the last quarter, which limited the continued accumulation of government revenue from that source. Consequently, economic growth slowed in 2008 compared to previous years and GDP is expected to post an expansion rate of close to 5.0% for the year overall. One of the economic authorities' main concerns in 2008 has been to check inflation, whose yearly rate is calculated to rise above 30%. Growth projections for 2009 are lower, owing to the drop in oil revenues,[1] and the government has announced that the exchange rate will be maintained at 2,150 bolívares to the United States dollar.

GDP increased by 5.6% during the first three quarters of 2008, compared to the same period of 2007, thanks to growth in both petroleum and non-petroleum sectors (4.1% and 5.9%, respectively). The strongest sectors were construction (7.6%), communications (21.3%) and community and personal services (9.1%). Financial services, which had posted double-digit growth since 2003, contracted by 5.2%. Domestic demand slackened sharply in this period, since gross fixed capital formation fell by 1.5%[2] and private consumption rose only moderately (8.3%). The volume of goods and services exports continued to decline (-0.4%), and goods and services imports were up just 3.8% by volume, after chalking up annual rates of over 30% between 2004 and 2007.

In April 2008, the government announced the nationalization of the cement companies operating in the country and of a large metallurgy firm, in the framework of the special powers granted to the President under the enabling law.[3] On 31 July the President announced the nationalization of Banco de Venezuela and issued 26

decrees with the force of law in the areas of labour, food production and supply, defence, economic planning, loans to the agricultural and tourism sectors, and development of what is termed the "popular economy". The executive branch and the cement companies failed to reach agreement by the August deadline on the price to be paid for the

BOLIVARIAN REPUBLIC OF VENEZUELA: GDP, INFLATION AND UNEMPLOYMENT

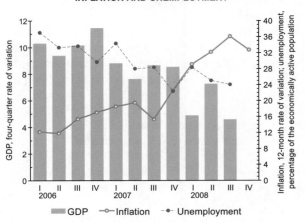

Source: Economic Commission for Latin America and the Caribbean (ECLAC), on the basis of official figures.

---

[1]   In the period January–November 2008, the average price of the Venezuelan crude oil basket rose by 43% compared with the average for 2007.

[2]   This aggregate had been expanding at rates of over 20% since the first quarter of 2004.

[3]   This legislation was adopted in January 2007 and remained in force until 31 July 2008.

nationalization, and the executive branch proceeded to expropriate the firms.[4]

The government continued to supply oil to a number of countries within the framework of the Bolivarian Alternative for Latin America and the Caribbean, the Petrocaribe energy cooperation agreement, Petrosur, and bilateral agreements signed with a number of countries.

In April 2008, legislation was adopted on the special contribution derived from extraordinary prices in the international hydrocarbon market. This law stipulates that oil companies must pay a special tax to the State when oil prices rise above US$ 70 per barrel of Brent crude. The tax operates at two rates: 50% of the price difference per barrel of crude when the barrel price rises above US$ 70 and 60% when it exceeds US$ 100. This tax must be paid in foreign exchange, not in bolívares, and the proceeds are deposited in the National Development Fund (FONDEN). In June, the government announced the elimination of the tax on financial transactions.

In the first seven months of 2008, the central government's ordinary income increased by 14.9%; the slower rate of increase may be attributed to a fall in income tax receipts (from both oil and non-oil sectors) and lower growth in VAT collection following the rate cut implemented in 2007. This lower rate of income growth was also despite a significant rise in takings from petroleum royalties. Operating costs increased by 40.1% in those seven months. As a consequence, during the first semester the central government is estimated to have run a deficit of almost 1%.

On 1 January 2008, a redenomination of the bolívar took place. Three zeros were cut from the currency unit, which was renamed the "bolívar fuerte" (Bs.F.) The minimum rates of interest for savings and time deposits were raised as of 1 May 2008, to 15% and 17%, respectively, and a ceiling of 33% was imposed on credit-card interest rates. For January-October, the average lending rate was 22.9%, while deposit rates averaged 13.6% and 15.6% (for savings and time deposits, respectively).

The growth of monetary aggregates slowed considerably in 2008. In September M2 and M1 were up by a nominal 11.7% and 9.9%, respectively, in relation to December 2007 (27% and 24.3% in relation to September 2007). Domestic credit to the private sector behaved in a like manner, with growth of 15.6% in December 2007-September 2008 (73.5% year-on-year at December 2007), reflecting a strong slowdown in business loans (which increased by 6%) and consumer loans (which increased by 28%).

BOLIVARIAN REPUBLIC OF VENEZUELA: MAIN ECONOMIC INDICATORS

	2006	2007	2008 [a]
	Annual growth rates		
Gross domestic product	10.3	8.4	4.8
Per capita gross domestic product	8.5	6.6	3.1
Consumer prices	17.0	22.5	32.7 [b]
Average real wage	5.1	1.2	-4.2 [c]
Money (M1)	83.4	24.6	20.8 [d]
Real effective exchange rate [e]	-6.1	-11.0	-17.6 [f]
Terms of trade	19.4	9.6	28.8
	Annual average percentages		
Unemployment rate	10.0	8.4	7.4 [g]
Central government overall balance / GDP	0.0	3.0	-1.8
Nominal deposit rate	10.1	10.6	15.9 [h]
Nominal lending rate	14.6	16.7	23.0 [h]
	Millions of dollars		
Exports of goods and services	66 782	70 838	95 938
Imports of goods and services	38 503	52 987	55 103
Current account	27 149	20 001	39 635
Capital and financial account	-22 011	-25 743	-36 135
Overall balance	5 138	-5 742	3 500

Source: Economic Commission for Latin America and the Caribbean (ECLAC), on the basis of official figures.
[a] Preliminary estimates.
[b] Twelve-month variation to November 2008.
[c] Estimate based on data from January to September.
[d] Twelve-month variation to October 2008.
[e] A negative rate indicates an appreciation of the currency in real terms.
[f] Year-on-year average variation, January to October.
[g] Estimate based on data from January to October.
[h] Average from January to November, annualized.

International reserves held by the Central Bank of Venezuela (including the resources in the Macroeconomic Stabilization Fund (FEM)) stood at US$ 40.468 billion in October 2008, and the authorities continued to transfer funds from Bank's international reserves to FONDEN (US$ 1.538 billion between February and March). A joint China-Bolivarian Republic of Venezuela fund was set up in May with contributions from both governments.[5] The Venezuelan government is also involved in efforts to set up a binational Russian-Venezuelan bank. In March, the government announced its intention to issue US$ 1.5 billion in structured notes during the year and in April launched a combined offer of US$ 3 billion in international sovereign bonds maturing in 2023 and 2028. This bond issue finally went ahead for US$ 4 billion.

The exchange rate remained at 2,150 bolívares to the dollar throughout 2008. Both the currency regime that has been in place since 2003 and restrictions on

---

[4] Negotiations to define the sum to be paid for the transaction of these firms' ownership are pending.

[5] This fund is to be used to fund projects in the country and consists of US$ 6 billion (US$ 2 billion contributed by the Venezuelan government and US$ 4 billion by the Chinese government).

capital outflows remained unchanged.[6] A law on foreign exchange offences entered into force on 28 January. As of 23 June, companies registered with the Foreign Exchange Board (CADIVI) prior to 11 June 2008 were exempted from requirements regarding foreign exchange requests, for amounts up to US$ 50,000 to be used for the importation of goods.

In January 2008, the Central Bank of Venezuela, together with the National Statistical Institute, began to publish a new national consumer price index (NCPI). Between January and October, this index rose by 24.7% in relation to December 2007,[7] driven by a faster rate of increase in the prices of food and drinks, restaurants and hotels, and medical and hospital services. Although price controls have been maintained for a wide range of goods and services, non-compliance has been on the rise, particularly in non-food segments. The wholesale price index rose by 23.5% during the same period (26.3% for national products and 13.2% for imported goods).

The general wage index showed an average increase of 22.8% in the first three quarters of 2008, in relation to the year-earlier period (21.2% in the private sector and 26.1% in the public sector). Both public sector wages and the minimum wage were raised by 30% as from 1 May. As an annual average, the unemployment rate came down to 7.7% during those three quarters (8.5% in 2007).

The current account surplus stood at US$ 44.325 billion for the period January-September; goods exports were up by 67.8% and goods imports rose by 6.4% during the same period.

---

[6]   Throughout 2008, there was a significant increase in the parallel exchange rate, however, which in November stood 137% above the official rate.

[7]   The consumer price index for the Caracas metropolitan area rose by 25.8% during the same period (35.6% year-on-year at October 2007). During the same period core inflation rose by 27.2%.

Bolivia

ECLAC estimates that GDP growth will reach 5.8% in 2008, an increase of about 1.2 percentage points over its 2007 level, and the urban unemployment figure will be 7.2%, 0.5 points down in relation to 2007. Inflation will stand at 13%, making 2008 the second consecutive year of two-digit price rises. The balance-of-payments current account and the non-financial public sector (NFPS) will close the year with surpluses, basically because of the high prices of natural gas in 2008. The political scene was dominated by a series of electoral processes: in the first half of the year, referendums on autonomy in various departments, and in the second semester, referendums on recalling the country's President and the prefects of certain departments. The Constituent Assembly, after more than a year of work, presented a draft for a new constitution which will be the subject of a referendum in January 2009 and which, if approved, will entail amendments to many laws to bring them into line with the new constitutional framework. This project would guarantee autonomy for departments, municipalities and indigenous peoples and would entail the holding of a presidential election in December 2009.

In the first half of 2008, the country's GDP was 6.5% higher compared to the same period in 2007. The five most buoyant sectors were metallic and non-metallic minerals (63.0%), construction (9.0%), crude oil and natural gas (6.8%), financial establishments (6.2%) and manufacturing (4.7%). The first of those had an incidence on GDP of 2.49 percentage points (38.3% of total growth), followed by manufacturing with 0.77% points. Growth in the production of metallic and non-metallic minerals was associated with the launching of a number of stages of the San Cristóbal mine project. The sector which had the least growth in the first half of 2008 (2.4%) was crop farming, livestock production, forestry, hunting and fishing, owing to the disastrous weather which struck the eastern part of the country in the first semester, associated with the La Niña phenomenon. On the demand side, GDP growth was based on households' final consumption expenditure and on gross fixed capital formation, which were up by 5.5% and 9.5%, respectively. Their incidence on GDP growth was 3.85 and 1.25 percentage points,

respectively. ECLAC estimates place the growth of the Bolivian economy close to 3% in 2009.

Monetary aggregates have expanded considerably over the past three years owing to rising international

BOLIVIA: GDP AND INFLATION

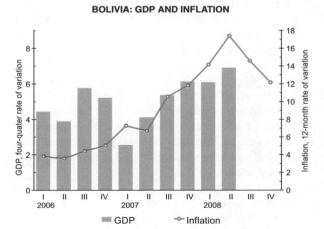

reserves and the replacement of the dollar by the boliviano.[1] Those aggregates followed the same trend in 2008, with the money supply rising by 14.1% to November, and by 35.7% from November 2007 to November 2008. M1, M2 and M3 increased by 19%, 28.6% and 32%, and by 33.6%, 46.4% and 49.3%, respectively, over those same two periods. Given the dedollarization of the Bolivian economy, the monetary liquidity growth figures for the M1, M2 and M3 aggregates including foreign currency were lower than the above figures. The central bank's goal since 2007 has been to hold down inflationary pressures on the economy, mainly by means of open-market operations; it had to deal with not only external inflationary pressures but also rising liquidity resulting from the positive performance of the export sector. Over the first 11 months of the year, open-market operations were up 118.1% to US$ 1.207 billion.[2] In reaction to the changing level of inflation, those operations ceased to grow, in contrast with their behaviour since January 2007. The main buyer in the open-market operations was the financial system.

Up to September 2008, the fiscal accounts recorded positive balances. At that date, the non-financial public sector (NFPS) had a surplus of 7.3% of GDP, an increase of 3.1 percentage points over September 2007. The revenue heading that showed the highest increase was that relating to hydrocarbons, which was up 2.7% of GDP. The national budget is expected to show an increase in public investment of close to 31.6% in 2009.

As for prices, the yearly cumulative inflation figure stood at 11.4% in November, and the 12-month figure was 12.1%. It should be noted that the latter peaked at 17.3% in June. The CPI component which showed the greatest variation was food. The slowing of inflation after July was due to falling world prices for food —of which Bolivia is a net importer— and to a double exchange-rate effect relating to the appreciation of the boliviano against the dollar and the latter's appreciation in international markets. This has resulted in reduced prices in internal markets for imported goods. The boliviano appreciated by 7.8% between December 2007 and October 2008 and by 9% compared with October 2007, contrasting with the behaviour in September and October of nominal exchange rates in neighbouring countries such as Brazil, Chile and Peru. Bolivia's real exchange rate appreciated by 10.8% from December 2007 to October 2007.

BOLIVIA: MAIN ECONOMIC INDICATORS

	2006	2007	2008 [a]
	Annual growth rates		
Gross domestic product	4.8	4.6	5.8
Per capita gross domestic product	2.6	2.4	3.7
Consumer prices	4.9	11.7	12.1 [b]
Average real wage	4.5	-1.3	-1.6
Money (M1)	42.9	58.1	52.8 [c]
Real effective exchange rate [d]	2.2	-1.0	-7.3 [e]
Terms of trade	20.4	3.6	5.7
	Annual average percentages		
Urban unemployment rate	8.0	7.7	...
General government overall balance / GDP	3.4	2.3	3.0
Nominal deposit rate [f]	2.4	2.4	3.6 [g]
Nominal lending rate [f]	7.8	8.2	8.8 [g]
	Millions of dollars		
Exports of goods and services	4 351	4 927	6 520
Imports of goods and services	3 459	4 082	5 496
Current account	1 317	1 763	2 053
Capital and financial account	121	117	247
Overall balance	1 439	1 880	2 300

Source: Economic Commission for Latin America and the Caribbean (ECLAC), on the basis of official figures.
[a] Preliminary estimates.
[b] Twelve-month variation to November 2008.
[c] Twelve-month variation to August 2008.
[d] A negative rate indicates an appreciation of the currency in real terms.
[e] Year-on-year average variation, January to October.
[f] Annual average of monthly rates in dollars.
[g] Average from January to November, annualized.

The current account registered a surplus for 2008, buoyed up once more by high average prices for hydrocarbons over the course of the year. In the period from January to September, the current account surplus stood at US$ 1.576 billion, 51.5% higher than in the same period in 2007. This was essentially due to increases in exports and in migrants' remittances, and a reduced deficit on the investment income account. During the same period, exports totalled US$ 4.694 billion, a 50.1% rise compared with the first three quarters of 2007. The leading sectors in that growth were mineral extraction (70.0%) and hydrocarbons (51.8%). Imports increased by 47.7% from January to September 2008 in relation to the same period in 2007.[3] Some 97.6% of those external purchases were made by manufacturing industry and essentially relate to industrial supplies and capital goods. The growth of imports was influenced by both economic growth and the appreciation of the boliviano. Over the same period, migrants' remittances increased by 8.1%.

---

[1]   Between November 2005 and November 2008, the central bank's international reserves swelled by US$ 5.967 billion, while deposits in bolivianos rose from 14.5% to 47.4%.
[2]   Between October 2007 and October 2008 they increased by 150.7% (US$ 1,361,400,000). As of October 2008, only 0.18% of the central bank's open-market operations were denominated in dollars.

[3]   The growth of imports in recent years has been significant; in comparison with January-September 2005, they have increased by over 100%.

As a result of the performance of the current account, as of late November 2008 the central bank's net international reserves were equivalent to US$ 7.547 billion, US$ 2.298 billion (42.3%) above their level at the end of December 2007 and US$ 2.538 billion (50%) higher than the October 2007 figure.

Two areas of concern are expected to arise in 2009 in relation to the country's exports. First, the worldwide slowdown in economic growth may lower the prices of the country's main export commodities. Second, the external sales of the manufacturing sector may fall because of the suspension of preferential tariffs which had been granted to Bolivia by the United States, following the decision taken in October by the Bolivian authorities to expel the representatives of the Drug Enforcement Administration (DEA).[4] The United States is the country's fourth largest export trade partner, accounting for 6.1% of Bolivia's external sales up to October 2008. Most of the goods benefiting from the preferential tariffs were craft products such as leather goods, jewellery and cloth. The government and the producers are seeking to redirect those exports to markets in the Bolivarian Republic of Venezuela and the Islamic Republic of Iran, in the framework of the country's cooperation agreements with those States.

---

[4] The preferential tariff regimes for which anti-drug certification is required are the Andean Trade Promotion and Drug Eradication Act (ATPDEA) and the Generalized System of Preferences (GSP). In November, the United States announced the suspension of preferential tariffs for Bolivia.

Brazil

In 2008, Brazil's GDP is estimated to have grown by around 5.9%. From September, the impact of the international financial crisis was reflected in a slowing economic growth rate. The slowdown is expected to continue in the months to come, with the GDP growth rate forecast to fall in 2009. Given the nature of the crisis and current economic conditions in Brazil, however, the authorities have a range of economic policy instruments at their disposal to help allay the adverse effects of the crisis.

Economic performance was highly positive in the first three quarters of 2008: GDP growth of 6.4% over the year-earlier period, 2 million more formal jobs over the year, the unemployment rate down to 7.6% of the economically active population (one of the lowest levels since 2002) and a 5.1% rise in real wages (comparing September 2008 with the same month in 2007).

Despite pressure from rising agricultural prices, the inflation rate stayed close to the set targets, with a cumulative rate of 6.4% in the 12 months to November. The fiscal balance continued to post a primary surplus, this time of 5.6% of GDP in the period January-October 2008. Overall, thanks to the lower cost of debt servicing, the public sector nominal deficit has narrowed to 0.33% of GDP.

The external accounts reflected the strong economic growth, with a steep climb in imports. Despite the central bank's intervention in the foreign-exchange market, the Brazilian currency continued to appreciate throughout the year and in August 2008, the exchange rate was 1.56 reais to the United States dollar, the lowest rate since 1999. Inflows of capital, in the forms of both foreign direct investment and portfolio investment, also remained strong.

In September 2008 the outlook changed as a result of the international financial crisis. The real depreciated by almost 50% and the exchange rate against the United States dollar, which had been highly volatile since September, reached 2.44 reais to the dollar in November. The strong devaluation was caused by the reduction in lines of credit for foreign trade, the withdrawal of foreign portfolio investors, remittances of the profits of transnational corporations' subsidiaries to their parent firms abroad and Brazilian firms' need for foreign exchange to cover exchange-rate derivative transactions.

In the first few weeks of the crisis, forward foreign-exchange contracts, the country's main source of export financing, were down by over 40%. In October outflows of portfolio investment (shares and securities) stood at US$ 7.8 billion and profit remittances between January and October amounted to US$ 30.5 billion, 67% more than in the same period of 2007.

A number of export firms that were relying on the continued appreciation of the real and that had engaged in derivatives arbitrage and related financial applications have been severely hit by the unforeseen plunge in the exchange rate. Their known losses in the derivatives market stand at over US$ 2 billion, and this figure may rise further yet, as the pre-crisis worth of this type of

BRAZIL: GDP, INFLATION AND UNEMPLOYMENT

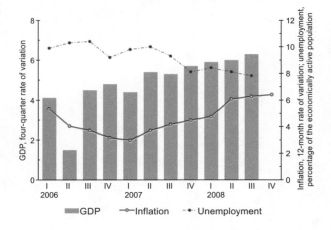

Source: Economic Commission for Latin America and the Caribbean (ECLAC), on the basis of official figures.

derivatives contracts was over US$ 37 billion (based on the August 2008 exchange rate).

The shortage of external credit has driven Brazilian banks to adopt a defensive stance and prefer to remain more liquid, thus creating particular difficulties for small and medium-sized banks, which relied most heavily on interbank operations.

Longer-term loans for big-ticket items such as consumer durables and automobiles have become smaller, shorter and more expensive. This is apparent in the figures for October 2008, which also showed a 38% reduction in the monthly supply of credit for agriculture compared with the year-earlier period. Personal and commercial loans dropped by 22% and 12%, respectively, in that period. In October 2008 the total balance of personal loans for automobile purchases shrank for the first time in several years, with monthly loan issues representing less than loan payments.

Starting in October, a number of sectors began to adjust their levels of production to cope with credit market difficulties. Seasonally adjusted data show that Brazilian manufacturing contracted by 1.7% in October as compared with September, as production of consumer durables and intermediate goods dropped by 4.7% and 3%, respectively. This followed the decision by automobile manufacturers to give their staff early vacations and suspend production for one or two weeks in order to avoid building up excess stock, after sales dropped by 11% in October. The mining and iron and steel sectors turned in similar performances, owing to falling international prices for metals and minerals, with production cuts announced for the coming months. Consequently, in 2008 automobile production is expected to be down by about 200,000 units on initial forecasts. Net monthly generation of employment was 61,000 jobs, which was the lowest October figure since 2004.

The Government of Brazil has adopted measures to soften the impact of the crisis. Its first steps were aimed at the credit market, with a view to guaranteeing greater liquidity in the interbank market. Between September and the end of November, the central bank used the large sums held in the form of compulsory deposits (259 billion reais in August) to reinject almost 85 billion reais into the financial system. This was enabled by the lowering of reserve requirements, specifically for large banks purchasing loan portfolios from smaller banks, which generated around 30 billion reais. Credit for agriculture was increased by 6 billion reais, while the remaining 50 billion reais were used to augment liquidity in the banking system, both for direct credit and for interbank operations.

Another economic policy priority was to provide foreign exchange to the market. To this end, the central

BRAZIL: MAIN ECONOMIC INDICATORS

	2006	2007	2008 [a]
	Annual growth rates		
Gross domestic product	4.0	5.7	5.9
Per capita gross domestic product	2.6	4.3	4.5
Consumer prices	3.0	4.5	6.4 [b]
Average real wage [c]	3.5	1.5	1.7 [d]
Money (M1)	20.4	32.7	7.4 [e]
Real effective exchange rate [f]	-11.5	-7.7	-8.8 [g]
Terms of trade	4.7	2.8	3.3
	Annual average percentages		
Urban unemployment rate	10.0	9.3	7.9 [h]
Central government operating balance / GDP	-2.9	-2.0	-2.6
Nominal deposit rate	8.3	7.7	7.8 [i]
Nominal lending rate	40.0	34.5	36.7 [j]
	Millions of dollars		
Exports of goods and services	157 283	184 458	229 918
Imports of goods and services	120 467	157 483	222 721
Current account	13 643	1 712	-27 752
Capital and financial account	16 927	85 772	54 752
Overall balance	30 569	87 484	27 000

Source: Economic Commission for Latin America and the Caribbean (ECLAC), on the basis of official figures.
[a] Preliminary estimates.
[b] Twelve-month variation to November 2008.
[c] Workers covered by social and labour legislation, private sector.
[d] Estimate based on data from January to September.
[e] Twelve-month variation to October 2008.
[f] A negative rate indicates an appreciation of the currency in real terms.
[g] Year-on-year average variation, January to October.
[h] Estimate based on data from January to October.
[i] Average from January to November, annualized.
[j] Average from January to October, annualized.

bank engaged in a variety of transactions, mainly swap contracts worth US$ 30 billion and direct sales of foreign exchange for US$ 6.7 billion.

The central bank set up direct credit lines to the value of US$ 11.3 billion to finance exports, to help banks to maintain or rediscount external trade operations. Between August and the end of November, international cash reserves shrank by 5.4% to stand at US$ 194 billion. In addition, the United States Federal Reserve announced that it was making available US$ 30 billion for swap operations with the central bank of Brazil, which brought the amount available in liquid reserves, including other operations of this type, to US$ 235 billion.

New legislation was introduced affording the central bank far-reaching powers to intervene in the banking system and broadening the scope of action and range of operations allowed to federal banks (such as Banco do Brasil and Caixa Econômica Federal). Between October and November, two major bank mergers took place: one between the private banks Itaú and Unibanco (that now form the largest South American bank); and the other between the State banks Banco do Brasil and Nossa Caixa (from the State of São Paulo), which enabled Banco do Brasil to expand considerably into major markets.

A number of production sectors received special credit lines to maintain the momentum of consumption; one example was 8 billion reais for the auto-finance portfolio purchase by Banco do Brasil and Nossa Caixa.

As far as interest rates are concerned, in October the central bank's Monetary Policy Committee decided to suspend the rises in the basic interest rate that had begun in March 2008 (when the basic interest rate in the Special System of Clearance and Custody (SELIC) had reached a historical low of 11.25%). The rate was thus held steady at 13.75%. On the financial market, annual lending rates rose by around 2.5 percentage points in October for all types of operation, while the average term for corporate loans was shortened (especially for working capital).

Another set of fiscal policy measures was implemented to boost domestic demand and improve expectations of adjustment to the crisis. In the short term, the federal government and some states, such as São Paulo, have legnthened the period for the monthly payment of taxes, reducing pressure on companies' cash flows. The federal government made a commitment to maintain its investment programme, which has been stepped up in recent months.

In the first 10 months of 2008 (compared with the same period of 2007), federal government revenues expanded strongly, with a nominal rise of 18.6%. Total expenditure increased by 11% during the same period. The Treasury's capital expenditure rose by over 40%. It is estimated that the crisis will have a negative impact on fiscal revenues, in the light of lower manufacturing sales (especially of automobiles) and reduced profits expected from State companies (owing to falling export prices).

Despite the performance of economic variables over the last few months of the year, economic activity in 2008 maintained a strong momentum. In the first nine months of the year, manufacturing was up 6.5% on the year-earlier period (boosted by a 17.6% rise in automobile production and an 18.9% increase in capital goods production), while commerce expanded by 10.4%. According to estimates by the National Confederation of Agriculture, agricultural production could be up by more than 10% in 2008.

In the first semester of 2008, gross fixed investment was 15% higher than in the year-earlier period, thereby continuing the rapid expansion observed in 2006 and 2007 (11% and 14%, respectively). Gross fixed investment as a percentage of GDP (in constant prices) rose from 14.3% in 2005 to 17.1% in the first half of 2008. Although these growth rates represent a recovery from extremely low levels, the fast pace of the expansion shows that Brazil's investment climate has improved considerably. Purchases of machinery and equipment (from home and abroad) also rose by about 19% in 2007 and 22% between January

and August 2008. This suggests that supply is responding quickly to demand pressures. Civil construction investment also expanded, albeit more modestly (by 5% and 11% in the two periods).

The strong increase in production and the impact of high interest rates combined to ease the pressure on prices caused by rising demand. From July, the increased supply of agricultural goods following the harvest helped to lower the average monthly variation of the extended national consumer price index from 0.69% in the second quarter of 2008 to 0.36% in the third quarter. This strengthened expectations that inflation would remain within two percentage points of the 4.5% target in 2008. In October, variation of the extended national consumer price index rose again to 0.45%, driven by the exchange rate. What remains uncertain is whether the lower levels of economic activity can offset the pressures of currency devaluation.

In the external sector, the cumulative current account deficit for January to October stood at US$ 24.8 billion (1.86% of GDP). This represented a departure from the surpluses recorded in recent years, and is attributable to the drop in the trade balance to US$ 20.8 billion (compared with US$ 34.4 billion in the year-earlier period) and to the deficit of US$ 48.9 billion on the services and income balance (compared with US$ 34.1 billion in the same period of 2007).

Merchandise exports and imports rose by 28% and 51.6%, respectively. Export performance reflected increased exports of commodities (48.7%) semi-manufactured products (29.9%) and manufactures (12.6%). The rise in export values breaks down into a 1.7% fall in volumes and a 29.7% jump in prices (47% for commodities, 27.5% for semi-manufactured products and 18.1% for manufactures). The value of imports was US$ 148 billion in this period, an unprecedented level that was underpinned by a surge in imports of consumer durables (67.1%), capital goods (53.1%) and intermediate goods (46.5%). There was a marked increase in import volumes for consumer durables (56.1%) and capital goods (40.3%), as well as a rise in imports of intermediate goods (20.9%).

Capital flows in the capital and financial account of the balance of payments posted a surplus of US$ 41.8 billion between January and October 2008, which was much less than the US$ 77 billion recorded in the same period of 2007. This was attributable to a major shift in the country's foreign direct investment position, from net inflows of US$ 850 million in the first 10 months of 2007 to net outflows of US$ 15.6 billion in the same period of 2008. Added to this was a significant reduction in inflows of foreign portfolio investment, which dropped from US$ 40.9 billion between January and October 2007 to just US$ 9.6 billion in the same period of 2008.

Total foreign direct investment inflows between January and October reached a record US$ 34.7 billion (up from US$ 31 billion one year previously). Direct investment represented 2.6% of GDP between January and October 2008 (compared with 2.9% one year earlier).

In October, total external debt stood at US$ 214 billion, of which US$ 165 billion was medium-term debt and US$ 49 billion was short-term debt. As a proportion of total export values, the cost of debt servicing fell from 32.4% in December 2007 to 18.4% in October 2008.

Chile

The Chilean economy is estimated to have grown by about 3.8% in 2008, less than the 5.1% posted the previous year. Since mid-2007, the main risks the economy faces materialized: the provision of natural gas from Argentina was suspended; international prices soared, first for food and then for fuel; and most recently, the crisis in the United States, despite alleviating inflationary pressure by bringing down commodity prices during the second semester, deepened and spread to other developed economies, which began to have a negative effect on Chile's exports. In short, the external boom that started in mid-2003 seems to have come to an end in 2008. In addition, the country has had to cope with internal upsets (droughts, technical and labour-related problems in natural-resource-based sectors) that also hindered growth. In response, the government has implemented a series of countercyclical measures, which, together with the fiscal and monetary policies applied since 2000 to stabilize growth and the vast external reserves accumulated during the recent boom, should help mitigate the crisis' negative impact on economic activity and employment in 2009.

Fiscal policy continued to pursue a structural surplus of 0.5% of GDP, which allows public expenditures to expand according to the medium-term values of its main determinants. Spending thus increased at a rate of just over 5% per year, in keeping with the growth pattern of the last few years.

Of the components of aggregate demand, gross fixed capital formation continued to be highly dynamic. During the first semester it expanded at an annual rate of 23% because high international commodity prices up to the middle of the year stimulated numerous investment projects in the energy and mining sectors. Total consumption in turn posted moderate growth of close to 6%, while private consumption, in particular of durables, slowed because the spike in inflation and the sluggish increase in employment slowed the expansion of the real pay-roll at a time when credit was tightening.

According to estimates, national unemployment stood at 7.9% in 2008, higher than in 2007; this was because, although the employment rate has risen, more people entered the workforce.

Monetary policy continued to pursue the target inflation range of between 2% and 4% within two years. Twelve-month inflation, as measured by the CPI and its

CHILE: GDP, INFLATION AND UNEMPLOYMENT

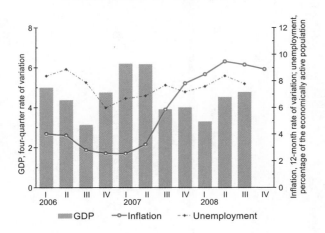

Source: Economic Commission for Latin America and the Caribbean (ECLAC), on the basis of official figures.

trend components, soared above target, however, reaching close to 10% during the second semester. This was the result of the sharp rise in international prices for food as of 2007 and for fuel in the first part of 2008, which spread to domestic prices thanks to indexation and the intense rise of demand.

The central bank reacted by incrementing the monetary policy rate on several occassions, from 5% when inflation began to climb in April 2007 to 8.25% in September 2008. In the last two months of the year, the drop in international prices partially alleviated inflationary pressure, and 12-month inflation is expected to end the year at around 8.5%.

The exchange rate appreciated steadily up to the middle of the year, which led the central bank, in anticipation of the effects of the external crisis, to implement a foreign-exchange purchasing programme aimed at boosting international reserves by US$ 8 billion by the end the year. Subsequently, as the crisis unfolded, the real exchange rate rose sharply and, towards the end of the year, reached levels comparable to those prior to the crisis. This counteracted efforts to reduce the inflationary pressure, however, and in the second semester, the bank suspended the foreign-exchange purchasing programme.

In 2009, the projected decline in world demand is expected to lower international prices, particularly for fuel and certain foodstuffs, and inflation is therefore expected to drop as well, especially in the second semester. Monetary authorities estimate that towards the end of 2009, inflation will once again be within the target range.

Exports of goods and services continued to slide in 2008, at first owing to technical and labour problems that reduced the volume of mining exports, and then because the prices and volumes of commodities traded on world markets slumped when the external crisis worsened in September that year. In October, a major credit crunch created serious liquidity shortages in several developed economies. This had two repercussions: on the one hand, without the necessary credit, export orders shrank; on the other, financial entities began to liquidate their commodity-related positions as these became unsustainable owing to the lack of liquidity. Commodity sales volumes and prices consequently plunged as the inventories on the world's main commodities markets swelled. According to information available up to October, copper export volumes were down by 29% and total mineral exports were down by 23% on the previous year.

Imports remained buoyant, especially machinery and equipment imports, whose rise of almost 25% was closely linked to investment dynamics. After three successive years of posting a surplus, the current account is therefore estimated to record a deficit in 2008 of about 2.7% of GDP.

CHILE: MAIN ECONOMIC INDICATORS

	2006	2007	2008 [a]
	Annual growth rates		
Gross domestic product	4.3	5.1	3.8
Per capita gross domestic product	3.3	4.0	2.8
Consumer prices	2.6	7.8	8.9 [b]
Average real wage [c]	1.9	2.8	-0.3 [d]
Money (M1)	13.2	18.1	13.4 [e]
Real effective exchange rate [f]	-2.2	1.3	-4.1 [g]
Terms of trade	31.4	3.8	-7.2
	Annual average percentages		
Urban unemployment rate	7.7	7.1	7.7 [d]
Central government overall balance / GDP	7.7	8.8	6.9
Nominal deposit rate	5.5	5.9	7.8 [h]
Nominal lending rate	14.4	13.6	15.2 [h]
	Millions of dollars		
Exports of goods and services	66 310	76 429	78 863
Imports of goods and services	44 351	53 938	70 502
Current account	6 838	7 200	-5 639
Capital and financial account	-4 841	-10 414	10 839
Overall balance	1 997	-3 214	5 200

Source: Economic Commission for Latin America and the Caribbean (ECLAC), on the basis of official figures.
[a] Preliminary estimates.
[b] Twelve-month variation to November 2008.
[c] General hourly wage index.
[d] Estimate based on data from January to October.
[e] Twelve-month variation to October 2008.
[f] A negative rate indicates an appreciation of the currency in real terms.
[g] Year-on-year average variation, January to October.
[h] Average from January to November, annualized.

The economy is expected to slow in 2009 in response to the projected reduction in external demand, tighter internal and external liquidity conditions and a significantly higher level of uncertainty. Growth is expected to remain positive, however, thanks to the countercyclical measures adopted by the authorities and the ongoing buoyancy of other emerging economies.

The country's fiscal and monetary authorities announced measures geared towards ensuring sufficient liquidity and stimulating domestic demand. The central bank increased the amounts and terms of its liquidity supply in dollars and pesos and authorized the use of bank deposits as additional collateral in these programmes. New temporary subsidies were created, and existing subsidies for buying homes were expanded. Capital was pumped into the Small Enterprise Guarantee Fund (FOGAPE) to boost its credit support capacity by US$ 2 billion, and medium-sized enterprises were granted access to the Fund. Some US$ 200 million was injected into the Production Development Corporation (CORFO) to support commercial bank loans to small and medium-sized enterprises. The capital of BancoEstado will be raised US$ 500 million to increase its capacity to lend to small businesses and home buyers.

In short, although the external context deteriorated in 2008, the Chilean economy is projected to continue recording positive, albeit modest, growth in 2009, and inflation is expected to fall, thanks to the recently adopted measures and the continued action of the set of macroeconomic policies implemented over a number of years to create countercyclical capacities, which have helped ensure the country's fiscal and external solvency.

Colombia

Colombia's economy is estimated to have grown by 3.0% in 2008. As well as the impact of the international financial crisis, a number of domestic factors had a hand in the economic slowdown. Despite a series of measures taken by the central bank to ease demand-side inflationary pressures, the inflation rate will end the year well over target at 7.5%. As often occurs during the first year in office of newly elected mayors and governors, there was a delay in programmed public investment, which was in addition to strikes in a number of sectors. Although exports remained flat in volume terms, they rose sharply in value during the year, thanks to high average prices for petroleum and other commodities. This is expected to bring about a small reduction in the balance-of-payments current account deficit, which should stand at 2.6% of GDP.

The economic growth rate is projected to slacken in 2009 to around 2%, mainly because of the effects of the international crisis on the country's exports, remittances, foreign direct investment and external borrowing.

The economic slowdown is expected to reduce fiscal revenues. According to calculations by the Ministry of Finance and Public Credit, a drop of one percentage point in growth reduces the tax take by the equivalent of 0.2% of GDP. In addition, the country's finances will be hurt by both the higher price of the dollar, which pushes up the local-currency cost of dollar-denominated debt, and the steeper cost of external borrowing resulting from the financial crisis. Some uncertainty therefore surrounds the possibility of meeting the deficit targets of 1.4% of GDP in the consolidated public sector and 3.3% of GDP in central government.

In the first semester of 2008 the board of the central bank decreed a series of 25-basis-point rises in the intervention rate in order to ease inflationary pressure, and this slowed growth in household lending and consumption. The intervention rate has remained unchanged at 10% since July. Towards the year's end, the central bank lowered the legal reserve requirement for current and savings accounts and fixed-term deposit certificates, in order to inject liquidity into the economy and loosen up the credit market.

The exchange-rate policy stance has been dictated by extreme volatility in the exchange rate, which started the year at 1,980 pesos to the dollar and ended it at an average of around 2,200 pesos to the dollar. The peso underwent a nominal devaluation of 27% in July-October alone, largely as a result of international market turbulence. In response to the shift in exchange-rate trends and the impact of the financial crisis, the authorities eliminated the deposit on foreign borrowing in October. In addition, a tax amnesty was approved for the repatriation of capital held abroad and shown to be free of links to illicit activities.

COLOMBIA: GDP, INFLATION AND UNEMPLOYMENT

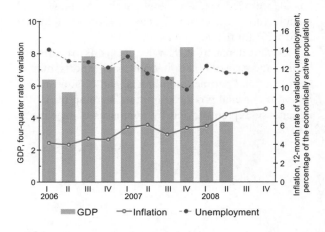

Source: Economic Commission for Latin America and the Caribbean (ECLAC), on the basis of official figures.

The economic growth the country has enjoyed in the last few years weakened in 2008, with the slowdown beginning in the first quarter and intensifying in the fourth. The economy expanded by 4.1% in the first semester, compared with 8.2% in the year-earlier period, with mining, transport and, to a lesser extent, agriculture, the main drivers in this period. Conversely, electricity, gas and water and manufacturing grew by less than 2.0% and construction, by 0.3%. Consumption, particularly private investment, which had been an engine of growth in previous years, continues to expand, albeit at much lower rates. Business and household confidence indicators trended downward over the course of the year, turning frankly negative in the second semester.

Inflation has been a concern for the authorities since 2006. Despite policy measures to contain inflationary pressures, the external price surge was passed through to domestic inflation, which is projected to reach 7.5%, well above the ceiling of the central bank's target range for 2008 of between 3.5% and 4.5%. The central bank hopes that slack global demand and falling commodity prices will ease inflationary pressures and thus expectations of inflation, which would enable it to loosen its policy stance in the medium term. The decline in demand and drop in commodity prices will help to contain inflation in 2009.

Urban unemployment rates, which had been trending downward since 2006, began to change direction mid-year, with a slight rise expected for the year overall. This shift is mainly a reflection of higher labour force participation since, at least until the third quarter, the employment rate continued to show positive year-on-year variation. Data on formal employment in manufacturing and commerce show signs of deterioration in formal job creation, however, with negative year-on–year rates for commerce in the third quarter. The higher inflation has also eroded wage-earners' purchasing power and manufacturing wages are expected to show a real loss of almost 2% for the year on average.

On the external front, the value of exports rose strongly, with an increase of 60.8% in traditional exports, mainly petroleum and petroleum products, and of almost 22% in non-traditional products. Imports were up by 19.1% in January-September, led by purchases of machinery

and equipment, fuels and mineral oils. The trade outlook for 2008 is not so bright and will depend, first, on the depth of the recession in the United States and the magnitude of the slowdown in the Bolivarian Republic of Venezuela, Colombia's two main trading partners. Another negative factor is the effect on export values of the drop in commodity prices that began in August. The current account deficit is expected to end the year at almost 2.6% of GDP. With respect to trade negotiations, the outcome of the elections in the United States does not appear to herald improved possibilities for approval of the free trade agreement with that country. Conversely, talks with the European Union are expected to prosper, since the requirement to negotiate as a bloc with the Andean countries has been dropped.

COLOMBIA: MAIN ECONOMIC INDICATORS

	2006	2007	2008 [a]
	Annual growth rates		
Gross domestic product	6.8	7.7	3.0
Per capita gross domestic product	5.3	6.3	1.7
Consumer prices	4.5	5.7	7.7 [b]
Average real wage [c]	3.7	-0.5	-1.8 [d]
Money (M1)	18.2	11.9	5.6 [e]
Real effective exchange rate [f]	-1.3	-10.7	-5.5 [g]
Terms of trade	3.8	8.0	13.1
	Annual average percentages		
Urban unemployment rate [h]	12.9	11.4	11.5 [i]
National central government overall balance / GDP	-3.8	-3.0	-2.7
Nominal deposit rate	6.2	8.0	9.7 [j]
Nominal lending rate	12.9	15.4	17.1 [k]
	Millions of dollars		
Exports of goods and services	28 558	34 213	41 832
Imports of goods and services	30 355	37 416	42 912
Current account	-2 982	-5 859	-6 442
Capital and financial account	3 005	10 572	9 053
Overall balance	23	4 714	2 611

Source: Economic Commission for Latin America and the Caribbean (ECLAC), on the basis of official figures.
[a] Preliminary estimates.
[b] Twelve-month variation to November 2008.
[c] Manufacturing-sector workers.
[d] Estimate based on data from January to August.
[e] Twelve-month variation to September 2008.
[f] A negative rate indicates an appreciation of the currency in real terms.
[g] Year-on-year average variation, January to October.
[h] Includes hidden unemployment.
[i] Estimate based on data from January to September.
[j] Average from January to November, annualized.
[k] Average from January to October, annualized.

Ecuador

Ecuador's GDP is estimated to have grown by 6.5% in 2008, with a slowdown projected for 2009 that will drag that rate down to 2%. The rate of inflation moved strongly upwards during the year, as international food prices reacted to the supply shock, and in October 2008 the yearly rate stood at 9.9%. Continuing with the process of change brokered by President Correa, the Constitutional Assembly drafted a new Constitution, which was approved by referendum on 28 September 2008.

Although fiscal policy was expansionary, thanks to buoyant petroleum revenues in the first three quarters, the non-financial public sector (NFPS) posted a surplus in 2008. In the first nine months of the year, the NFPS primary surplus was 6% of GDP and the overall position showed a surplus of 4.9% of GDP. Those results represent a significant improvement on the performance rendered in the same period of 2007, basically thanks to the strong upturn in oil prices during the period and to the government's efforts to secure a higher percentage of petroleum revenues. The ratio of public debt to GDP has continued to fall, as a result of this positive fiscal performance combined with GDP growth in 2008. As of the third quarter, Ecuador's total public debt amounted to US$ 12.98 billion, or the equivalent of 24.5% of GDP, while external public debt was US$ 10.012 billion, or 18.9% of GDP.

NFPS petroleum income was up by 222% in the first nine months of 2008, which accounted for the 69.2% rise in NFPS revenue in that period. Non-petroleum revenues also rose, especially receipts from income tax (up 33.5%) and VAT (13.4%), which benefited from more buoyant economic activity and higher export prices during those months. Income from the surpluses of state-owned companies rose by 63.6% during the high-price period.

NFPS spending rose by 69.5% in the first nine months of 2008, as compared with the year-earlier period. Particularly notable was the increase in capital spending (accrual basis), especially gross fixed capital formation, which was up by 116.2%. Current expenditures also increased (55.6%), however, during that period.

The most significant changes to the legal framework of fiscal policy in 2008 had to do with the tax reform applied following the Constituent Assembly's adoption in December of the law on tax equity which, among other things, abolished revenue pre-allocations; the approval, in April 2008 of legislation abolishing petroleum funds (law on the recovery of the use of State petroleum resources), which were absorbed into the central government budget; and the approval at the end of July 2008 of the legislation to reform and interpret the tax equity law. In November 2008 the government also announced a package of economic and financial measures aimed at reducing the impact of the international financial crisis in Ecuador.

In November 2008 Ecuador's yearly inflation rate stood at 9.1%. This reflected the impact of the external shock on food prices in the first half of the year. The real effective exchange rate depreciated by an average of 2.2% in the first 10 months of 2008, owing to the

ECUADOR: GDP, INFLATION AND UNEMPLOYMENT

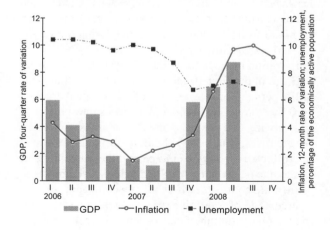

Source: Economic Commission for Latin America and the Caribbean (ECLAC), on the basis of official figures.

weakness of the United States dollar against the currencies of Ecuador's main trading partners, including Colombia, in the first semester, which started to be reversed as of September 2008.

Generally speaking, interest rates were lower in October 2008 than a year earlier. For example, the effective benchmark lending rate for corporate loans dropped from 10.7% in October 2007 to 9.2% a year later, while the rate for loans to SMEs came down from 14.1% to 11.6%.

The financial sector continued to grow in 2008. In the first 10 months of the year, the assets of open private banks continued to increase, with an expansion of 19.1% to October. The composition of the private banks' loan portfolio tended towards liquid assets held abroad between October 2007 and April 2008, when these represented 26% of the sector's total assets. Since then, turbulence in the international markets has led the banks to reduce their foreign deposits, although holdings in United States Treasury bonds have been maintained. Conversely, from April 2008 growth in the portfolio of loans to companies and other residents began to outpace that of total assets. This trend was fuelled by high domestic liquidity and falling interest rates, as well as the withholding tax on interest payments abroad introduced under the tax reform, in those cases where the retention is not treated as a credit in the country of origin. Holdings of State bonds were minimal during the period, representing 0.6% of total assets in September 2008.

In 2008 GDP growth was driven mainly by household consumption and gross fixed capital formation, stimulated, in the latter case, by a significant increase in public works undertaken by the government during the period. Central government consumption also rose.

Services and construction were the economy's two most dynamic sectors in 2008. Both benefited from the higher public spending in the period, although private demand also spurred the construction sector. Commerce and manufacturing also registered a buoyant performance on the back of surging domestic demand during the year.

Oil extraction by the State-owned Petroleum Corporation of Ecuador (PETROECUADOR) was up by 3.2% in the first 10 months of 2008 over the year-earlier period. The total volume of oil extracted dropped by 0.1%, however, compared to the same period in 2007, owing to a decrease of 4.2% in oil extraction by private firms. Since 2007 the Ecuadorian government has followed a policy of increasing the percentage of oil income received by the State, which also applies to partnership contracts (where private companies receive a percentage of total oil extracted) with private firms and the renegotiation of concessions; a recent example is the modification of the partnership contract with REPSOL-YPF.

ECUADOR: MAIN ECONOMIC INDICATORS

	2006	2007	2008 [a]
	Annual growth rates		
Gross domestic product	3,9	2,5	6,5
Per capita gross domestic product	2,4	1,0	5,0
Consumer prices	2,9	3,3	9,1 [b]
Real minimun wage	3,3	3,9	8,2
Money (M1)	19,1	18,6	37,2 [c]
Real effective exchange rate [d]	1,2	5,1	2,2 [e]
Terms of trade	7,3	2,8	15,6
	Annual average percentages		
Unemployment rate [f]	8,1	7,4	6,9 [g]
Central government overall balance / GDP	-0,2	-0,1	-0,1
Nominal deposit rate	4,4	5,3	...
Nominal lending rate	8,9	10,1	...
	Millions of dollars		
Exports of goods and services	14 213	16 070	20 723
Imports of goods and services	13 749	15 619	20 363
Current account	1 618	1 650	1 568
Capital and financial account	-1 748	-263	1 132
Overall balance	-131	1 387	2 700

Source: Economic Commission for Latin America and the Caribbean (ECLAC), on the basis of official figures.
[a] Preliminary estimates.
[b] Twelve-month variation to November 2008.
[c] Twelve-month variation to September 2008.
[d] A negative rate indicates an appreciation of the currency in real terms.
[e] Year-on-year average variation, January to October.
[f] Includes hidden unemployment.
[g] Estimate based on data from January to September.

The nationwide unemployment rate was 7.1% in September 2008, remaining stable with respect to the previous year. At the same time, the employment rate rose slightly, from 40.2% in September 2007 to 41.1% in September 2008.

The balance-of-payments current account posted a surplus in 2008. This reflected a substantial upswing in petroleum exports as a result of the higher prices for crude in 2008.

In the first nine months of 2008, the value of exports increased by 51.8%, of which 85% was attributable to the upturn in petroleum exports. The volume of crude oil exports rose 4.8%, while the average export price surged by 85.8%. Non-petroleum exports were up by 17.5% in the period, particularly those of bananas and plantains, followed at a distance by exports of tinned fish.

The value of imports jumped by 43% in the first nine months of 2008, driven largely by raw materials, whose imports were up by 45.9%. Rising investment in Ecuador in 2008 fuelled imports of capital goods, which climbed by 41.5% in those nine months, while imports of consumer goods rose 42% thanks to higher private and public consumption.

Remittances from emigrants slowed in 2008. In the first semester these rose by a meagre 1.6% over the year-earlier period and fell as a percentage of GDP, from

3.2% to 2.8%. This was due to problems in the United States economy and to the loss of momentum in Spain in 2008, since almost 90% of remittances into Ecuador are sent from those two countries.

Foreign direct investment (FDI) remained sluggish throughout the period, rising from 0.6% of GDP in the first semester of 2007 to 1% of GDP a year later. Unlike the pattern seen up to 2007, in 2008 FDI rose faster in business services and commerce than in the traditional sector of mining and quarrying (oil). In fact, despite the high oil prices in the second half of 2007 and the first three quarters of 2008, FDI in mining and quarrying remained at 0.5% of GDP in the first semester of 2008, similarly to the figure for the first half of 2007.

Paraguay

The Paraguayan economy expanded by about 5% in 2008, its sixth consecutive year of growth. This performance was driven mainly by brisk growth in domestic demand, marked by substantial upturns in gross fixed capital formation and private consumption. The best-performing sectors were construction, agriculture and livestock. A slight fiscal surplus and a positive primary balance of around 1.2% of GDP are expected for the end of the year. The cumulative rise in consumer prices to November stood at 6.9%, so the final inflation rate should fall within the target range (5%, with a margin of 2.5% on either side) although closer to the upper limit. The current account deficit is expected to close the year at US$ 335.2 million, equivalent to 2.1% of GDP. The presidential election in April was won by Fernando Lugo, the candidate of the Alianza Patriótica para el Cambio (Patriotic Alliance for Change), resulting in a new government after 61 years with the Colorado Party in power. The expansion of economic activity is projected to slow in 2009, with an estimated growth rate of 2%.

A positive primary balance of around 1.2% of GDP is expected for the end of 2008, with a small fiscal surplus equivalent to 0.5% of GDP, this being the fifth consecutive year of balanced fiscal accounts. The standby agreement signed in 2006 with the International Monetary Fund (IMF) expired in August. The latest IMF assessment indicated that all fiscal goals would be met. The cumulative surplus to September reached 2.03 trillion guaraníes, while cumulative revenue over the same period rose to 9.4 trillion guaraníes, 70% of which was from tax receipts. The largest component of tax revenue is value added tax (VAT), followed by taxes on income and foreign trade. Personal income tax, due to be introduced in January 2009, is expected to boost revenue and increase the tax burden, which is comparatively low (estimated at 12.1% for 2008). The largest component of government expenditure was staffing costs, which made up 49.1% of the total to September. Sound fiscal performance was reflected in a lessening of public-sector debt, which was down 2.8% by late October 2008. The external public financial debt recorded in the Debt Management and Financial Analysis System (DMFAS) dropped by 3.4% during the same period.

After holding the interest on monetary regulation instruments unchanged for four months, the central bank raised benchmark rates in March. In June, it began to auction the instruments and the legal reserve requirement

PARAGUAY: GDP AND INFLATION

Source: Economic Commission for Latin America and the Caribbean (ECLAC), on the basis of official figures.

in national currency was raised. There was a slowdown in the growth of monetary aggregates from the second quarter onward, while the process of "guaranization" continued: in September 2008 the ratio of local- to foreign-currency deposits was 1.42, compared with 1.12 in September 2007. The effect was even more pronounced in the area of lending, where the same ratio reached 1.55 in September 2008 as against 1.16 in September 2007. In October, in reaction to the financial crisis in the international markets and the sharp devaluation of the guaraní, much of this process was reversed and the ratios were then 1.15 for deposits and 1.4 for loans. On 9 October the central bank loosened its monetary policy, reducing the legal reserve requirements for deposits in local and foreign currency, lowering by one percentage point the yield curve of the benchmark interest rate for the sale of monetary regulation instruments and establishing a credit line for local financial entities in the form of a facility for short-term liquidity through the repurchase of monetary regulation instruments (FLIR). On 14 November the central bank lowered the benchmark interest rate for the instruments by a further percentage point and created a facility for their early payment for up to 50 billion guaraníes per entity.

To July, the guaraní recorded a year-on-year real appreciation against the dollar of 27.95%. In order to soften the appreciation, the central bank intervened vigorously in the currency market; in late July, cumulative net purchases of dollars reached US$ 459.7 million, causing an increase in international reserves to US$ 3.187 billion or 21.1% of GDP. With respect to the country's main trading partners, the real effective exchange rate index dropped by 19.76% during the same period. From August onward the dollar strengthened, forcing the central bank to sell foreign exchange in order to stabilize the exchange rate. From August to October US$ 389 million were sold and the guaraní depreciated sharply against the dollar. Between August and November the guaraní fell heavily against the dollar, by 21.6% in nominal terms. The level of international reserves fell to US$ 2.737 billion by the end of October.

The economy continued to expand in 2008. From January to September, GDP increased by 6.5% compared to the same period in 2007. Total growth for 2008 is estimated to reach 5%. Domestic demand was particularly influenced by gross fixed capital formation, which rose by 20.9% between January and September in relation to the same period in 2007, driven by dynamic growth in construction (in housing, and work on the binational Yacyreta hydroelectric dam project) and the machinery and equipment sector. As for production, the performance of the livestock, forestry and fishing sector was driven by increases in external demand and prices, and agriculture

PARAGUAY: MAIN ECONOMIC INDICATORS

	2006	2007	2008 [a]
	Annual growth rates		
Gross domestic product	4.3	6.8	5.0
Per capita gross domestic product	2.4	4.9	3.0
Consumer prices	12.5	6.0	8.3 [b]
Average real wage	0.6	2.4	-0.8 [c]
Money (M1)	10.8	46.1	18.3 [d]
Real effective exchange rate [e]	-10.4	-10.4	-13.5 [f]
Terms of trade	-1.9	4.8	4.7
	Annual average percentages		
Urban unemployment rate	8.9	7.2	...
Central administration			
overall balance / GDP	0.5	1.0	0.5
Nominal deposit rate	9.8	5.9	5.8 [g]
Nominal lending rate	16.6	14.6	13.6 [h]
	Millions of dollars		
Exports of goods and services	5 154	6 324	8 830
Imports of goods and services	5 406	6 486	9 421
Current account	120	45	-335
Capital and financial account	263	678	527
Overall balance	383	723	192

Source: Economic Commission for Latin America and the Caribbean (ECLAC), on the basis of official figures.
[a] Preliminary estimates.
[b] Twelve-month variation to November 2008.
[c] Figure for June.
[d] Twelve-month variation to October 2008.
[e] A negative rate indicates an appreciation of the currency in real terms.
[f] Year-on-year average variation, January to October.
[g] Average from January to September, annualized.
[h] Average from January to October, annualized.

benefited from increased production as well as rising food prices on international markets during the first semester. The manufacturing and mining sectors saw strong growth in machinery and equipment, mineral production (cement), meat production and paper and printing. Commerce and services increased by 5.4% between January and September, thanks to the good performance of transport and the financial services. Data are still not available for employment rates in 2008, so it is not yet known whether the economic growth has led to job creation.

Inflation measured as the year-on-year variation of the consumer price index (CPI) rose from 8.8% in January to 13.4% in July. Inflation began to fall in August, and in November the year-on-year variation stood at 8.3%. In the same month core inflation (which excludes fruit and vegetables) recorded a year-on-year rate of 8%, as did core X1 (which also excludes regulated services and fuels). Variations in prices for foods, raw materials and fuels have had a significant impact on CPI. There was a 12.9% increase in the index for wages and salaries during the first semester over the same period in 2007. The minimum wage, however, remained unchanged between October 2007 and 2008.

Rising international prices for commodities, and especially for agricultural goods, had a considerable impact on foreign trade. In October, the value of recorded exports was up by a year-on-year figure of 74.1%; particularly dynamic were soybean, vegetable oils, meat and flour, which were up 86.5%, 178.7%, 186.2% and 88.3%, respectively. Imports increased by 62.7%, principally among intermediate goods (fuels) and capital goods. As of October, the trade deficit stood at US$ 3.381 billion, 51.2% higher than the previous year. The current account is expected to post a deficit of US$ 335.2 million, the first negative result since 2001.

Peru

The economic performance of Peru was characterized by buoyant domestic demand and a deterioration in external conditions. This included inflationary pressure, a fall in the terms of trade, strong capital movements that pushed up exchange-rate volatility and —towards the end of the year— a worsening of financing conditions and considerable uncertainty surrounding the future of global markets. Be that as it may, GDP growth once more accelerated to over 9%, spearheaded by investment and private consumption. Inflation, which had already exceeded the target range by the end of the previous year, rose throughout the year and is expected to stand above 6% in December.

Buoyant imports and the worsening terms of trade resulted in a current account deficit equivalent to close to 4% of GDP. However, high foreign investment led to another expansion of net international reserves. The difficult global situation and higher interest rates point to a smaller expansion of economic activity of about 5% in 2009. Inflation is expected to decline gradually and approach the target range by late 2009.

In the first half of the year, the main challenges of economic policy were the rise in inflation and currency appreciation. In the second half, the authorities endeavoured to contain the impact of the international financial crisis on the Peruvian economy.

To ensure that price rises in mainly imported products such as fuel and food were prevented from generating expectations of across-the-board increases in consumer prices, the benchmark interest rate was raised several times from 5.0% at the beginning of the year to 6.5% in September. As interest rates were lowered in the United States at the same time, this attracted short-term capital inflows that brought down the exchange rate. To offset this trend and halt the credit expansion, on several occasions the authorities increased the legal reserve requirement (from 6% to 9%) and the marginal reserve requirement (to 25% for local currency and 49% for foreign currency), while the fee for transactions by non-residents was raised as well. Also in the first half of the year the central bank acquired US$ 8.7 billion, bringing its reserves to US$ 35.5 billion.

This successfully put an end to short-term capital inflows and to the appreciation of the new sol. However, in a context of high economic growth and the swelling ranks of debtors, those measures failed to stop the financial system's credit to the private sector from expanding rapidly (28.5% in mid-October).

Using fiscal policy to curb inflation, the authorities raised the target for the surplus of the non-financial public sector (NFPS) to 2.7% of GDP. High economic growth contributed to a new real increase in fiscal receipts (8%

PERU: GDP, INFLATION AND UNEMPLOYMENT

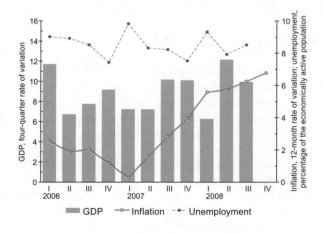

GDP, four-quarter rate of variation

Inflation, 12-month rate of variation; unemployment, percentage of the economically active population

■ GDP   ─○─ Inflation   ─•─ Unemployment

Source: Economic Commission for Latin America and the Caribbean (ECLAC), on the basis of official figures.

up to October), although this was less dramatic than in previous years. Total receipts from the general sales tax expanded by 20% in this period, while real receipts from income tax edged up only slightly (mainly on account of lower prices for exports of natural resources). As a result, the central government's income as a proportion of GDP is expected to fall moderately for the year as a whole.

Efforts to step up public investment continued. Up to October, central government capital expenditure grew by 32% in real terms, while current expenditure as a proportion of GDP fell owing mainly to lower interest payments. This development boosted the resources of the fiscal stabilization fund, which will in turn facilitate the implementation of counter-cyclical policies in case the external crisis has a higher-than-expected impact on the Peruvian economy.

The deepening of the United States financial crisis and the contagion of other markets were reflected from September in a sharp downturn of stock-market indicators, more expensive external credit (higher country risk rating) and an increased preference for liquidity in dollars, which increased their proportion of total liquidity in the financial system from 29.6% in August to 36.2% in October. In a bid to increase the financial sector's liquidity, the authorities adopted a number of measures: by November they had sold off US$ 5.685 billion of previously accumulated reserves; long-term credit from abroad was exempted from the reserve requirement; and the marginal reserve requirement was eliminated for local currency and reduced to 35% for foreign currency.

Nonetheless, the new sol depreciated in the second half of the year, and in October the real bilateral exchange rate against the dollar was similar to the level recorded in the same month of the previous year, although the average for the year shows an appreciation. As for the real effective exchange rate, the appreciation was more significant (around 4% in October) and held steady until the end of the year.

Approval by the Congress of the United States has paved the way for the entry into force of the free trade agreement with that country in 2009, when a similar agreement with Canada will also come into effect. Negotiations with China were being concluded towards the end of the year.

Despite slower growth in the final quarter, GDP has expanded by more than 9% on the strength of domestic demand, fuelled by a strong increase in private investment (around 25%) and public investment (over 50%) and a significant rise in household consumption (about 8%). In addition, export figures were higher than in the previous year, although some loss of dynamism could be seen towards the

PERU: MAIN ECONOMIC INDICATORS

	2006	2007	2008 [a]
Annual growth rates			
Gross domestic product	7.6	8.9	9.4
Per capita gross domestic product	6.3	7.6	8.2
Consumer prices	1.1	3.9	6.7 [b]
Average real wage	1.2	-1.8	2.6 [c]
Money (M1)	22.4	30.7	27.3 [d]
Real effective exchange rate [e]	2.8	1.0	-3.3 [f]
Terms of trade	26.5	3.6	-7.0
Annual average percentages			
Urban unemployment rate	8.5	8.4	8.3 [g]
Central government			
overall balance / GDP	1.5	1.8	2.3
Nominal deposit rate	3.4	3.5	3.3 [h]
Nominal lending rate	17.1	16.5	16.7 [h]
Millions of dollars			
Exports of goods and services	26 447	31 298	35 868
Imports of goods and services	18 295	23 870	34 772
Current account	2 757	1 505	-5 635
Capital and financial account	-30	8 082	9 095
Overall balance	2 726	9 588	3 460

Source: Economic Commission for Latin America and the Caribbean (ECLAC), on the basis of official figures.
[a] Preliminary estimates.
[b] Twelve-month variation to November 2008.
[c] Figure for June.
[d] Twelve-month variation to October 2008.
[e] A negative rate indicates an appreciation of the currency in real terms.
[f] Year-on-year average variation, January to October.
[g] Estimate based on data from January to October.
[h] Average from January to November, annualized.

end of the year. Meanwhile, rising domestic demand boosted imports, which expanded by over 20% in real terms.

Higher prices for imported food and fuel contributed to a steeper rise in the consumer price index (CPI), which in November stood at 6.75% (clearly exceeding the inflation target ceiling of 3%). The fall in international prices and a moderate slackening of domestic demand are expected to help bring down inflation gradually during 2009.

High economic growth stimulated labour demand and between January and September employment in formal enterprises climbed by 8.9%, albeit with decreasing rates from the middle of the year. There was a decline in employment in microenterprises and own-account work, such that the employment rate in metropolitan Lima dropped by 0.4 percentage points in the first three quarters of the year and the unemployment rate only remained virtually unchanged thanks to a fall in labour-force participation. Despite the rise in inflation, real wages grew by 2.6% (June).

The buoyancy of merchandise imports and the widening deficit on the commercial services account contributed to the significant narrowing of the trade surplus from 6.9% of GDP in 2007 to approximately 1% in 2008; another contributing factor was the worsening of the terms of trade (down an estimated 7% for the year as a whole), which was a turnaround of the trend observed since 2002. Given the continuing high transfers from the factor income account, the current account surplus of the last four years gave way to a deficit equivalent to approximately 4% of GDP.

The private sector received considerable capital inflows (particularly in the form of foreign direct investment), while the public sector continued the policy of reducing its external debt, with advance payments made to the Andean Development Corporation and in Brady bonds. The net effect of rising private external debt and shrinking public external debt was a drop in total external debt from 30.3% of GDP in late 2007 to 27.8% at the end of the third quarter of 2008.

Uruguay

The Uruguayan economy grew by 11.5% in 2008. This was the fifth consecutive year in which GDP grew much more quickly than the historical average, with a cumulative increase of 55% for the period. Annual inflation remained at around 8.5%, owing to higher international commodity prices during the first half of the year and to the rise in import prices that was in turn a result of appreciation of the United States dollar in the final quarter. According to ECLAC estimates, given current international uncertainty, the growth rate is expected to be 4% in 2009.

The fiscal situation of the non-financial public sector recorded a primary surplus of some 2.0% of GDP and interest payments on debt of 3.0%. This resulted in a deficit of 1.0% of GDP in the rolling 12-month period to September 2008. The deficit is expected to close the year at about 1.2 percentage points of GDP. Fiscal revenues swelled as State-owned corporations recorded a rise in the primary balance and fiscal receipts expanded. Spending by the non-financial public sector increased by a similar proportion to income, which was attributable to purchases of petroleum and transfers carried out as part of social policy.

The gross-debt-to-GDP ratio of the non-financial public sector fell once again, to stand at 43% in mid-2008. External debt restructuring continued by means of bond issues and buy-back operations in the market. Country risk, which had been around 200 base points in the first half of the year, rose to about 700 base points in October 2008 as a result of international financial volatility. At the end of October, gross reserves amounted to US$ 6.0 billion (approximately 20% of GDP), which was US$ 2.0 billion more than in the year-earlier period. Of this increase, 38% was attributable to the higher reserve requirements adopted for short-term deposits in local and foreign currency in the national banking system, following the liquidity control measures introduced in October 2007 and reinforced in June 2008.

Measures put in place in June 2008 consisted of raising the reserve requirement for local-currency deposits of less than one month to 25% and raising the requirement for foreign-currency deposits of residents and non-residents of up to six months to 35%. For public-sector deposits with the Banco de la República Oriental del Uruguay, reserve requirements were set at 100%. Also, yields on reserve requirements were eliminated, rules were introduced for the daily monitoring of reserve requirements and fines introduced for non-compliance.

Monetary policy continued to aim at preserving price stability, and maintained the system to set the short-term interbank interest rate. At the beginning of October, the rate set by the Monetary Policy Committee of the Uruguay Central Bank was raised to 7.75%, following 12 months at 7.25%.

Monetary policy measures combined with the implementation of price agreements in the main production chains of basic consumer goods. The agreements were in force principally between May and September 2008, but subsequently became unnecessary as prices for those products fell at the international level.

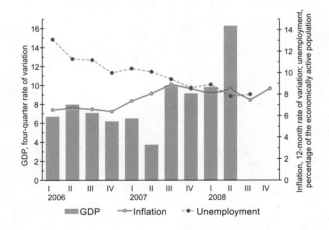

URUGUAY: GDP, INFLATION AND UNEMPLOYMENT

Source: Economic Commission for Latin America and the Caribbean (ECLAC), on the basis of official figures.

In June, credit to the resident private sector expanded by 31.5% (dollar equivalent) compared with the same month in 2007, with slightly higher growth of 33% for credit in foreign currency. The default rate was at a record low of around 1%. In the same period, deposits increased by 21.2% (dollar equivalent), with significant growth in local-currency deposits (43%). Deposits in current and savings accounts represented 75% of the total, which provided considerable liquidity for the system. The lending rate in United States dollars was an annual 5.9%, while the annual borrowing rate was 1.1% for fixed-term deposits in foreign currency.

The nominal exchange rate continued to float. In the 12-month period up to June 2008, the local currency registered a 19% nominal appreciation, although this was mainly reversed in September and October, when the currency depreciated by 14% in relation to June. Meanwhile, the real effective exchange rate appreciated by an average of around 10% in the first 10 months of 2008 compared with the year-earlier period.

In 2008, the economic growth rate of 11.5% was attributable to increased output in almost all sectors. This was especially true of manufacturing (16%) and transport and communications (33.7%), which grew by more than the average for the economy. Growth in other sectors, such as commerce, restaurants and hotels (7.2%), agriculture (6%), construction (4.7%) and other branches of activity (5.3%), was below the average for the economy. Electricity, gas and water declined by 23%, as severe drought affected hydroelectric power generation.

In the first half of the year, external demand for goods and services held steady in the course of the year, while internal demand rose because of the rise in household incomes (4.9%) and increased credit. Investment grew by 25% during the year, and represented 2.2 percentage points of GDP growth.

In 2008, goods exports are estimated to have risen by 25.1% compared with the year-earlier period. The main destinations were Brazil (16.5%), Argentina (8.4%) and the Russian Federation (6.3%). Goods imports, f.o.b. expanded by 35.6% for the year, with a surge in imports of machinery and equipment and of intermediate goods. In the first half of the year, the balance-of-payments current account deficit represented 2.1% of GDP, mainly because of the trade deficit of US$ 391 million (in contrast to the US$ 292 million surplus posted in the first six months of 2007). The current account is expected to close the year with a deficit of around 3.5 percentage points of GDP. The financial account recorded capital inflows of US$ 2.2 billion between January and July, as a result of inflows to the private sector.

URUGUAY: MAIN ECONOMIC INDICATORS

	2006	2007	2008 [a]
	Annual growth rates		
Gross domestic product	7,0	7,4	11,5
Per capita gross domestic product	6,8	7,2	11,2
Consumer prices	6,4	8,5	8,5 [b]
Average real wage	4,3	4,7	3,3 [c]
Money (M1)	20,0	31,8	12,0 [d]
Real effective exchange rate [e]	-4,4	-1,0	-10,0 [f]
Terms of trade	-2,2	1,9	-4,4
	Annual average percentages		
Urban unemployment rate	11,4	9,6	7,9 [c]
Central government overall balance / GDP	-1,0	-1,7	-1,0
Nominal deposit rate	1,7	2,3	3,0 [g]
Nominal lending rate	10,7	10,0	12,0 [g]
	Millions of dollars		
Exports of goods and services	5 785	6 796	8 310
Imports of goods and services	5 882	6 840	9 037
Current account	- 400	- 235	-1 096
Capital and financial account	2 798	1 245	3 388
Overall balance	2 399	1 010	2 291

Source: Economic Commission for Latin America and the Caribbean (ECLAC), on the basis of official figures.
[a] Preliminary estimates.
[b] Twelve-month variation to November 2008.
[c] Estimate based on data from January to October.
[d] Twelve-month variation to October 2008.
[e] A negative rate indicates an appreciation of the currency in real terms.
[f] Year-on-year average variation, January to October.
[g] Average from January to October, annualized.

Inflation up to November stood at 8.5%, which means that it will end the year higher than the rate set in the monetary programme (a target range of between 4.5% and 6.5%). The inflationary trend was the result of higher export prices, especially for derivatives of wheat, meat and dairy products, as well as rising international oil prices in the first half of 2008. In the third and fourth quarters, the prices of these goods fell, although local-currency prices of imported products rose as the dollar appreciated. Wholesale inflation stood at an annual rate of around 20% in the first six months of the year, although this was followed by deflation which brought down the annual rate to 8.6% in November.

The labour market remained in a growth phase at the national level, with the employment rate rising from 56.5% in the first 10 months of 2007 to 57.3% in the same period of 2008. The participation rate remained stable at around 62%. Unemployment dropped from an average of 9.4% between January and October 2007 to 7.8% in the same period of 2008. The average wage index posted a real increase of 3.1% between January and October, with rises of 2.9% in the private sector and 3.8% in the public sector. The national minimum wage was adjusted upwards by 28% in nominal terms in relation to the previous year, which means it now represents the equivalent of about US$ 175 per month in prices of early November.

Wage councils completed their third round of collective negotiations since they were reintroduced in 2005, reaching agreements through tripartite consensus in 80% of sector groups and subgroups. In the remaining 20%, agreements were reached thanks to the support of government representatives for a given position. These agreements represent a significant recovery of wage levels and increases in real wages, and will remain in force for between a 24 and 30 months.

Mexico and Central America

Costa Rica

The rise in international food and fuel prices, as well as the slowdown in the world economy, had a negative impact on the growth of the Costa Rican economy, with the growth rate down to 3.3% compared with 7.3% in 2007. At the same time, national open unemployment edged up slightly to 5% (bucking the trend of the last three years). The current account deficit is expected to represent the equivalent of 8% of GDP, while the fiscal deficit of the central government should weigh in at around 0.5% of GDP. Inflation, for its part, posted an increase and will probably stand at around 15% at the end of the year.

According to ECLAC estimates, GDP will grow by 1% in 2009. Economic performance will continue to be influenced by weak external demand. The slowdown in the world economy and recession in the country's main trading partner (United States) will result in low growth in: merchandise exports, tourism revenues and inflows of foreign direct investment (FDI) (particularly investment in the property sector). Lower international prices for fuel and raw materials will ease pressure on the current account deficit and on inflation, with the latter expected to be lower than in 2008 but nonetheless close to 10%.

The implementation agenda for the Dominican Republic-Central America-United States Free Trade Agreement (CAFTA-DR) dominated economic policy in 2008. In the context of this agenda, several laws were adopted including a telecommunications act and an insurance act, which laid the foundations for opening the two sectors up to competition. The final bill was approved in November, and CAFTA-DR is therefore expected to enter into force on 1 January 2009. Throughout the year, macroeconomic policy squared up to the external shocks through increases in social spending and changes to monetary and foreign-exchange policy.

The slightly negative balance of the central government in 2008, following the positive balance of around 0.6% of GDP recorded in 2007, was mainly the result of higher investment in infrastructure and increased social spending to tackle the impact of price rises throughout the year. Despite a reduction in the amount of tax evasion, the current revenues of the central government posted moderate growth, owing to the slowdown in receipts from taxes on consumers, income and car imports (as a consequence of slower economic growth).

Exchange-rate and interest-rate patterns in 2008 fall into two contrasting periods. In the first four months of the year, the nominal exchange rate against the United States dollar posted an appreciation of over 5% to reach 494 colones to the dollar in April, mainly as a result of capital inflows. In response to the lower interest rate in the United States and other trading partners, and to discourage such inflows, the monetary policy rate was reduced from 6% to 3.25% in January (and remained at this level until 28 May).

There was a turnaround in the exchange rate from May, as it moved towards the upper limit of the exchange-rate band. Between May and December, the exchange

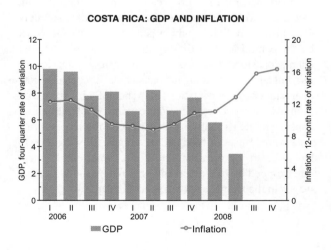

COSTA RICA: GDP AND INFLATION

Source: Economic Commission for Latin America and the Caribbean (ECLAC), on the basis of official figures.

rate depreciated by over 10%. Upward pressure on the exchange rate is attributable to less favourable short- and medium-term expectations in the wake of weaker external accounts. With a view to offsetting the pressure on the exchange rate, the central bank intervened on the foreign-exchange market by reducing its net reserves by 27% between April and October. The exchange-rate band was also adjusted: the selling rate was reduced from 572.49 colones to the dollar to 555.37, while the buying rate was increased from 488.73 colones to the dollar to 500 colones (with a daily increase of 6 centavos to the upper limit of the band). In terms of the real effective exchange rate, the average variation recorded up to October was a 3% appreciation. In the face of upward pressure on the exchange rate and rising inflation, the authorities increased the monetary policy rate on four occasions to reach 10.87% in early August (at which level it remained subsequently). Despite the increase, the real borrowing rate ended the year in negative figures.

Slower growth in the Costa Rican economy (3.3%) was partly due to the slowdown in consumption (4%, which was two percentage points less than in 2007), which itself was a result of rising inflation. The other contributing factor was the smaller expansion of the world economy (particularly in the United States), which had a negative impact on external demand (an estimated real decline of 3% for exports). Gross fixed investment continued to grow (by around 15%), but at a slower rate than the 16.7% recorded in 2007. The sectors that turned in the best performances were construction, transport and communications, and financial services, although they all posted lower growth rates than in 2007. In contrast, manufacturing and agriculture showed negative growth rates.

Inflation, as measured by the consumer price index, climbed sharply in 2008. Year-on-year inflation from December to December is expected to be approximately 15% (10.8% in 2007), which is above the 9% target set by the central bank at the beginning of the year. Higher international food and fuel prices are partly responsible for this rise, but other contributing factors include the exchange-rate depreciation and expectations of higher inflation (based on monthly surveys of expectations carried out by the central bank). The items that have experienced the largest price rises were transport, food and beverages. Slowing growth has affected job creation, and the national employment rate dropped by half a percentage point. Meanwhile, real wages in the formal sector dipped slightly.

COSTA RICA: MAIN ECONOMIC INDICATORS

	2006	2007	2008 [a]
	Annual growth rates		
Gross domestic product	8.8	7.3	3.3
Per capita gross domestic product	6.9	5.5	1.6
Consumer prices	9.4	10.8	16.3 [b]
Average real wage [c]	1.6	1.4	-1.5 [d]
Money (M1)	37.9	22.6	7.9 [e]
Real effective exchange rate [f]	-1.1	-2.2	-3.1 [g]
Terms of trade	-2.9	-1.0	-3.8
	Annual average percentages		
Unemployment rate	6.0	4.6	4.9
Central government			
overall balance / GDP	-1.1	0.6	-0.5
Nominal deposit rate	11.4	7.1	5.1 [h]
Nominal lending rate	22.7	17.3	16.3 [h]
	Millions of dollars		
Exports of goods and services	11 073	12 859	13 883
Imports of goods and services	12 449	14 103	16 099
Current account	-1 023	-1 639	-2 442
Capital and financial account	2 053	3 096	1 992
Overall balance	1 031	1 457	-450

Source: Economic Commission for Latin America and the Caribbean (ECLAC), on the basis of official figures.
[a] Preliminary estimates.
[b] Twelve-month variation to November 2008.
[c] Average wages reported by workers covered by social security.
[d] Estimate based on data from January to August.
[e] Twelve-month variation to October 2008.
[f] A negative rate indicates an appreciation of the currency in real terms.
[g] Year-on-year average variation, January to October.
[h] Average from January to November, annualized.

The balance-of-payments current account deficit widened considerably from 6.2% of GDP in 2007 to around 8% of GDP in 2008. In the light of less buoyant manufacturing exports from free zones and the inward processing procedure, merchandise exports grew by around 3% (14.9% in 2007). Merchandise imports, on the other hand, expanded by about 15% (13.4% in 2007), mainly thanks to a surge in the oil bill and in imports of other intermediate goods.

Exports of services, spearheaded by "other services" including business support and data processing services and software, are expected to grow by around 20%. Growth in tourism, measured in visitor numbers, has slowed down in recent months, as has growth in revenues from family remittances. Foreign direct investment (FDI) should close the year at around US$ 2.0 billion, which represents annual growth of 8%.

El Salvador

According to ECLAC estimates, GDP growth in El Salvador should stand at 3% in 2008, some 1.5 percentage points below the 2007 figure. Despite a slowdown, family remittances (17.5% of GDP) nonetheless helped to mitigate the negative impact of higher oil and food prices on the current account, which showed a deficit equivalent to 6% of GDP. The global fiscal deficit of the non-financial public sector stood at 0.9% of GDP, and annual inflation came in at around 5%.

In 2009, owing to the worldwide slowdown, GDP growth in El Salvador will be around 1%, held back by falls in exports, remittances and foreign direct investment (FDI). Positive contributions to growth are expected from agriculture and the services sector, as well as the positive impact of the use of resources from the Millennium Challenge Account and increased public investment resulting from the holding of elections (legislative and municipal elections will take place in January and the presidential election in March). All these factors will tend to compensate for declining external demand. The falls in economic activity and world oil prices should reduce inflation, and the current account deficit is likely to be close to its 2008 level.

The current income of the non-financial public sector (NFPS) in 2008 stood at 17% of GDP (8% higher than in 2007). Tax receipts were up 12% and were equivalent to 13.6% of GDP, close to the 2007 figure. This was due to the positive impact of improvements in tax administration adopted as part of the reform of 2005. Current expenditure (16% of GDP) expanded by 13.6% as a result of increased transfers. Public transport and the consumption of electric power, water and liquefied gas were subsidized to the tune of about US$ 400 million (1.8% of GDP).

This pressure on the fiscal accounts led to an overall NFPS deficit equivalent to 0.9% of GDP (0.7 percentage points above the 2007 figure). The overall central government deficit stood at 0.6% of GDP. The balance of the external public debt remained relatively stable but internal public debt rose by almost 12%. Treasury notes were issued totalling US$ 450 million (2% of GDP, barely 0.3 percentage points more than in 2007). In November 2008, the political parties and the government agreed on

a US$ 950 million increase in external debt in the form of loans provided by the Inter-American Development Bank (IDB) and the World Bank. Of that total, US$ 650 million will be used to restructure the debt in Eurobonds maturing in 2011, and the remainder will be devoted to social development. The challenges facing the State in 2009 in terms of public resources will be to improve the targeting of subsidies and to streamline public spending.

Nominal interest rates remained relatively steady in 2008, resulting in negative real interest rates. Limited liquidity in the system led to a slowing of growth in bank

EL SALVADOR: GROWTH AND INFLATION

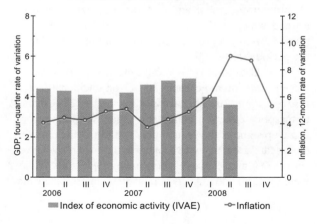

Source: Economic Commission for Latin America and the Caribbean (ECLAC), on the basis of official figures.

lending to the public and private sectors. The main financial indicators remained stable. In October, the net international reserves of the central bank stood at US$ 2.344 billion (about 7% more than in 2007), equivalent to 2.5 months of goods and services imports.

Favourable prices for certain products boosted the performance of the agricultural sector for the fourth consecutive year, with growth of 8.4%, almost identical to the 2007 figure. Growth in other productive activities was positive, but less so than in 2007. Construction, manufacturing and mining expanded by 1.7%, 3.6% and 4.5%, respectively. Remittances accounted for 3.7% of the growth of private consumption, which was three points below the previous year's level. Public investment (11% of total gross fixed investment) increased by 13.7%, but did not make up for a 0.9% fall in private investment. The latter was due to worldwide financial uncertainties and the slowdown in the United States economy, which led to greater caution in investments and caused a fall in growth in 2008.

Owing to upward pressure on the prices of food and petroleum products, the annual inflation rate exceeded 9% in mid-2008. Between September 2007 and September 2008, the monthly cost of the basic food basket rose by 34.5% in rural areas and by 27.8% in urban areas. To attenuate this negative impact, the government raised its subsidies on public transport in mid-2008, strengthened the Solidarity Network programme in order to reduce absolute poverty and launched the Family Alliance programme, which aims to improve the standard of living of middle-income families through discounts on school fees, expanded health-care coverage and pension increases. Inflation moderated in the second half of the year, with the year-on-year rate approaching 5%. In June 2008, nominal minimum wages were increased by 5%, as a result of which the annual average for the real minimum wage remained constant. Open unemployment and underemployment also rose, a trend which will strengthen in 2009. The number of families living in poverty may therefore increase during the period 2008-2009.

Goods exports were strong, increasing by 17%, 10 percentage points more than in 2007. Non-traditional exports rose by 24% and traditional exports soared by 28%, thanks to the price effect on coffee and sugar. Maquila exports made up some of the ground they had lost in the previous three years, growing by 12% (a figure they had not achieved since 2000), and services exports rose by 6%. Goods imports were up 15%, and imports of consumer, intermediate and

EL SALVADOR: MAIN ECONOMIC INDICATORS

	2006	2007	2008 [a]
	Annual growth rates		
Gross domestic product	4.2	4.7	3.0
Per capita gross domestic product	2.4	2.9	1.3
Consumer prices	4.9	4.9	5.3 [b]
Real minimun wage	-0.7	2.5	-0.0
Money (M1)	15.2	16.5	6.3 [c]
Real effective exchange rate [d]	0.4	1.3	2.4 [e]
Terms of trade	-1.3	-0.9	-4.6
	Annual average percentages		
Urban unemployment rate	5.7	5.8	...
Central government			
overall balance / GDP	-0.4	-0.2	-0.6
Nominal deposit rate	4.4	4.7	4.0 [f]
Nominal lending rate	7.5	7.8	7.6 [f]
	Millions of dollars		
Exports of goods and services	5 186	5 527	6 320
Imports of goods and services	8 805	9 842	11 201
Current account	-675	-1 119	-1 342
Capital and financial account	747	1 399	1 639
Overall balance	72	280	297

Source: Economic Commission for Latin America and the Caribbean (ECLAC), on the basis of official figures.
[a] Preliminary estimates.
[b] Twelve-month variation to November 2008.
[c] Twelve-month variation to October 2008.
[d] A negative rate indicates an appreciation of the currency in real terms.
[e] Year-on-year average variation, January to October.
[f] Average from January to October, annualized.

capital goods rose by 9.8%, 27% and 3.5%, respectively. The oil bill reached a record level of US$ 2 billion, 9% of GDP and 18% of total imports. Services imports rose by 7%, eight percentage points less than in 2007.

The economy benefited from inflows of family remittances (US$ 3.943 billion), although their growth rate fell to 6.7% because of the economic crisis and the hardening of migration policy in the United States. Remittances covered almost 81% of the trade deficit (22% of GDP). These trends led to a balance-of-payments current account deficit of 6% of GDP (half a percentage point above the 2007 figure), which may expand if the inflow of remittances continues to decline. Foreign direct investment (FDI), totalling US$ 463 million (2% of GDP), was mainly oriented towards electric power generation, the maquila industry, telecommunications and the financial sector, with the latter making up a third of total FDI in 2007.

Guatemala

The Guatemalan economy grew by around 3.3% in 2008, a marked slowdown from the 5.7% posted for 2007. Growth was driven by external demand and private consumption. The yearly inflation figure is expected to rise from 8.7% to 10.9%, mainly owing to supply factors, and the fiscal deficit should drop to around 1.2% of GDP. Although the trade deficit is projected to be high (16% of GDP), the inflow of current transfers should limit the balance-of-payments current account deficit to 5% of GDP, which is expected to be financed by capital flows which will also increase international reserves.

The new government which took office in January 2008 emphasized social and rural development policies, support for small and medium-sized enterprises, public security and the justice system. It is also seeking to establish legal standards that ensure access to stable and sufficient revenue.

According to ECLAC estimates, the economy will grow by 2% in 2009. The budget for the coming year includes increased allocations in the government's priority areas. The authorities are predicting a central government deficit of 2% of GDP, although increased expenditure will help soften the impact of the slowdown in the United States economy. The main consequences for economic growth will be slower expansion of export income, remittances and foreign direct investment (FDI).

The central government deficit for 2008 is projected at 1.2% of GDP, representing a fall for the second year running. In the first eight months of 2008, total real government revenues were down by about 3.5% compared to the same period in 2007, owing to slower growth and increased inflation. Total spending fell by 13%, mainly because spending on public works was held back by new budgetary standards implemented at the beginning of the year to provide greater transparency in fiscal management. Increased budget performance is expected in the fourth quarter. The tax burden stood at 12% of GDP, well below the average for the region.

At the end of 2008, the national congress adopted a solidarity tax to replace the extraordinary tax imposed temporarily to support the peace agreement. A specific tax on the first registration of imported vehicles was also proposed, to replace import tariffs. An income tax reform

bill, to be implemented in stages, is expected to be placed before parliament in 2009.

Like others in the region, the central bank had to deal with complex monetary policy issues in 2008. A significant part of the inflationary trends were caused by external supply problems which were largely beyond the bank's control, but it had to try to curb pressures caused by second-round effects. The authorities were also aware of the initial consequences for the country's economy of slowing growth in the United States. The monetary-policy interest rate was raised only twice in 2008, in March and July, rising from 6.5% to 7.25%, compared to 2007 when six adjustments were made and the rate climbed from 5% to 6.5%.

GUATEMALA: MONTHLY INDEX OF ECONOMIC ACTIVITY (MIEA) AND INFLATION

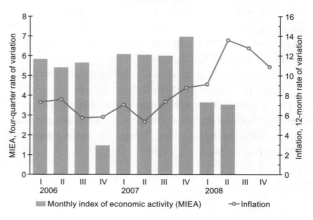

■ Monthly index of economic activity (MIEA)   —○— Inflation

Source: Economic Commission for Latin America and the Caribbean (ECLAC), on the basis of official figures.

The increased interest rate differential with respect to the United States caused an inflow of short-term capital which led to a real appreciation of the quetzal. In April 2008, to mitigate this appreciation, the monetary authorities invoked the rule that allows them to intervene in the foreign-exchange market and by October they had purchased US$ 242 million. Consequently, international reserves rose by a similar amount.

Real monetary aggregates suffered a decline in 2008 (between 2% and 3%) caused by steep cuts in fiscal expenditure, increasing monetary sterilization operations and depressed growth in loans offered by the commercial banks. The real rise of credit to the private sector is expected to fall to 4% compared to the 16% posted in 2007. In 2008, real interest rates on loans and deposits averaged 2% and -6%, respectively. Although in the first quarter three major international banks that were already operating in the region joined the national financial system, by mid-year the assets of foreign banks made up only 8% of the total assets of the Guatemalan banking system.

Economic growth is expected to slow to 3.3% for 2008, as a result of the downturn in private consumption caused by a reduced inflow of remittances. The strong expansion of external demand, however, should prevent a sharper fall in growth. All sectors other than construction are expected to expand. While transport, communications and banking are projected to grow at two-digit rates, construction, which recorded 12% growth in 2007, is predicted to slow somewhat owing to the postponement of private-sector projects and public infrastructure initiatives during the new government's first year in office. Agriculture and manufacturing are projected to grow by around 2%.

Inflation rose in 2008, reaching a year-on-year variation of 14.2% in July but falling back to 10.9% in November (in 2007 it had stood at 8.7%). This was down to supply factors such as the rise in fuel and food prices, partially counteracted by the nominal revaluation of the currency. Food prices are expected to record a year-on-year increase of around 15%, partly because of crop losses caused by the heavy rainfall that hit the country in October.

No employment survey data were available for 2008, although in March the Ministry of Labour and Social Security estimated the unemployment rate at around 5.5%. Up to October, there had been no nominal adjustments to the daily minimum wage, which dropped by almost 10% in real terms.

GUATEMALA: MAIN ECONOMIC INDICATORS

	2006	2007	2008 [a]
	Annual growth rates		
Gross domestic product	5.3	5.7	3.3
Per capita gross domestic product	2.7	3.2	0.8
Consumer prices	5.8	8.7	10.9 [b]
Average real wage	3.2	-1.6	-11.0
Money (M1)	18.4	14.1	-0.5 [c]
Real effective exchange rate [d]	-2.9	-0.0	-4.7 [e]
Terms of trade	-1.9	-1.9	-0.9
	Annual average percentages		
Central administration			
overall balance / GDP	-1.9	-1.5	-1.2
Nominal deposit rate	4.7	4.9	5.1 [f]
Nominal lending rate	12.8	12.8	13.3 [f]
	Millions of dollars		
Exports of goods and services	7 601	8 721	9 914
Imports of goods and services	12 719	14 511	16 166
Current account	-1 512	-1 697	-1 823
Capital and financial account	1 765	1 913	2 123
Overall balance	252	216	300

Source: Economic Commission for Latin America and the Caribbean (ECLAC), on the basis of official figures.
[a] Preliminary estimates.
[b] Twelve-month variation to November 2008.
[c] Twelve-month variation to October 2008.
[d] A negative rate indicates an appreciation of the currency in real terms.
[e] Year-on-year average variation, January to October.
[f] Average from January to October, annualized.

Thanks to prices higher than those of previous years, the value of goods exports is expected to record an increase of about 15%, the same as in 2007. This result was influenced by the increased value of non-traditional exports (42%), particularly those of food and chemicals. Sales of traditional products were dominated by coffee, cardamom and petroleum, while sugar exports fell by 16%, mainly because of a drop in export volumes caused by maritime transport difficulties. An 11% rise was recorded for imported goods, driven by purchases of intermediate and consumer goods, while capital goods imports became sluggish. Up to October 2008, income from family remittances had stood at US$ 3.657 billion. The annual growth rate for these remittances dropped to 6.7% (14.4% in 2007) influenced by the problems in the economy of the United States and the hardening of its immigration policy. Net foreign direct investment inflows were equivalent to 2% of GDP, slightly above the figure recorded in 2007.

Honduras

The Honduran economy grew by 3.8% in 2008, which was slower than the 6.3% recorded in 2007. Growth remained driven by private consumption sustained by income from family remittances. Annual inflation rose from 8.9% in 2007 to approximately 12%, partly owing to supply factors. The balance-of-payments current account deficit reached a fairly unsustainable level of 12% of GDP. The trade deficit was also extremely wide (29% of GDP), although this was partly offset by incoming current transfers and capital inflows. Nevertheless, up to October international reserves shrank by US$ 160 million. In August, Honduras joined the Bolivarian Alternative for Latin America and the Caribbean (ALBA).

For 2009, ECLAC forecasts GDP growth of 2%. The economy will be less buoyant as a result of recession in the United States economy, which will hit the real economy in the form of lower demand for Honduran exports, a fall in income from family remittances and reduced inflows of foreign direct investment (FDI). A stand-by agreement was approved with the International Monetary Fund (IMF) in April 2008. This funding is a precautionary arrangement for the authorities. The priority aims of the agreement are to consolidate and reorient the fiscal position and strengthen the energy sector.

The fiscal deficit narrowed from 2.9% of GDP in 2007 to around 2% of GDP in 2008. In real terms, total revenues are expected to grow by 2% for the year, while current expenditure should fall by 3% and capital expenditure is predicted to grow by 0.5%. Between January and May 2008, the fiscal accounts worsened. Total real government revenues dropped by 2%, although they appeared to have recovered somewhat in the second half of the year, thanks to the implementation of the law against Tax Evasion Act. Total expenditure expanded by 16% in the first five months, before declining in the second half of the year as a result of reduced fuel and electricity subsidies. Across-the-board subsidies for electricity consumption and transfers to State-owned electricity enterprises were maintained. In September, the National Congress approved a reform to the Income Tax Act that raised the tax threshold from 70,000 lempiras to 130,000 lempiras (equivalent approximately to US$ 6,900).

In the first half of 2008, the monetary policy rate was raised on four occasions to stand at 9%, and remained at this level for the second half of the year. Up to August, real monetary aggregates posted annual declines of 11% (in the case of M2) and 7% (for M3). The real growth rate of credit to the private sector is predicted to close the year at 5% (compared with growth of 21% in 2007). To tackle the international financial crisis, in October the monetary authorities reduced the legal reserve requirement from 12% to 10%, thereby freeing up 1.8 billion lempiras (equivalent to US$ 95 million) for the national banking system. That measure improved the availability of credit in a banking system affected by restricted external credit, and also provided resources to cover damage caused by floods. In 2008, the inflation target rose to a range of 8% to 10%. Up to November, the nominal exchange rate remained stable at 18.9 lempiras to the dollar. Between December 2007 and September 2008, the lempira appreciated by 5% in real terms.

The country's financial sector appears relatively solid, with limited exposure to contamination and contagion from the international financial crisis. However, the parent companies of the main foreign banks have urged their subsidiaries in Honduras to maintain a higher level of liquidity, which will reduce the amount of credit available in the future. In mid-2008, the assets of foreign banks represented 20% of total assets in the Honduran banking system.

Between December 2007 and August 2008, public external debt climbed by 9%, while internal debt rose by 15%. In response to the drastic reduction in liquidity, the Government of Honduras is requesting a range of soft credit lines. The agreements with the Government of the Bolivarian Republic of Venezuela remain in force, with US$ 30 million requested for the National Bank for Agricultural Development (BANADESA) and US$ 100 million through the Bolivarian Alternative for Latin America and the Caribbean (ALBA). In addition, the Government of Honduras (along with other Central American governments) has requested financing from the Central American Bank for Economic Integration (CABEI). Honduras and other countries also have access to a joint fund of the Inter-American Development Bank (IDB) for tackling hikes in food prices.

The country's economy expanded by 3.8% in 2008, which was much lower than the 6.3% growth rate recorded in 2007. The only sector to have bettered its performance from the previous year was agriculture, which grew by 5.5% compared with 5.0% in 2007. In contrast, up to August 2008 construction posted year-on-year growth of 13%, compared with 23% in 2007. Growth was driven by internal demand, and investment was also buoyant this year. In the wake of the heavy rains that fell in October, farmers stopped planting bean crops, which will cause supply problems over the months to come. Losses were also recorded in maize crops.[1]

Up to October, consumer prices posted a year-on-year increase of 13.1%, pushed up mainly by higher food and oil prices throughout the year. In July, year-on-year variation in food prices was 24%, before dropping to 20% in October. Thanks to subsidies, the prices of transport remained about average. High inflation cancelled out the increase in minimum wages, so that these remained stable in real terms.

As of August, exports of traditional products benefited from good prices to display solid growth of 21%, which was four percentage points higher than the growth rate observed in 2007. Non-traditional exports were also more buoyant: 11% compared with 6% in 2007. The growth rate of goods for processing (maquila sector) continued to decrease to stand at 1.5%. Up to August, merchandise imports increased by 25%, on the strength of the stable exchange rate of the lempira, the rising oil

bill and capital goods imports (as imports of consumer goods slowed). However, the balance-of-payments current account deficit will stand at around 12% of GDP, and would have been wider if oil prices had not dropped from July onwards. By the end of 2008, the growth rate of remittances is expected to be 8%, which is two percentage points lower than in 2007. In October 2008, the United States authorities agreed to extend the Temporary Protection Status (TPS) for 75,000 Hondurans until June 2010, which will help mitigate any impact on remittances.

HONDURAS: MAIN ECONOMIC INDICATORS

	2006	2007	2008 [a]
Annual growth rates			
Gross domestic product	6.3	6.3	3.8
Per capita gross domestic product	4.2	4.2	1.7
Consumer prices	5.3	8.9	10.9 [b]
Real minimun wage	5.1	2.8	-0.0
Money (M1)	24.0	16.3	5.1 [c]
Real effective exchange rate [d]	-2.5	-1.8	-2.9 [e]
Terms of trade	-4.6	-1.9	-2.7
Annual average percentages			
Urban unemployment rate	4.9	4.0	...
Central government			
overall balance / GDP	-1.1	-2.9	-1.9
Nominal deposit rate	9.3	7.8	8.9 [f]
Nominal lending rate	17.4	16.6	17.4 [f]
Millions of dollars			
Exports of goods and services	5 881	6 344	6 639
Imports of goods and services	8 301	9 594	10 789
Current account	-509	-1 225	-1 683
Capital and financial account	820	1 063	1 457
Overall balance	311	-162	-225

Source: Economic Commission for Latin America and the Caribbean (ECLAC), on the basis of official figures.
[a] Preliminary estimates.
[b] Twelve-month variation to November 2008.
[c] Twelve-month variation to September 2008.
[d] A negative rate indicates an appreciation of the currency in real terms.
[e] Year-on-year average variation, January to October.
[f] Average from January to September, annualized.

---

[1]   According to official data, as a result of the heavy rains, there were at least 34 deaths, 16 people missing, 69,000 people affected and losses amounting to almost US$ 154 million.

Mexico

Mexico's GDP shrank from 3.2% in 2007 to an estimated 1.8% in 2008 owing to the general weakening of domestic demand coupled with a steep decline in export growth, especially in the second semester. A slightly restrictive monetary policy limited the supply of credit during the first part of the year, reining in private consumption. The expansion of the real wage bill slowed, remittances from migrant workers decreased, and the gradual worsening of the international financial crisis lowered expectations in general, which had a negative effect on investment. Annual inflation is expected to reach 6% in 2008 on the back of the rise in international food prices and domestic electricity and housing prices. The fiscal balance will remain close to equilibrium; the current account deficit of the balance of payments is estimated to reach about 1.5% of GDP, twice the size of the deficit posted in 2007.

The manufacturing industry suffered the effects of the slowdown in demand in the United States market, which absorbs 80% of Mexico's exports, most of which are manufactures. The trade deficit widened thanks to buoyant imports, especially gasoline, cereals (whose import values were driven up by high international prices), machinery and electrical material imports.

The Mexican economy will slow down further in 2009. The government measures being taken to mitigate the impact on the financial and the real sector will help ensure liquidity and stimulate production. Nonetheless, GDP growth is projected to fall to less than half that recorded in 2008 as a result of declining manufacturing exports, a depressed domestic market, less credit and reduced inflows of foreign direct investment and remittances from Mexicans working abroad.

Public-sector revenues rose 11.5% in real terms between January and September thanks to the increase in both oil income (19.7%) and non-oil income (7.2%). Oil revenue was boosted by the relatively high prices obtained for petroleum exports and domestic gas sales. The favourable impact of these prices was partially offset, however, by the drop in production volumes and crude oil exports and the rise in petroleum imports. Non-oil tax revenues expanded 11.3% mainly thanks to higher receipts of income tax, VAT and the special tax on production, services and imports. The collection of the flat-rate business tax that came into force in 2008 also increased non-oil revenues.

Higher-than-expected receipts made it possible to step up public-sector budget spending between January and September by 13.2%: current non-financial expenditure increased 13.8% and capital expenditures 25.5%. Physical investment expanded to account for 15.9% of programmed spending. Public-sector borrowing requirements are expected to reach 2% of GDP, slightly more than in 2007.

In order to soften the impact of the slowdown of the world economy, the government launched a growth

MEXICO: GDP, INFLATION AND UNEMPLOYMENT

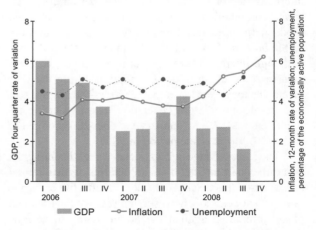

Source: Economic Commission for Latin America and the Caribbean (ECLAC), on the basis of official figures.

and employment stimulation programme, which aims to use public resources representing about 1% of GDP to stimulate the economy. The programme consists of five lines of action: the expansion and reallocation of public expenditure to promote infrastructure spending in particular; procedural changes to streamline public spending, particularly in infrastructure, and to avoid under-implementation; the construction of a refinery; an extraordinary support programme for small and medium-sized enterprises; and the simplification of procedures for foreign trade and customs operations to ensure access for more products and at better prices and to make it easier to establish companies in Mexico.

In the second semester, the Ministry of Finance and Public Credit announced the acquisition of US$ 8 billion of international reserves from the central bank to ensure the liquidity of the national treasury and cover the government's operating expenses in the ensuing months. Up to September 2008, US$ 3.649 billion in external liabilities were amortized. That same month, net external public debt stood at 2.9% of GDP for 2008, while net internal public debt reached 15.5% of GDP.

In the wake of falling crude oil prices, the government performed a number of hedging operations in financial markets in the second semester of 2008 at a total cost of US$ 1.5 billion and using a base price of US$ 70 per barrel of Mexican crude. If prices in 2009 average close to those in force in November 2008, (less than US$ 40 per barrel), the federal government will receive compensation of US$ 9.553 billion, enough to avoid having to make adjustments to the national budget.

The central bank had to deal with a number of issues in 2008. High international prices for certain food items, commodities and energy products drove up inflation, and the interest rate was therefore raised three times between June and August by 25 basis points, finally targeting an interbank rate of 8.25%. From September on, however, private consumption and employment levels worsened, and food, energy and other commodity prices began to drop, so the bank decided to leave the interest rate at 8.25%. Although interest rates were nominally higher in 2008 than in 2007, the episodes of inflation during the year meant that they were lower in real terms. The average real interest rate of the 28-day Federation Treasury Certificates (CETES) was 2.3% for January-October 2008 compared with 4.2% for the same period in 2007.

The real exchange rate appreciated slightly during the first three quarters of 2008, both in terms of the bilateral rate with the United States dollar and the effective exchange rate. In October 2008, however, the value of the Mexican peso plummeted against the dollar owing to various derivative operations carried out by companies established in Mexico. The central bank was forced to intervene to

MEXICO: MAIN ECONOMIC INDICATORS

	2006	2007	2008 [a]
	Annual growth rates		
Gross domestic product	4.8	3.2	1.8
Per capita gross domestic product	3.7	2.0	0.6
Consumer prices	4.1	3.8	6.2 [b]
Average real wage [c]	0.4	1.0	0.7 [d]
Money (M1)	15.1	11.7	8.9 [e]
Real effective exchange rate [f]	0.0	0.6	-0.3 [g]
Terms of trade	0.5	0.9	2.8
	Annual average percentages		
Urban unemployment rate	4.6	4.8	4.9 [h]
Public sector			
overall balance / GDP	0.1	0.0	0.0
Nominal deposit interest rate	6.1	6.0	6.7 [i]
Nominal lending interest rate	7.5	7.6	8.3 [j]
	Millions of dollars		
Exports of goods and services	266 146	289 492	323 703
Imports of goods and services	278 015	305 506	345 689
Current account	-2 231	-5 813	-15 136
Capital and financial account	1 228	16 099	17 636
Overall balance	-1 003	10 286	2 500

Source: Economic Commission for Latin America and the Caribbean (ECLAC), on the basis of official figures.
[a] Preliminary estimates.
[b] Twelve-month variation to November 2008.
[c] Manufacturing sector.
[d] Estimate based on data from January to September.
[e] Twelve-month variation to October 2008.
[f] A negative rate indicates an appreciation of the currency in real terms.
[g] Year-on-year average variation, January to October.
[h] Estimate based on data from January to October.
[i] Average from January to November, annualized.
[j] Average from January to October, annualized.

prevent an overreaction triggering more inflation. By November, 14% of reserves had been auctioned off in a move to prop up the peso. Between July and the end of November 2008, the average exchange rate of the peso rose from 10.2 to 13.0 pesos per dollar, and at the end of October, the bilateral real exchange rate was almost 15% lower than at the end of the same month in 2007.

In October 2008, the Mexican congress approved a first set of energy reforms aimed at improving the efficiency of Petróleos Mexicanos (PEMEX), the parastatal oil company. The company was granted greater autonomy in its decision-making regarding project investment and the allocation of resources for maintenance and operations.

The downturn in the Mexican economy, especially during the last two quarters of the year, was triggered by the recession in the United States. The modest increase recorded in annual GDP in 2008 is the combined result of growth in the agricultural sector and services (especially basic services) and the stagnation, particularly from May onwards, of industrial activity, a trend that worsened towards the last quarter of the year. Growth in the services sector also waned towards the end of 2008 as private consumption growth fell even lower. The weak performance of the industrial sector reflects a significant contraction of mining activity, limited growth in the manufacturing sector and a sharp drop in construction activity.

Manufacturing started to decline in August 2008 and is expected to continue to do so until the end of the year. Automobile production was down in July and August but increased 5.1% in September compared with the same month the previous year. Automobile exports fell in July-September compared with the same period in 2007.

Despite slower economic growth, open unemployment remained at about 4% of the economically active population in January-September, a similar level to that recorded in 2007, thanks to the absorption of some of the workforce by the informal sector. The number of people affiliated to the Mexican Social Security Institute (IMSS) increased at a slower pace and rose by barely 0.9% in October 2008 compared with the same month the previous year. The worst employment trends were detected in the processing and construction industries (4.6% and 2.2% fewer jobs, respectively).

The slowdown in the world economy, and particularly in the United States, put the brakes on export growth in Mexico as well. Exports remained buoyant up to the end of the first semester, but falling oil prices and the drop in demand in the United States market curbed Mexican sales dramatically. In January-September, the growth of goods exports diminished drastically to only 1.6%, compared with the same period of the previous year. Sales to the United States shrank 1.3%.[1] In current dollars, sales kept increasing until the third quarter but were clearly trending downwards. Automobile exports recorded the second largest drop after petroleum exports, which were also down compared with the first semester.

Import values rose 15.4% in the first three quarters owing in part to high oil and grain prices and increased machinery and electrical material purchases. In real terms, import growth far outpaced export growth. The trade deficit therefore widened by US$ 1 billion since the end of 2007 to stand at US$ 8.38 billion in September 2008. Excluding oil, the trade deficit exceeded US$ 50 billion in the same period.

The economic-financial crisis in the United States had a severe impact on remittance flows to Mexico. Up to September 2008, the accumulated value of these flows was US$ 17.526 billion (3.7% less than in 2007). Foreign direct investment is expected to reach U$ 18 billion in 2008. Most of this investment will be in the manufacturing industry, financial services and trade.

---

[1] Estimates based on current deflated figures for the export prices index (see INEGI).

Nicaragua

According to ECLAC estimates, Nicaragua's grew 3% in 2008, which is 0.3 percentage points lower than the figure for 2007. Although exports remained buoyant (having expanded by 19%), the current account deficit is expected to widen to the equivalent of 26% of GDP as a result of the even greater increase in imports (24%). The fiscal deficit of the central government after grants should widen to represent 1.3% of GDP. Inflation closed the year at around 15%.

The country's economic performance was negatively affected by a surge in the prices of food, fuel and raw materials, which reduced available income and pushed up imports significantly. On the other hand, the impact of adverse factors was mitigated by the rise in public spending and the international aid received in the context of the Bolivarian Alternative for Latin America and the Caribbean (ALBA). Municipal elections were held on 9 November. The periods prior to, during and following the elections were marked by disputes among the various political and social stakeholders.

In 2009, the Nicaraguan economy will be impacted by slower world economic growth, particularly in the United States. According to ECLAC forecasts, GDP will grow by 2%, in the light of slower export growth and lower remittances and foreign direct investment (FDI). Although the growth rate of inflation will fall as a result of reduced pressure from international food and fuel prices, inflation will remain in double figures.

Total central government outlays in 2008 climbed by around 8% in real terms. The significant increase in expenditure was due to investment to rebuild infrastructure in the wake of hurricane Felix and the torrential rains in the north west of the country, higher social spending (on education, health and housing) and the cost of organizing the municipal elections. In addition, the central government also used non-recurring expenditure to tackle the rise in international prices by introducing electricity and fuel subsidies and purchasing food to stabilize prices and strengthen supply networks.

Total central government revenues improved by around 0.5% in real terms. Despite higher receipts thanks to the introduction of new auditing software, the increase in revenues was limited by the reduction or temporary suspension of

the import tariffs on various products (including edible oils, beans, pasta and barley), designed to offset the impact of rising international food prices. The fiscal budget of the central government does not include the hundreds of millions of dollars in aid estimated to have been received through the cooperation of the Bolivarian Republic of Venezuela, estimated at several hundreds of millions of dollars, and the use made of those funds has not been disclosed either. In 2009, the fiscal budget could come under pressure as a result of reductions in international cooperation following friction that has arisen between the donor community and the Government of Nicaragua.

In 2008, monetary policy generally continued to feature the measures that had been in place throughout 2007. The effectiveness of monetary policy remained

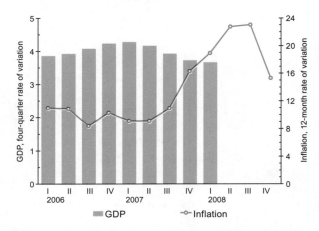

NICARAGUA: GDP AND INFLATION

Source: Economic Commission for Latin America and the Caribbean (ECLAC), on the basis of official figures.

somewhat compromised by the high level of dollarization of the economy.[1] The legal reserve requirement was maintained at 16.25%, while the nominal deposit rate for local currency deposits remained relatively stable throughout the year (at levels close to 6.5%). The nominal lending rate in national currency also remained largely the same during the year, with an annual average of nearly 13%. The real lending rate was in negative figures, which fostered an expansion of domestic credit (about 26% higher than in 2007). In 2008, the authorities continued with their policy of pre-announced mini-devaluations at an annual rate of 5%, as an anchor for inflationary expectations. Owing to the difference in inflation with the United States, the real bilateral exchange rate appreciated by around 8%. With a view to supporting the foreign-exchange regime, the central bank continued to accumulate net international reserves, although at a slower pace than in 2007.

As far as trade policy is concerned, negotiations were ongoing towards an Agreement of Association between Central America and the European Union. In 2008, five rounds of talks were held, with a view to concluding negotiations in 2009. In January, the agreement with Taiwan Province of China entered into force. The Government of Nicaragua has also been seeking closer political and economic ties with the Islamic Republic of Iran and the Russian Federation.

In 2008, economic activity maintained the trend of slower growth that had begun in mid-2007. Private consumption suffered the effects of rising inflation. In contrast, external demand and fixed gross investment grew more quickly than in 2007 (the latter thanks to increased public spending). The agricultural sector picked up considerably (with growth of almost 7% compared with 1.4% in 2007), thanks to the recovery of production following the adverse climatic conditions in 2007, rising international food prices and the positive phase of the biannual coffee cycle. The growth rate of the manufacturing industry slowed down (with growth of around 4%, compared with 7.6% in 2007), as a result of weaker external demand.

December-to-December inflation, measured through variation in the consumer price index, stood at around 15% (16.9% in 2007). Year-on-year inflation in August reached a record 23.9%, before decreasing in the last few months of the year amidst falling international food and fuel prices. The sectors that posted the largest price increases in 2008 were food and beverages and transport.

The balance-of-payments current account deficit widened from 18.3% of GDP in 2007 to around 26% of

NICARAGUA: MAIN ECONOMIC INDICATORS

	2006	2007	2008 [a]
	Annual growth rates		
Gross domestic product	3.9	3.8	3.0
Per capita gross domestic product	2.5	2.4	1.7
Consumer prices	10.2	16.2	15.2 [b]
Average real wage	1.4	-1.8	-5.1 [c]
Money (M1)	17.5	23.6	15.5 [d]
Real effective exchange rate [e]	-1.2	2.1	-4.5 [f]
Terms of trade	-2.4	-1.0	-3.6
	Annual average percentages		
Urban unemployment rate	7.0	6.9	...
Central government			
overall balance / GDP	0.0	0.6	-0.8
Nominal deposit rate	4.9	6.1	6.5 [g]
Nominal lending rate	11.6	13.0	13.1 [g]
	Millions of dollars		
Exports of goods and services	2 375	2 685	3 168
Imports of goods and services	3 928	4 673	5 798
Current account	-679	-1 048	-1 750
Capital and financial account	740	1 140	1 802
Overall balance	62	92	52

Source: Economic Commission for Latin America and the Caribbean (ECLAC), on the basis of official figures.
[a] Preliminary estimates.
[b] Twelve-month variation to November 2008.
[c] Estimate based on data from January to September.
[d] Twelve-month variation to October 2008.
[e] A negative rate indicates an appreciation of the currency in real terms.
[f] Year-on-year average variation, January to October.
[g] Average from January to October, annualized.

GDP in 2008, owing to worsening terms of trade: the oil bill rose by around 58%, while imports of raw materials and intermediate goods for agriculture and construction increased by 19% and 57%, respectively.

Merchandise exports and remittances expanded more significantly than in 2007 (by around 19% and 7%, respectively). The slower world economic growth did have an effect on these items in the last few months of 2008. Traditional exports increased substantially (by around 19%, compared with 4.4% in 2007), as coffee, sugar and meat exports soared in a context of higher international prices and better weather conditions than in 2007. Exports from free zones expanded by about 11%, in a continuation of the slowdown observed in the last three years. Flows of FDI represented approximately US$ 400 million, or 5% more than in 2007. The pressure on the balance of payments in 2009, due to reduced inflows of remittances and FDI, could be partially offset by a lower import bill, caused by falling international prices for fuel and other raw materials.

---

[1]   In 2008, approximately 65% of the broad money supply (M3) was in the form of deposits in United States dollars.

Panama

Despite deteriorating conditions in the world economy, Panama's real GDP is expected to rise by 9.2%, completing five consecutive years of growth in excess of 7%. Per capita GDP will be up by 7.5%. The balance-of-payments current account deficit will be close to 10% of GDP owing to the impact of rising food and oil prices, and the central government deficit will remain below 1% of GDP. The year-on-year rise of the consumer price index peaked at 10% in September, but began to decline from October onwards.

Under existing agreements, public and private investments of about US$ 20 billion will continue to be executed in 2008-2010. These projects include the construction of a third set of locks for the Panama Canal, road works to expand and improve the coastal highway, and the second stage of the toll highway known as the North Corridor. In 2009, these projects are expected to make up to some extent for the slowdown in growth caused by the expected fall in housing construction and the slowing demand for services resulting from the international crisis. Consequently, economic growth is forecast at 4.5% for 2009, a fairly robust level despite the worldwide situation.

Central government spending crept up slightly in 2008 as a result of measures taken to hold back the rising cost of living, while tax revenue in real terms showed no significant variation. In response to high food and oil prices, the government launched a US$ 100 million plan to support the crop-growing sector, including soft loans, purchases of inputs at wholesale prices, subsidized sale prices and tax exemptions for low-income households. The aims of these measures, reflected in an increase in the areas sown and in swelling crop volumes, include an end to rice imports in 2009. The government has also strengthened its programme of transfers to low-income sectors.

In the first 10 months of 2008, public debt rose by about US$ 500 million, two thirds of which corresponded to the increase in internal debt. Since public debt increased at a lower rate than output, it once again showed a decrease as a proportion of GDP.

With the United States Congress having not yet ratified the free trade agreement (FTA) with Panama signed in 2007, and given the economic slowdown in the United States, there will be few chances of expanding bilateral trade in 2009. Nonetheless, exploratory talks with the government of Canada towards a bilateral trade treaty have been fruitful and the open-skies agreement for the two countries' airlines has been implemented.

The financial sector suffered little from the worldwide crisis in 2008 because it had little exposure to high-risk financial instruments. Still, by the end of the year the nominal interest rate had risen to an average of 18% for credit cards and 8.25% for motor-vehicle loans. The rate of growth of total banking-sector credit fell to 12% compared with 19.6% in 2007. Up to August 2008 the interest rate had been fluctuating between 80 and 150 basis points above the LIBOR, but thereafter, it rose to the LIBOR plus 300 basis points. This interest-rate trend, together with relatively high levels of indebtedness among the population, may become a problem in future if the world economic situation deteriorates further.

PANAMA: GDP AND INFLATION

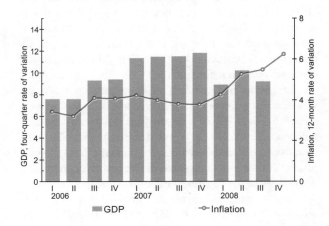

Source: Economic Commission for Latin America and the Caribbean (ECLAC), on the basis of official figures.

Although the expansion of economic activity in 2008 was more than two percentage points down on that of 2007, while GDP was up 11.5%, the economy of Panama performed remarkably well despite the worsening world economic situation.

The main engines of its growth in 2008 were the construction, commerce and transport sectors. The expansion of internal demand reflected consumption growth in real terms of about 6.5%. The rate of gross fixed capital formation is expected to stand at 22% by the end of the year, thanks to a number of major infrastructure projects still under way. The construction sector enjoyed growth of 22.7%, compared with 20.3% in 2007, owing to strong gross investment in housing construction by the private sector. An indicator of the upswing in this sector is the production of premixed concrete, which exceeded the indices for 2007 in every month in 2008. Despite layoffs at the end of 2008, employment in the construction sector remained above 75,000 jobs.

Traffic on the Panama Canal showed no significant downturn, and the daily average for ship transits was still around 36. In income terms, increased toll prices made up for a fall in tonnage. The Panama Canal Authority, jointly with the Government of Panama, is planning to implement projects to enhance the value of the route and take advantage of economies of scale, consolidating freight handling, storage, packing and logistics services; these improvements should maximize the economic benefits spilling over into related sectors.

Inflation shot up during the early months of the year to its highest levels in 20 years, with a peak of 10% in September 2008. With petrol prices now on the decline, however, the year-on-year increase in the consumer price index (CPI) started to moderate in October.

The open unemployment rate fell from 6.4% in 2007 to 5.6% in August 2008. Owing to the high inflation rate, average real wages in the urban sector declined by 0.9% in the first half of the year. Nonetheless, labour intermediaries and international businesses continue to experience bottlenecks in recruiting skilled labour.

PANAMA: MAIN ECONOMIC INDICATORS

	2006	2007	2008 [a]
Annual growth rates			
Gross domestic product	8.5	11.5	9.2
Per capita gross domestic product	6.7	9.7	7.5
Consumer prices	2.2	6.4	7.7 [b]
Real minimun wage	2.0	1.0	-0.8 [c]
Money (M1)	36.9	17.0	35.8 [d]
Real effective exchange rate [e]	1.3	1.5	-0.5 [f]
Terms of trade	-2.9	-1.0	-1.1
Annual average percentages			
Unemployment rate [g]	8.7	6.4	5.6
Central government			
overall balance / GDP	0.2	1.2	-1.0
Nominal deposit rate	3.8	4.8	3.6 [h]
Nominal lending rate	8.1	8.3	8.2 [h]
Millions of dollars			
Exports of goods and services	12 416	14 263	16 193
Imports of goods and services	11 918	14 627	17 007
Current account	-527	-1 422	-2 121
Capital and financial account	699	2 044	2 775
Overall balance	172	622	654

Source: Economic Commission for Latin America and the Caribbean (ECLAC), on the basis of official figures.
[a] Preliminary estimates.
[b] Twelve-month variation to November 2008.
[c] January-June average.
[d] Twelve-month variation to August 2008.
[e] A negative rate indicates an appreciation of the currency in real terms.
[f] Year-on-year average variation, January to October.
[g] Includes hidden unemployment.
[h] Average from January to October, annualized.

The current account is expected to show a deficit of some US$ 2.1 billion, around 10% of GDP, which is mainly due to an increase of over 15% in the import bill resulting from higher prices for foodstuffs, oil and other construction inputs, while total goods exports will be up 10%, with almost 12% growth in sales from the Colón Free Zone. As a result, the trade gap was expected to widen to almost 4% of GDP by late 2008. Despite the worldwide slowdown, the tourism sector saw an increase of around 12% in tourist arrivals in 2008. The financial account would reach a US$ 1.8 billion surplus by the end of the year.

The Caribbean

Bahamas

The slowdown in the United States has resulted in a marked deceleration of the growth rate of the Bahamian economy, which will stand at 1.5% for 2008 compared with 2.8% in 2007. Tourism and construction have lost momentum and foreign direct investment (FDI) inflows have also slackened. The government introduced fiscal stimulus measures to boost the flagging level of private-sector activity, maintain growth and create employment. Consequently, the fiscal stance deteriorated slightly during the early part of the 2008/2009 financial year. Growth for 2009 is forecast at 1.5%. However, the outcome will depend to a great extent on the length and depth of the slowdown and financial crisis in the United States, the principal market for the Bahamas.

The macroeconomic policy adopted by the authorities has sought to balance the competing aims of improving government finances, providing a fiscal stimulus in the wake of depressed conditions in major export markets, and maintaining the soundness and competitiveness of the fixed exchange-rate regime. Structural polices have remained focused on diversifying tourism by expanding the industry's activities to include the Family Islands and revitalizing the financial services sector.

The overall fiscal deficit came to 1.7% of GDP in fiscal year 2007/2008, down from 2.5% of GDP the previous fiscal year. The fiscal stance was positively affected by an increase in revenues that was attributable to improved tax administration and collections, which outpaced growth in expenditure. Although current spending rose by 2.1%, capital outlays and net lending to public enterprise were reduced during the period. Current revenues were bolstered by higher tax receipts associated with increased import duties and business and professional fees, which were in turn linked to vibrant growth in the offshore financial services sector in the earlier part of the year. Some of these gains were eroded during the latter part of the year; import taxes, however, remain the major source of revenue. In fiscal 2008/2009, government finances are expected to be buffeted by fallout from the global financial crisis, reduced demand for tourism and sluggish activity in the offshore sector. In addition, government borrowing and economic stimulus measures are expected to lead to a weakening of the fiscal

position. As a result, the overall fiscal deficit is expected to rise to 2.5% of GDP, while the debt-to-GDP ratio is expected to increase during the year, although it should remain favourable by Caribbean standards.

Even though monetary policy has been relatively conservative, with the discount rate of the central bank remaining unchanged, government borrowing of US$ 100 million on the external market has boosted liquidity in the banking system. Excess liquid assets, i.e., assets in excess of required reserves, showed a 50% gain of $182.2 million in Bahamian dollars (B$) for the first three quarters of the year compared with the same period in 2007. The fall in demand in the United States market has been reflected in a sharp slowdown in the supply of credit to the private sector, especially consumer credit and mortgages. The quality of bank assets have deteriorated during the year, with non-performing balances (payments over 90 days past due) increasing by over 30%. An evaluation prepared by the central bank has revealed that domestic banks have no exposure to subprime mortgages, while offshore banks have no more than minimal exposure to these instruments. Nevertheless, the international financial crisis has led to an increase in loan arrears as the slowdown reduces the ability of borrowers to repay their loans. Exchange-rate policy remains geared towards maintaining the stability of the Bahamian dollar and its parity with the United States dollar. Meanwhile, little progress has been made in removing exchange controls.

Activity has slowed in the tourism and financial services sectors, the drivers of the economy, particularly during the latter part of the year. Real growth of 1.5% is expected, compared with 2.8% in 2007. During the first seven months of 2008, total visitor arrivals declined by 3.2%, when the 2.2% increase in visitors arriving by air was offset by the 5.9% fall in visitors arriving by sea. The outlook for the full year is somewhat less promising, as travel demand continues to weaken in the wake of more intense fallout from the financial crisis originating in the United States, which is the point of departure of around 87% of tourists heading to the Bahamas. This is a particular cause for concern, since the tourism sector accounts for around 50% of GDP and employs about 60% of the labour force. In 2009, GDP growth is expected to drop to 0.5% as weakened global demand affects the domestic economy.

Reflecting the softening of the market, Atlantis Resort has laid off some 800 workers, while Baha Mar Ltd has laid off about 40 workers. The government plans to accelerate some capital projects to counter the slowdown and cushion the contraction of the labour market. Unemployment has risen from 7.9% in 2007 to an estimated 8.7% in 2008. Year-on-year, the inflation rate up to June climbed to 5.1% in 2008.

For the first semester, the current account deficit narrowed from 17% of GDP in 2007 to 8.7% of GDP in 2008. The merchandise deficit contracted by 10.6%, as reduced consumer demand led to a sharp decline in net non-oil imports, which compensated for the hike in non-discretionary spending on fuel. Exports also

BAHAMAS: MAIN ECONOMIC INDICATORS

	2006	2007	2008 [a]
	Annual growth rates		
Gross domestic product	4.6	2.8	1.5
Per capita gross domestic product	3.4	1.5	0.3
Consumer prices	2.3	2.7	5.1 [b]
Money (M1)	1.2	3.4	5.7 [c]
	Annual average percentages		
Unemployment rate [d]	7.6	7.9	8.7
Central government			
overall balance / GDP	-1.2	-3.2	-1.7 [e]
Nominal deposit rate [f]	3.4	3.7	4.0 [g]
Nominal lending rate [h]	10.0	10.6	11.2 [g]
	Millions of dollars		
Exports of goods and services	3 101	3 401	3 643
Imports of goods and services	4 374	4 536	4 262
Current account	-1 439	-1 314	-692
Capital and financial account	1 360	1 269	912
Overall balance	-79	-46	220

Source: Economic Commission for Latin America and the Caribbean (ECLAC), on the basis of official figures.
[a] Preliminary estimates.
[b] New Providence. Twelve-month variation to June 2008.
[c] Twelve-month variation to October 2008.
[d] Includes hidden unemployment.
[e] Fiscal year 2007-2008.
[f] Deposit rate, weighted average.
[g] Average from January to June, annualized.
[h] Lending and overdraft rate, weighted average.

expanded owing mainly to re-exports. The services account weakened as a 3.3% reduction in travel receipts and lower local spending by offshore companies cut into the surplus. Meanwhile, the capital and financial account surplus expanded, bolstered by government borrowing, FDI inflows and capital inflows.

Barbados

Economic performance in Barbados during 2008 has shown a clear decline from the previous year, with GDP growth slowing from 3.2% in 2007 to an estimated 1.5% in 2008. Key sectors, such as tourism and sugar production, face mounting challenges, while inflation is expected to accelerate to 8% (December-December) and the current account deficit is likely to increase from 7% to 8% of GDP. In 2009, a widening external deficit and mounting domestic demand for public expenditure will put strong pressure on public policies and finances, while the impact of the global recession will translate into slower rates of activity for key economic sectors.

During 2008 public finances worsened due to the adverse economic environment, with an accumulated fiscal deficit equivalent to 3.4% of GDP being registered for the first three quarters of the calendar year. This was a significant deterioration with respect to the situation in the same period of 2007, when the cumulative deficit amount to 1.7% of GDP. Under the heading of government current expenditure, interest payments, subsidies and other current transfers recorded the largest increases. Although fiscal revenues also expanded, principally due to higher receipts of import duties and corporate tax payments, this increase was not large enough to offset the upswing in government expenditure. The stock of public debt has risen further, with the total (external and domestic) debt outstanding as of year-end being estimated by the Central Bank at the equivalent of 101% of GDP.

In order to stimulate the economy, monetary policy has been aimed at boosting liquidity and encouraging lending. The Central Bank of Barbados lowered the benchmark deposit rate to 4.5% in April. Given the international financial crisis, there is concern that foreign investment flows and deposit accumulation will slow down. A shortage of external credit which may force the government to look for further domestic funding is therefore expected.

The steady rise in retail prices has been a major concern during 2008, especially in the case of food items. In the first half of the year, cumulative headline inflation topped 5.7% (almost four times higher than it was in the first half of 2007). These developments prompted the implementation of government measures designed to alleviate inflationary pressures, such as the provision of price subsidies for flour, an exemption from the environmental levy for basic goods, the reinforcement of price controls, and a review of port charges and processing fees. December-December inflation is estimated at approximately 8%. Inflation is expected to gradually subside somewhat in 2009 in response to lower international food and oil prices, although it will remain high by historical standards.

The unemployment rate rose to 8.6% in the second quarter of 2008. This was a slight increase over the same period of 2007, but the rate is still lower than it was in previous years.

Barbados' economic growth flagged, with GDP growth for the period January-September amounting to just 1.7% as compared with 3.5% for the same period in 2007. The index of industrial production up to July indicated a 5.7% fall in overall output compared to the corresponding months of 2007, with textile manufacturing, the sugar industry, construction, chemicals, and electricity, gas and water being the most severely affected sectors. In contrast, there were some industrial sectors, such as electronic components, beverages and tobacco, and mining and quarrying, that actually increased their production levels. The tourism sector turned in mixed results. There was a slight decline in the number of stopover arrivals for the first half of 2008 but, surprisingly enough, even though cruise ship calls also fell, the number of cruise ship passengers rose by 13.2%. Overall, tradable sectors grew less than non-tradable sectors did during this period.

In view of these factors, the GDP growth rate for 2008 is expected to be just 1.5%. This development is directly related to the global financial crisis, which has dampened tourism activity and investment flows. Prospects for 2009 are not much brighter, with GDP growth being estimated at 0.5%, as a result of waning consumer demand, a slowdown in investment in tourism projects and the exacerbation of the sugar industry's chronic losses. In particular, the decline of the sugar industry, once a key component of Barbados' economy, is a major concern, especially in the light of the forthcoming termination of the European Union's Sugar Protocol, under which price guarantees have been provided for Caribbean sugar exports to European markets. Under the terms negotiated in the Economic Partnership Agreement between the European Union and the Caribbean Forum of African, Caribbean and Pacific (ACP) States (CARIFORUM), these price guarantees are to be completely phased out by 2012. It is widely feared that, without such preferential treatment, the national sugar industry will become unviable and will be forced to close down. The costs of such an event in political, labour and environmental terms would be very high, and further export diversification is therefore needed.

Higher international prices have also had an adverse impact on the balance of payments, mainly through increased food and oil import bills. The trade deficit is expected to have widened from 31% of GDP in 2007 to 32% of GDP in 2008, while the current account deficit has risen significantly (77% in January-September 2008 over the same period of 2007) and is likely to reach 8% of GDP by year's end (compared to 7.0% of GDP in 2007).

BARBADOS: MAIN ECONOMIC INDICATORS

	2006	2007	2008 [a]
Annual growth rates			
Gross domestic product	3.3	3.2	1.5
Per capita gross domestic product	3.0	2.9	1.2
Consumer prices	5.6	3.9	8.9 [b]
Money (M1)	-1.0	20.5	1.9 [c]
Annual average percentages			
Unemployment rate [d]	8.7	7.4	8.3 [e]
Non-financial public-sector overall balance / GDP	-2.0	-2.8	-3.4 [f]
Nominal deposit rate [g]	5.0	5.5	5.1 [h]
Nominal lending rate [i]	10.0	10.4	10.1 [h]
Millions of dollars			
Exports of goods and services	1 994	2 149	661 [j]
Imports of goods and services	2 186	2 310	1 808 [j]
Current account	-277	-245	-286
Capital and financial account	320	523	325
Overall balance	43	278	39

Source: Economic Commission for Latin America and the Caribbean (ECLAC), on the basis of official figures.
[a] Preliminary estimates.
[b] Twelve-month variation to June 2008.
[c] Twelve-month variation to August 2008.
[d] Includes hidden unemployment.
[e] January-June average.
[f] Cumulative to september 2008.
[g] Interest rate for savings.
[h] Average from January to August, annualized.
[i] Prime lending rate.
[j] In 2008, goods only.

Thanks to additional official borrowing, the capital and financial surplus has been large enough to counterbalance the current account deficit, despite the higher level of capital outflows associated with public and private debt payments and profit repatriation. Consequently, international reserves, declined only marginally over the first nine months of 2008.

Belize

The economy is expected to post a significant recovery in 2008 by growing 6% as compared with 1.2% in 2007. After the negative effects of Hurricane Dean in 2007, activity picked up on account of higher production of oil and some agricultural commodities, foremost fishery products. Economic policy is constrained both on the domestic and the external front. A high debt burden and a tight fiscal position, which have been worsened by the international financial crisis, are reducing policy leverage, and the likely fall-out in export demand and tourism is hampering efforts to improve the balance of payments. Although the new administration has returned to fiscal prudence, the slowdown in external demand might push the authorities to use fiscal stimuli to shield growth and employment.

Public finances improved in 2008, with the overall balance moving from a deficit of 1.1% of GDP in 2007 to an estimated surplus of 0.7% of GDP in 2008. The primary surplus will increase marginally to 4.7% of GDP. Petroleum revenue has expanded on the back of higher production in established fields. A windfall tax of 50% on oil revenues, when the price of oil exceeds US$ 90 per barrel, was implemented in September. However, the downward trend in oil prices means that revenues will be lower than expected. Public finances also benefited from significant grant inflows, including BZ$ 50 million from Taiwan Province of China. Despite higher allocations for flood rehabilitation and development expenditure, total public spending will fall to 28.9% of GDP linked to lower external interest payments and reduced outlays on goods and services. Public debt remains a major concern notwithstanding a comprehensive debt restructuring programme and a super bond issued at the beginning of 2007. Central government debt stood at 79% of GDP at the end of September 2008. Weakened global demand is likely to slow growth in receipts from the general sales tax, import duties and business taxes, and an overall fiscal deficit of 4.6% of GDP is therefore expected in 2009.

The monetary stance was relatively neutral in 2008. The central bank left its reserve requirement unchanged, while year-on-year growth in broad money slowed in October to 13.8% from 15.4% in 2007, in spite of the increase in activity. Credit to the private sector slowed moderately as demand was constrained by adverse global conditions.

The central government reduced its borrowing from the banking system as foreign debt replaced domestic debt to some extent. However, central bank net credit to the government is projected to increase in 2009 as access to external borrowing becomes more difficult and its cost increases. The central bank is also planning to move towards a more market-driven monetary policy, including the use of open market operations, a repo rate and other indirect instruments. In the longer term, the policy change might facilitate the deepening of the nascent capital market and improve the financing of businesses.

Domestic supply rebounded following the fall-out from Hurricane Dean in 2007. Output of shrimp, bananas, citrus fruits, the wholesale and retail trade, transport and communications and petroleum boosted growth to 6.0% in 2008 from 1.2% the previous year. Momentum also came from distribution activities, buoyed by dynamic imports and telecommunications, which benefited from a medium-term roll-out plan for service expansion. Activity in the Free Zone picked up strongly in the first half of the year. Nevertheless, an unfavourable external environment has led to reduced activity in tourism and construction. The closure of Williamson Industries, the country's leading manufacturer, led to a sharp fall in the production of clothing and textiles. Economic growth was also hampered by flood damage to food crops and lower electricity generation and is expected to decline to approximately 3% during 2009 as downside risks for tourism, construction and distributive trades posed by the global financial crisis materialize. However, the effect will be partly offset by recovery in sugarcane output, moderate growth in shrimp production and dynamic petroleum output.

Inflation picked up significantly. For the period August-August it stood at 9.5% fuelled by price hikes in basic food products, such as flour and rice, transport and communication, fuel and power. With the fall in international fuel and food prices in the latter part of the year and the global slowdown affecting demand for a range of other commodities, however, inflation is expected to fall to 5.0% by the end of 2008 (December-December). Wage demands have eased as the unions allow the government a grace period for settling in.

The structural current account deficit is expected to double to 7.4% of GDP but will be offset by foreign direct investment, especially in fisheries, tourism and real estate and higher capital grant receipts. This will lead to an improvement in the overall balance-of-payments surplus from 2.2% of GDP in 2007 to 3.7% of GDP in 2008. Domestic exports rebounded following the dampening effects of Hurricane Dean in 2007. Banana export receipts increased on account of higher volumes and prices, and exports of marine products also benefited from increased volumes. The year saw substantial outlays on imports of oil and capital goods for major projects such as the Vaca dam and the Belcogen sugar-based electricity plants. Overall developments led to an increase in reserves to US$ 157.4

BELIZE: MAIN ECONOMIC INDICATORS

	2006	2007	2008 [a]
	Annual growth rates		
Gross domestic product	4.7	1.2	6.0
Per capita gross domestic product	2.4	-0.9	3.8
Consumer prices	2.9	4.1	9.5 [b]
Money (M1)	19.7	14.0	6.8 [c]
	Annual average percentages		
Unemployment rate [d]	9.4	8.5	...
Central government overall balance / GDP	-1.9	-1.1	0.7
Nominal deposit rate [e]	5.8	5.9	...
Nominal lending rate [f]	14.2	14.3	...
	Millions of dollars		
Exports of goods and services	801	824	900
Imports of goods and services	775	810	930
Current account	-25	-51	-105
Capital and financial account	75	74	158
Overall balance	50	23	53

Source: Economic Commission for Latin America and the Caribbean (ECLAC), on the basis of official figures.
[a] Preliminary estimates.
[b] Twelve-month variation to August 2008.
[c] Twelve-month variation to October 2008.
[d] Includes hidden unemployment.
[e] Deposit rate, weighted average.
[f] Lending rate, weighted average.

million, representing 2.8 months of imports. Due to the global financial crisis it is expected that external payments in 2009 will be affected by reduced tourist arrivals and receipts and lower foreign direct investment, as some investors hold off on projects.

Cuba

In 2008, the Cuban economy posted GDP growth of 4.3%, with a similar growth rate in per capita GDP. The fiscal deficit is estimated to have widened to the equivalent of 4.2% of GDP.

The year got off to an auspicious start, buoyed by a 15% increase in tourism during the high season, which took the first-semester economic growth rate to 6%. In the second semester, however, higher international prices for food and petroleum were added to considerable losses caused by an unusually active hurricane season, along with a drop in the price of nickel, Cuba's principal export product. With respect to political affairs, in February Raul Castro was appointed President of the Council of State of Cuba.

An economic growth rate of 4% is projected for 2009. The reconstruction work in hurricane-damaged areas will boost growth in the construction sector, particularly housing. The drop in international food and oil prices will free up resources to increase imports of intermediate and capital goods, which are necessary to step up investment. The Cuban authorities also hope that the change of administration in the United States in January will lead to a softening of that country's embargo, particularly regarding the prohibition on travel to the island and on family remittances, which would benefit the Cuban economy.

The overall deficit of the central government increased from the equivalent of 3.2% of GDP in 2007 to 4.2% in 2008, owing to a combination of negative factors on the income and expenditure sides alike.

Growth in revenues was healthy in the first semester, but then slowed as a result of slacker economic activity and losses caused by the hurricanes, and a drop of 2% in real terms has been estimated for the year overall. Income from circulation and sales taxes was down slightly in 2008, after being driven in the previous two years by massive purchases within the framework of the energy modernization programme. Income from other taxes also grew little or even fell.

Total spending was slightly down as a percentage of GDP, reflecting a significant drop —of almost 40%— in capital spending. Current spending expanded by 10% owing to expenditure on evacuations and rehabilitation work in the hurricane-struck areas, higher subsidies to the population to cover the differences between the higher cost of food, particularly imports, and the subsidized basic food basket;

and a rise in storage prices for a number of agricultural products aimed at stimulating production.

The monetary authorities adopted a policy of moving gradually towards the elimination of monetary duality. Monetary aggregates grew slightly above the nominal increase in GDP. In the first three quarters M1 recorded a nominal rise of 10%, while M2 was up by around 15% owing to the large increase in fixed-term deposits.

Since financial equilibrium was sustained, inflationary pressures occurred on the supply side. Shortages of some agricultural products in the wake of the hurricanes pushed up their prices. In response, the economic authorities were forced to impose price controls on these products, using as a ceiling the last price reached prior to the storms.

Lending rates for business loans in convertible pesos dropped from 9.1% to 9%, equalling the maximum rates in Cuban pesos. Interest rates fell in real terms, given the inflation rate of 4.9%. Exchange-rate policy remained unaltered in 2008.

Trade policy was directed towards deepening established ties with the Bolivarian Republic of Venezuela and the People's Republic of China, as well as strengthening trade and investment links with other countries. Close ties were also forged during 2008 with Brazil and the Russian Federation, two very important emerging economies. With both Cuba signed cooperation agreements heralding enhanced economic links in the future. Full diplomatic relations were also re-established with Mexico in 2008, which is expected to lead to an increase in bilateral economic relations.

The economic growth rate (4.3%) fell short of both the figure for 2007 (7.3%) and the authorities' initial estimate for the year (8%). This performance was partly attributable to five extreme weather events (tropical storms Fay and Hanna and Hurricanes Gustav, Ike and Paloma), which caused large-scale damage and losses, estimated at around US$ 10 billion. Three million people, representing almost a third of the island's total population, were evacuated and more than 500,000 homes were damaged or destroyed.

Agriculture was badly hit by the storms, with around 113,000 hectares damaged and losses of at least 53,000 tons of food. Consequently, the agricultural sector grew by just 1.5%, well below the 18% growth registered in 2007. Production of ground provisions, vegetables, cereals and fruit dropped, while that of sugar cane grew by around 33% and livestock production expanded strongly.

Growth in manufacturing slumped from 9.9% in 2007 to 1.1% in 2008. The production of metal products and some non-metal goods fell by close to 30%. Construction expanded by 3.3%, thus reversing the contraction witnessed in 2007. Transport, storage and communication grew by almost twice the average for the economy as a whole, thanks to considerable investment in road and rail transport. Commerce sustained a decline, while tourism improved on its 2007 performance.

In 2008, the rate of inflation, measured by the consumer price index, reflected external shocks, such as that caused by international food and oil prices, as well as the reduced supply of agricultural products in the wake of the hurricanes and storms. The surge in inflation eased off in the course of the year, however. The unemployment rate dropped by 0.2 percentage points to 1.6%, while real average wages declined by 1.8% and the minimum wage by 3.2%.

Exports and imports of goods recorded opposite trends to the previous year. The value of exports grew by just 9.3% (compared to 26.6% in 2007), mainly because of a drop in prices, particularly for nickel, whose prices slipped by 30%. In contrast, imports increased by 43.8%, following a much lower rate of 6.2% in 2007. A significant leap was posted for intermediate and consumer goods (65% and

20%, respectively), reflecting the increase in the prices of food and petroleum. Even with the large drop in food prices in the second semester, the food bill is estimated to have increased by a third in 2008.

Cuba's external debt rose from US$ 8.9 billion to US$ 9.9 billion, with 80% of this increase corresponding to medium- and long-term debt.

CUBA: MAIN ECONOMIC INDICATORS

	2006	2007	2008 [a]
Annual growth rates			
Gross domestic product	12.1	7.3	4.3
Per capita gross domestic product	12.0	7.3	4.3
Consumer prices [b]	5.7	2.8	0.4 [c]
Average real wage	11.6	-0.9	-1.8
Money (M1)	-2.6	5.6	...
Real effective exchange rate [d]	2.1	3.0	2.7
Terms of trade	26.3	5.2	...
Annual average percentages			
Urban unemployment rate	1.9	1.8	1.6
Central government overall balance / GDP	-3.2	-3.2	-4.2
Nominal deposit interest rate [e]	4.0	4.0	...
Nominal lending interest rate [f]	9.4	9.1	...
Millions of dollars [g]			
Exports of goods and services	9 834	12 022	...
Imports of goods and services	9 709	10 375	...
Current account	-215	488	...

Source: Economic Commission for Latin America and the Caribbean (ECLAC), on the basis of figures from the National Statistics Office.
[a] Preliminary estimates.
[b] Local-currency markets.
[c] Twelve-month variation to October 2008.
[d] A negative rate indicates an appreciation of the currency in real terms.
[e] Average of minimum and maximum rates on time deposits.
[f] Average of minimum and maximum rates on loans to enterprises by the country's main banks.
[g] Calculated using the official rate of one peso to the dollar.

Dominican Republic

The economy of the Dominican Republic is estimated to have grown by 4.5% in 2008. While this is the lowest figure in four years, it still exceeds the rate of demographic growth, producing a 3% rise in per capita GDP. Annual inflation is estimated at 7% and the deficits of the non-financial public sector (NFPS) and the current account are equivalent to 3.2% and 12.6% of GDP, respectively. Against the background of international financial crisis and the contraction of the world economy, the growth rate of the country's GDP is expected to fall to 1.5% in 2009. The annual inflation rate is expected to decline because of slower economic growth and falling international oil prices.

As in 2007, GDP growth in 2008 was mainly driven by internal demand. It was particularly strong in the first half of the year, with annualized real growth of 13%. Over the year as a whole, private consumption and gross fixed investment were the main engines of growth.

The growth of public spending is estimated to have picked up in 2008, with an annual expansion of 18.6% in real terms. As a result, it is expected to be equivalent to 20.3% of GDP, an increase of about three percentage points over 2007; this represents a considerable change in the country's fiscal situation. The factors underlying this trend include higher central government spending in the context of the electoral process which culminated with the presidential election in May and, above all, increased subsidies granted to several productive and social sectors to mitigate the effects of rising world prices of foodstuffs and fuels and the impacts of tropical storm Hanna and hurricane Ike. During the period from January to November 2008, the real value of central government transfers was 32% above the level recorded a year earlier.

As a proportion of GDP, total central government revenue were down about one percentage point, from 17.9% to 17.1%, as a result of a fall in receipts caused by slower economic growth. By the end of 2008, the real value of tax revenue was around 5.6% lower than in 2007. Corporate income taxes, the second-largest component of tax revenue, showed a real-terms fall of 15% against the previous year's figure, and receipts from the Tax on the Transfer of Industrialized Goods and Services (ITBIS), which generates a quarter of the total tax take, were stalled in real terms. Tax receipts from personal incomes, property taxes and oil taxes were expected to be higher.

As a result, the fiscal situation of the non-financial public sector in the Dominican Republic experienced a drastic change in 2008, with a deficit equivalent to 3.2% of GDP compared with a surplus of 0.4% in 2007. Together with the quasi-fiscal deficit inherited from the banking collapse of 2003, the consolidated public-sector deficit at the end of 2008 is forecast at 5.3% of GDP.

DOMINICAN REPUBLIC: GDP AND INFLATION

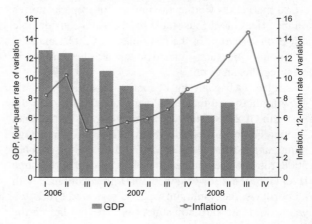

Source: Economic Commission for Latin America and the Caribbean (ECLAC), on the basis of official figures.

External inflationary pressures forced the monetary authorities to cut back on liquidity in order to reduce the impact of the external shock on the levels of domestic prices. The interest rate for interest-bearing short-term deposits, which stood at 7% in January 2008, was gradually adjusted upwards, reaching 9.5% in November. These changes were gradually passed on to other interest rates in the financial system from the second quarter of 2008. Furthermore, beginning in the second half of the year, the monetary authorities decided that commercial banks must keep 20% of their deposits in their central-bank accounts as part of the reserve requirement. The interest rate on three-year non-redeemable bonds issued by the central bank was increased to 18%, two points above its initial level.

The nominal exchange rate remained stable in 2008. Its level in late November was 6.2% higher than the average rate in late December 2007. Deteriorating fiscal balances and the worsening international situation, as well as rising domestic inflation, have put some pressure on the currency market, but this has been effectively defused by the monetary authorities thanks to the managed-float policy followed since 2004.

In the first half of the year, productive activity continued the upward trend seen over the previous three years (with an annualized growth rate of 7.5%), but from July onwards there were clear signs that growth was slowing. It is estimated that at the end of the year, above-average rates of growth will be recorded in energy and water production (9%), transport, storage and communications (10%), commerce, hotels and restaurants (6%) and financial and business services (5.5%). Growth in construction (2%), manufacturing (1%) and community, social and personal services (2%) is expected to lag behind that of the economy as a whole, while the agricultural sector and mining will experience negative growth of 7% and 9%, respectively.

The continuing price rises for food and oil in the world market, as well as the impacts of tropical storms on the prices of various staple foods, had a considerable effect on inflation. In the last quarter of 2008, external inflationary pressures trended downwards because world oil prices began to fall.

Against a background of continuing strong economic growth, the broad unemployment rate fell again in the first half of 2008. The April figures from the National Labour Force Survey showed a fall of 1.6 percentage points against the October 2007 figure. As of October 2008, the rate is estimated to have remained at the same level (14%), the lowest since 2000. In accordance with labour laws, the minimum wage is reviewed every two years, so no upward adjustment is expected before the first quarter of 2009.

DOMINICAN REPUBLIC: MAIN ECONOMIC INDICATORS

	2006	2007	2008 [a]
	Annual growth rates		
Gross domestic product	10.7	8.5	4.5
Per capita gross domestic product	9.0	6.9	3.0
Consumer prices	5.0	8.9	7.2 [b]
Real minimun wage	-7.1	4.8	-7.3
Money (M1)	10.0	26.9	...
Terms of trade	-1.0	3.3	-5.6
	Annual average percentages		
Urban unemployment rate [c]	16.2	15.6	14.0 [d]
Central government overall balance / GDP	-1.1	0.6	-3.2
Nominal deposit rate [e]	9.8	7.0	10.4 [f]
Nominal lending rate [g]	15.7	11.7	15.5 [h]
	Millions of dollars		
Exports of goods and services	11 153	11 927	12 162
Imports of goods and services	13 731	15 540	19 442
Current account	-1 262	-2 231	-5 824
Capital and financial account	1 452	2 888	5 508
Overall balance	190	657	-316

Source: Economic Commission for Latin America and the Caribbean (ECLAC), on the basis of official figures.
[a] Preliminary estimates.
[b] Twelve-month variation to November 2008.
[c] Includes hidden unemployment.
[d] Figure for April.
[e] 90-day certificates of deposit.
[f] Average from January to October, annualized.
[g] Prime rate.
[h] Average from January to November, annualized.

The value of total goods exports will remain at the 2007 level. The main factor in this result has been the sharp decline in the value of ferronickel exports which resulted from a 38.3% nosedive in world prices for that product. Exports from the free trade zones fell once more, although less steeply than in 2007 (-1.5%), owing to a further steep fall in textile manufactures (-19%). The value of imports saw another annual increase (27%). This was mostly due to the country's growing oil bill, which rose by a cumulative 58.5% over the first three quarters compared with the same period in 2007. The balance-of-payments current account deficit is estimated at US$ 5.8 billion, and as a proportion of GDP, it grew considerably in 2008, from 5.3% to 12.6%.

The net current transfers of the balance of payments are estimated at almost 4% more than those in 2007. Family remittances during the period will come in at close to US$ 3.1 billion, a 5% increase. The balance-of-payments capital account was positive. The cumulative figure for foreign direct investment (FDI) to September stood at US$ 2.353 billion, 133% above the figure for the same period in 2007. External investment flows were mostly focused on new projects in manufacturing and telecommunications. At the end of the third quarter, available net reserves stood at US$ 2.088 billion, equivalent to 1.5 months' worth of goods imports.

Guyana

Guyana's economy continued to grow steadily in 2008 (by 4.8% compared with 5.3% in 2007), fuelled by a strong performance in the mining and service sectors, and significant public and private investments in infrastructure. This positive growth is, however, counterbalanced by high inflation, which is expected to reach 9% by the end of the year, and a widening trade and current account deficit; both of these factors may be attributed to the increasingly adverse international environment. Forecasts for 2009 point to more moderate growth (2,5%), recurrent inflationary pressures and a similarly large current account deficit.

As recommended in the poverty reduction strategy paper (PRSP) agreed on with international financial institutions, the government adopted policies designed to preserve economic growth, stabilize financial markets and fight inflationary pressures. Thus, the excise tax on fuel was lowered, while valued added tax was eliminated on some basic items. A collateral effect was the deterioration of the primary balance, with current revenue rising by just 4.9% during the first half of 2008, while current expenditure expanded by 24%. This was offset, however, by a strong increase in capital receipts. During 2008, public debt swelled following the higher issuance of treasury bills, increased disbursements from multilateral agencies, and the impact of bilateral credits coming from the PETROCARIBE Energy Cooperation Agreement; at the same time, debt relief increased slightly under the Heavily Indebted Poor Countries (HIPC) Debt Initiative and the Multilateral Debt Relief Initiative (MDRI). By mid 2008, the total stock of public debt was approximately 96% of GDP.

The Bank of Guyana centred efforts on keeping the foreign exchange market stable, allowing a moderate depreciation of the national currency. Similarly, it kept interest rates steady with only marginal increases during the year; the Bank of Guyana's rate has remained at the same level (6.5%) since February 2007 while the Treasury Bill discount rate was set at 3.94% in September, slightly higher than in December 2007. Commercial interest rates were also relatively stable during the year. Domestic credit has been tighter overall, with the public sector bearing the brunt of the reduction, while credit to the private sector has continued to grow, albeit at a slower

pace than in 2007. Simultaneously, the Bank strove to increase international reserves, which topped US$ 320 million in July.

Economic growth remained positive, at an estimated rate of 4.8%, down from 5.3% in 2007. As in previous years, the mining sector was the main contributor to economic expansion, with 15.2% growth during the first half of 2008 compared with the first half of 2007, fuelled by higher prices for commodity exports and significant investments in bauxite and gold mining. Services and construction also recorded positive performances. Meanwhile, the agriculture sector, which is a major employer, grew only marginally during the same period; while rice and sugar output increased moderately and benefited from investment and restructuring processes, fishing and forestry output contracted sharply.

Sugar production is expected to expand in 2009, once the upgraded Skeldon sugar factory, soon to be completed, becomes operational. However, the overall outlook for 2009 is for moderate GDP growth (2.5% for 2009) due to the impact of the global economic slowdown and the resulting fall in international prices and demand for Guyana's main exports.

A major economic issue is the gas and oil exploration that started during the third quarter of the year with the launch of seismic surveys in several offshore blocks. Exploratory drilling is expected to begin towards the end of 2009. In addition, several private proposals for biofuels production are currently being considered by the government.

Inflation, particularly the steep increase in food prices, has been a serious concern throughout 2008.

Accumulated headline inflation for January-June was 5.8% while accumulated food inflation stood at 8.9% during the same period. Although price increments are expected to have moderated during the last few months of 2008, reflecting falling food and oil international prices as well as the VAT exemption on several staple food items, it is still expected that headline inflation will reach 8%-9% by the end of the year.

External accounts deteriorated as a result of the negative evolution of the terms of trade, rising demand for imports and higher payments for services. While the value of goods exports grew by 22% during the first half of 2008 (compared with the first half of 2007), imports expanded at a higher rate: 29.2%. Even with the reduction in international commodity prices during the second half of the year, the trade and current account deficits are expected to widen in 2008, with the goods import bill forecast to be around 95% of GDP, and the current account deficit expected to be equivalent to 35% of GDP. Although workers' remittances from abroad increased during the first half of 2008, they are expected to diminish because of the global economic slowdown. The capital and financial account surplus was strengthened by capital inflows mainly from official sources and from foreign direct investment in telecommunications, mining and forestry. Since this surplus is sufficient to finance the current account, international reserves should remain steady.

A landmark event in 2008 was the signing of the Economic Partnership Agreement (EPA) between

CARIFORUM States and the European Union. Despite strong reservations by the Guyanese government, the entry into force of the EPA should have a positive impact on exports, preserving preferential trade access to European markets for sugar, rice and other products.

GUYANA: MAIN ECONOMIC INDICATORS

	2006	2007	2008[a]
	Annual growth rates		
Gross domestic product	5.1	5.4	4.8
Per capita gross domestic product	5.2	5.5	5.1
Consumer prices	4.2	14.1	7.4[b]
Money (M1)	27.0	12.8	28.3[c]
	Annual average percentages		
Central government overall balance / GDP	-13.1	-7.4	-4.8[d]
Nominal deposit rate[e]	3.3	3.2	3.1[f]
Nominal lending rate[g]	14.9	14.1	13.9[f]
	Millions of dollars		
Exports of goods and services	733	854	831[h]
Imports of goods and services	1 130	1 335	1 372[h]
Current account	-250	-232	-416
Capital and financial account	293	231	74
Overall balance	43	-1	-342

Source: Economic Commission for Latin America and the Caribbean (ECLAC), on the basis of official figures.
[a] Preliminary estimates.
[b] Twelve-month variation to June 2008.
[c] Twelve-month variation to September 2008.
[d] Official target in the 2008 budget.
[e] Small savings rate.
[f] Average from January to September, annualized.
[g] Prime rate.
[h] In 2008, refers to goods only.

Haiti[1]

Preliminary estimates indicate that in 2008 the Haitian economy registered GDP growth of just 1.5%, a surge in the inflation rate to 19.8% at the end of the fiscal year in September, and an increase in both the overall fiscal deficit (2.1% of GDP) and the balance-of-payments current account deficit (2.4% of GDP).

Consequently, the performance of the Haitian economy in 2008 was substantially worse than expected owing to internal and external shocks. Among the former were those of a social and political nature, such as the climate of institutional uncertainty which prevailed from April to August pending the appointment and confirmation in office of a new Prime Minister and cabinet, and the natural disasters that struck the country, causing considerable damage. On the external front, as with other small economies highly dependent on food and petroleum imports, the escalation in both food and fuel prices up to July 2008 created an extremely serious problem for the country's economy.

The adverse international climate, dominated by the recession in the United States economy and the still-uncertain consequences of the global financial crisis are expected to have a negative impact on the country's economy during 2009. The impact of the crisis on multilateral institutions (which hold 77% of the country's debt) and bilateral bodies could put paid to commitments or disbursements of international aid, which provides funding for most of Haiti's public investment programmes (90%).

Within the framework of agreements with the international financial community (the 2006-2009 three-year Poverty Reduction and Growth Facility with the International Monetary Fund), the authorities wish to reach completion point of the debt cancellation stage, involving around US$ 900 million, by June 2009. This target has been maintained in spite of the non-fulfilment of some of the criteria agreed with the IMF owing to the extraordinary shocks that have disrupted the economy.

In 2008, the authorities maintained a policy of prudence and fiscal discipline, generally adhering to the performance criteria agreed under the three-year programme. Between April and June, in order to mitigate the effects of external shocks, they applied subsidies to lower the price of rice and contain rising fuel prices, using budget funds obtained through the financial agreement with the Bolivarian Republic of Venezuela (PETROCARIBE) and other donors.

Tax income declined by 0.8% in real terms. Budgetary targets could not be met because production levels were down and because the suspension of the mechanism for automatic adjustment of local fuel prices in line with oil prices on the international market resulted in a loss of revenue from the tax on fuel imports.

However, a significant increase was recorded for grants (82.3%) and some categories of direct taxation (income tax) and indirect taxation (VAT), which increased by 3.6% and 4.8%, respectively, thanks to new enforcement mechanisms and other measures.

In spite of the reduction of operating expenditure in real terms (-44%) and investments (-12,5%), total expenditure was up by 8.5%, reflecting a higher wage bill (16%) and subsidies (287%); the latter were equivalent to 2.2% of GDP. The increase in the total fiscal deficit (2.1% of GDP) was financed by non-recurring external contributions, without resort to monetary financing.

Regarding external public debt (27.3% of GDP), the most significant developments were a reduction in debt-servicing (from US$ 75 million to US$ 49 million), and a new debt agreement for US$ 135 million with Petróleos de Venezuela S.A. under the fuel arrangement with that country, which has been fully operational since March.

The monetary policy implemented by the Bank of the Republic of Haiti (BRH) sought to reduce liquidity in order to curb inflation. The Bank increased the interest rate on 91-day BRH bonds from 4% to 8% and also increased from 27.5% to 37.5% the local currency proportion of the legal reserve requirement. In September, despite expanding private credit (25.1%), net domestic credit

---

[1]   The present study relates to fiscal year 2008 (October 2007 to September 2008); however, in some cases, in order to facilitate comparison with other regional data, the reported statistics correspond to the calendar year.

increased by only 3.4% compared with the same month of the previous year, owing to the significant reduction in public credit (-32.3%).

Net international reserves grew by 7% compared with the previous year, despite net sales of dollars made by the central bank in an attempt to curb depreciation of the local currency. Nominal currency depreciation was 10.5% for fiscal year October 2007 to September 2008, increasing by an average of just 2.3%. Owing to the above as well as high domestic inflation, the real exchange rate still recorded an appreciation of 6.6% compared with 2007.

The low level of GDP growth (1.5%) in 2008 is attributable to the shocks suffered by the Haitian economy. The sharp rise in international prices eroded the purchasing power of households and pushed up costs. Nevertheless, remittances, albeit less buoyant, helped to mitigate the direct effects on consumption.

Investments rose up to March, but then dried up in the wake of the institutional crisis in April. Purchases of machinery and equipment, in particular, were affected. The construction industry grew by 4%.

Haitian exports are expected to contract in 2008 (despite favourable prices for agricultural products) owing to a significant reduction in the volume of maquila exports. The high cost of food and fuel is likely to lead to a real increase in the import bill.

In 2008, the average rate of inflation (14.4%) was almost double that for 2007 (8.9%). There were two main causes for this upsurge: food and fuel imports. Differential inflation rates for local goods (14.7%) and imported goods (27.2%) reflected this asymmetry up to September. These shocks were also accompanied by a drastic reduction in the purchasing power of wages, which over the past five years has accumulated a loss of 70%.

The fall in the value of exports (9%) contrasts with the increase in imports (21%). The trade deficit was even wider and was accompanied by a sharp deterioration in the country's terms of trade (-23%). Despite current transfers —grants and above all remittances (US$ 429 million and US$ 1.258 billion, respectively)— the current account deficit increased (2.4% of GDP compared with 0.5% of GDP in 2007).

The balance-of-payments financial account surplus (US$ 239 million, including errors and omissions) doubled and net inflows of funds increased thanks to new disbursements and a reduction in debt-servicing by one third.

HAITI: MAIN ECONOMIC INDICATORS

	2006	2007	2008 [a]
	Annual growth rates		
Gross domestic product	2.3	3.2	1.5
Per capita gross domestic product	0.7	1.5	-0.2
Consumer prices	10.3	10.3	18.0 [b]
Real minimun wage	-12.0	-7.6	-14.2
Money (M1)	2.7	12.7	17.4 [c]
Terms of trade	-3.8	-2.8	-22.9
	Annual average percentages		
Central government overall balance / GDP [d]	0.3	-1.6	-2.1
Nominal deposit rate [e]	6.0	5.2	2.4 [f]
Nominal lending rate [g]	29.5	31.2	23.3 [f]
	Millions of dollars		
Exports of goods and services	695	782	818
Imports of goods and services	2 136	2 319	2 686
Current account	- 73	- 29	- 168
Capital and financial account	166	188	239
Overall balance	93	159	70

Source: Economic Commission for Latin America and the Caribbean (ECLAC), on the basis of official figures.
[a] Preliminary estimates.
[b] Twelve-month variation to October 2008.
[c] Twelve-month variation to September 2008.
[d] Fiscal year.
[e] Average of minimum and maximum rates on time deposits.
[f] Average from January to October, annualized.
[g] Average of minimum and maximum lending rates.

Together with the factors previously mentioned, which by themselves are cause for concern, the floods caused by the four hurricanes that struck the country in August and September (Fay, Gustav, Hanna and Ike), had disastrous consequences for the country: 900 deaths, more than 800,000 people affected and total damage equivalent to 15% of GDP.

Apart from the immediate effects (such as shortages, worsening food insecurity and a deterioration in public finance owing to heavy outlays and expenditure restructuring), the most severe socio-economic consequences of these disasters will be felt in the fiscal year ending in September 2009, threatening already meagre advances in production and social conditions. The scope of these repercussions could be mitigated by reactivating key sectors such as infrastructure and construction, and promoting the generation of jobs and income. Recovery programmes focused on the agricultural sector, which sustained losses of around US$ 200 million, will play a determining role.

Jamaica

2008 has been a year of challenges for the Jamaican economy. With its heavy dependency on food and oil imports, the importance of the tourism sector for its economy and the considerable weight that workers' remittances have for thousands of households, Jamaica is extremely vulnerable to external shocks. The global financial crisis has therefore had a significantly negative impact on macroeconomic indicators. The forecast for real GDP growth in 2008 has been substantially reduced to 0%, while inflation is expected to stand at 20% by the end of the year. Furthermore, there are fears that the poor performance of the trade balance could be aggravated by a further deterioration in the terms of trade, while the surplus in the services balance has declined because of higher transportation and freight costs. This, in turn, has resulted in a significant deterioration in the current account balance. In 2009, GDP growth will be marginal at best (estimated at around 0.5%).

The Jamaican fiscal and monetary authorities have concentrated their efforts on economic stabilization, attempting to control inflationary pressures and maintaining a stable foreign-exchange market. The Government introduced several measures aimed at curbing inflation, preserving the population's purchasing power and promoting private investment and business. These measures included a rise in the income tax threshold, reductions of the transfer tax and stamp duty on property and securities transactions and elimination of the withholding tax on dividends (the latter takes effect from January 2009). Moreover, during 2008 the Government implemented a tax amnesty programme, waiving up to 80% of interest and penalties on unpaid taxes in exchange for the full payment of the principal. This amnesty, aimed at increasing the tax net and bringing in additional income, resulted in a slight increase in fiscal revenues during the second quarter of 2008, thereby offsetting the shortfall in receipts from the bauxite levy and other sources.

Although the central government accumulated a primary surplus equivalent to 3.7% of GDP for the period April-October of the fiscal year 2008/2009, the overall fiscal balance during the same period recorded a deficit equivalent to 4.1% of GDP. With debt servicing already claiming over 50% of the budget, the status and evolution of external and domestic debt remains a major concern and a constraint on public policies. Total public debt was the equivalent of about 112% of GDP in August 2008. During the first eight months of 2008, the total public debt stock increased by 3.7%, while the external debt, which accounts for 44.3% of total public debt, grew by 4.9%. The domestic debt stock grew by 3.1%.

JAMAICA: GDP, INFLATION AND UNEMPLOYMENT

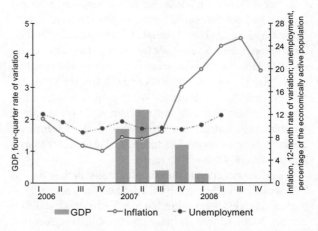

Source: Economic Commission for Latin America and the Caribbean (ECLAC), on the basis of official figures.

Monetary policy has been tightened, with the monetary base contracting at a faster pace than originally programmed by the monetary authorities. The Bank of Jamaica raised interest rates from 13.5% to 14% in June to mitigate inflationary expectations. So far, the policies implemented by the Jamaican Government and central bank to mitigate inflationary pressures and speculative expectations have produced a mixed outcome. The exchange rate was fairly stable for most of the year, with the Jamaican dollar recording a small accumulated nominal depreciation of 1.48% vis-à-vis the dollar by September 2008. However, increased pressures on the exchange market during October-November prompted the Bank to intervene to reduce excess liquidity in local currency. It also has programmed increasing interest rates in December to mitigate the demand for foreign currency. Price inflation has been considerable, with headline inflation of 16.9% accumulated up to September (one of the largest increases in the Caribbean), while food inflation topped 19% during the same period.

However, the most pressing issue for Jamaica's economy is the decline in GDP growth: real GDP contracted by 0.3% between January and September compared with the same period of 2007. The productive sector that suffered the most dramatic decline was agriculture, forestry and fishing, reflecting the impact of hurricanes Dean (August 2007) and tropical storm Gustav (August 2008), dry spells, fire damage and a reduction in the use of essential inputs such as fertilizers. Other sectors posting weak performances were transport, storage and communication, manufacturing and construction. On the other hand, mining and quarrying and most service sectors still managed to post positive growth rates. Although agriculture, electricity and mining are expected to gradually recover from the damage caused by hurricanes, this will not be sufficient to boost domestic output during 2008: growth is forecast at 0%.

Regardless of the global economic slowdown, tourist arrivals had not decreased by mid-2008. On the contrary in fact: by June 2008 accumulated tourist arrivals totalled 1.6 million, which was a slight increase on the same period of 2007. However, this increase is mainly attributable to a strong rise in stop-over arrivals by both foreign nationals and non-resident Jamaicans. On the other hand, cruise arrivals (a key indicator for tourism activity) declined significantly during the same period. The Jamaican government has lowered its forecast of growth for tourist arrivals in 2009 from 30% to 6%.

The deterioration of the current account deficit, fuelled by a widening deficit in the trade balance, has been one of the main issues threatening Jamaica's economic stability during 2008. Although the volume of goods exported increased marginally during the first half of the year, principally thanks to buoyant alumina exports, this was

completely offset by a huge expansion in the import bill, which represented approximately 55% of GDP by June. Such a development is due to the steep increase in expenditure on fuel, food and chemical imports. Consequently, the accumulated trade deficit amounted to the equivalent of 35% of GDP during the first half of the year, a rise of 50% compared with the same period in 2007. However, the import bill is expected to stabilize gradually, thanks to the fall in international prices for fuel, food and other essential supplies during the final quarter of 2008.

Unlike in recent years, the tourism-driven services surplus and the current transfers surplus (boosted by workers' remittances) failed to offset the trade deficit. As a result, by June the accumulated current account deficit had more than doubled (compared with June 2007) and amounted to US$ 1.391 billion or 20% of GDP. This deficit was compensated by a capital and financial account surplus, driven by considerable growth of private investment inflows, which grew by 95.6% in the first half of 2008 (led by the foreign acquisition of Jamaica's largest rum producer). This enabled the Bank of Jamaica to increase its net international reserves, during the first half of the year. However, its intervention in the exchange market during the last quarter translated into a substantial reduction of international reserves (US$ 1.8 billion by November).

JAMAICA: MAIN ECONOMIC INDICATORS

	2006	2007	2008 [a]
Annual growth rates			
Gross domestic product	2.5	1.2	0.0
Per capita gross domestic product	1.9	0.6	-0.5
Consumer prices	5.8	14.3	19.6 [b]
Money (M1)	19.3	14.8	10.6 [c]
Real effective exchange rate [d]	0.2	3.1	-5.7 [e]
Annual average percentages			
Unemployment rate [f]	10.3	9.9	11.1 [g]
Central government overall balance / GDP [h]	-5.4	-4.9	-4.1 [i]
Nominal deposit rate [j]	5.3	5.0	5.0 [k]
Nominal lending rate [l]	22.0	22.0	22.1 [k]
Millions of dollars			
Exports of goods and services	4 782	4 939	5 297
Imports of goods and services	7 098	7 902	10 025
Current account	-1 183	-1 800	-3 422
Capital and financial account	1 413	1 390	4 486
Overall balance	230	-410	1 065

Source: Economic Commission for Latin America and the Caribbean (ECLAC), on the basis of figures from the International Monetary Fund and national sources.
[a] Preliminary estimates.
[b] Twelve-month variation to November 2008.
[c] Twelve-month variation to September 2008.
[d] A negative rate indicates an appreciation of the currency in real terms.
[e] Year-on-year average variation, January to October.
[f] Includes hidden unemployment.
[g] Average of the January and April figures.
[h] Fiscal year.
[i] Data for April to October in fiscal year 2008-2009.
[j] Interest rate for savings, average.
[k] Average from January to September, annualized.
[l] Average interest rates on loans.

Suriname

Suriname's economy continued to grow in 2008, bolstered especially in the first half of the year by a booming commodities market. Real GDP growth is estimated to stand at 5% for the year. Credit continued its expansionary route, with deposit rates remaining stable and lending rates falling even in the face of the global financial crisis and high inflation rates (17.8% October-October). The current account surplus is expected to decrease as a percentage of GDP, while continuing to benefit from mineral output. The fiscal position remains solid, thanks to increased revenue from minerals and indirect taxes. Uncertainty about commodity prices and inflation are the major challenges for economic policy in 2009.

The Government's fiscal position remained comfortable, at least during the first half of 2008, while the decline in commodity prices in the second six months of the year is affecting related fiscal revenue and expenditure. For the year as a whole, revenue is expected to stand at approximately 36% of GDP, while expenditure is expected to represent around 32% of GDP. Taxation revenues and royalty payments from the increased production of bauxite, gold, alumina and new oil production streams are expected to have increased significantly in 2008 (from an already high level of 26% of total fiscal revenue in 2007). While wage increases did occur in the public sector early in 2008, these were below prevailing rates of inflation and are not expected to compound the inflation problem. The primary balance at the end of the third quarter stood at 3.7% of GDP, while the overall balance posted a surplus of 1.7% of GDP. The overall balance is expected to remain positive, although at a lower level than in 2007. The fiscal accounts continue to be strengthened by multilateral and bilateral project funds. A recent infrastructure loan from China has increased the debt stock, but it remains clearly within the mandated limits of 45% of GDP for foreign debt and 15% of GDP for domestic debt.

Monetary policy remained loose, even in the light of high inflation. Year-on-year M1 increased by 18.3% in the third quarter of 2008, to reach 20.4% of GDP. Deposit rates dipped slightly to 6.3%, and the lending rate dropped from 14.9% in the first quarter of 2007 to 12.6% in the first quarter of 2008. The central bank's policy aims at making credit available, attracting foreign direct investment

and accumulating reserves to sustain the currency. The exchange rate remained within a quasi-fixed regime at approximately SRD$ 2.745 to US$ 1.

Inflation will average approximately 15% for 2008, which is nearly 3% above the projected annual average and therefore a major cause for concern. In October, the rate of inflation stood at 17.8%. The main drivers of domestic inflation were prices of food and non-alcoholic beverages, which as of September 2008 displayed a 29% year-on-year increase. The internal causes of inflation, such as Suriname's expansionary monetary policy, also compounded the externally generated factors.

GDP is expected to grow by about 5% during 2008, fuelled by continued growth in the mining industry, the alumina processing industry and new investment in the petroleum industry. Agriculture, with the restructuring of the banana sector and international interest in palm oil and biofuel investments, also boosted the economy after its recovery in 2007. The rice industry is the exception, with increasing associated costs as well as heavy indebtedness. The combined effects of falling commodity prices, as well as the effects of the financial crisis on Suriname's major trading and investment partners (the United States and the European Union), are expected to slow down GDP growth and foreign direct investment (FDI) in the latter half of 2008 and into 2009. There is also uncertainty regarding the long-term sustainability of the mining industry, especially considering that BHP-Billiton pulled out of the Bakhuys development project in October and plans to leave Suriname altogether by 2010.

The current account position was boosted by strong aluminium, gold and oil prices in the first half of 2008, even though imports increased. Second-quarter estimates show a positive current account position: a surplus of approximately 14% of GDP. Mid-year export earnings represented approximately 65% of GDP, and import payments approximately 52% of GDP. However, the drop in commodity prices and the slowdown in the global economy are expected to have a significant impact on Suriname's export earnings and thus reduce its current account surplus.

Suriname has guardedly embraced the Economic Partnership Agreement (EPA) signed with the European Union. The country continues to have good relations with international donors thanks to prudent debt management, solid economic growth and a facilitative fiscal framework. Bilateral obligations concerning arrears with Brazil and the United States have yet to be resolved. The uncertainty about the volatility of the commodity prices on which Suriname's macroeconomic success depends, will be decisive for economic growth in 2009 (estimated to slow to 3%) and the country's ability to maintain this favourable debt position.

SURINAME: MAIN ECONOMIC INDICATORS

	2006	2007	2008 [a]
	Annual growth rates		
Gross domestic product	5.8	5.3	5.0
Per capita gross domestic product	5.1	4.7	4.4
Consumer prices	...	5.6	17.8 [b]
Money (M1)	21.8	25.1	18.3 [c]
	Annual average percentages		
Unemployment rate	12.1	12.0	...
Central government			
overall balance / GDP	1.6	3.1	1.7 [d]
Nominal deposit rate [e]	6.7	6.4	6.3 [f]
Nominal lending rate [e]	15.7	13.8	12.5 [f]
	Millions of dollars		
Exports of goods and services	1 408	1 604	...
Imports of goods and services	1 278	1 502	...
Current account	115	187	...
Capital and financial account	-21	-10	...
Overall balance	94	177	...

Source: Economic Commission for Latin America and the Caribbean (ECLAC), on the basis of official figures.
[a] Preliminary estimates.
[b] Twelve-month variation to October 2008.
[c] Twelve-month variation to September 2008.
[d] Cumulative to september.
[e] Deposit and loan rates published by International Monetary Fund.
[f] Average from January to May, annualized.

Trinidad and Tobago

The global financial crisis marks a turning point for Trinidad and Tobago's economy, after several years in which the surge in global hydrocarbons prices had helped to create a highly favourable external context. In 2008 growth is estimated to have slowed to 3.5%, compared with 5.5% in 2007. The turmoil also resulted in a reduction in the trade and current account surpluses and a significant rise in inflation (15.4% year-on-year in October). In 2008 the economic policy mix again consisted of an expansionary fiscal stance based on dynamic public investment, combined with a monetary focus on absorbing excess liquidity generated by public spending, within a quasi-fixed exchange rate regime. Economic policy will continue to be guided by the "Vision 2020" national development plan and 2009 will undoubtedly pose a number of economic challenges, especially in terms of reducing the country's dependence on the energy sector, which generates more than 45% of output, between 85% and 90% of merchandise exports and over 55% of fiscal revenue. Growth is projected at around 2% for 2009.

The central government surplus increased significantly in fiscal year 2007-2008,[1] reaching 6.5% of GDP. This reflects more rapid nominal increases in revenue than in spending, with both energy and non-energy tax receipts coming in above budget projections. The 2007-2008 budget assumed an average oil price of US$ 50 per barrel, far below the actual average of US$ 93.15. This price differential resulted in energy tax collections of some 8 billion Trinidad and Tobago dollars (TT$) over budget projections and explains the apparent contradiction of deeming fiscal policy expansionary even with a large gain in the fiscal surplus. The excess of revenue over spending was mainly transferred to the Heritage and Stabilisation Fund and the Infrastructure Development Fund. Meanwhile, public debt stood at 28% of GDP at the end of fiscal year 2007-2008, while external debt was 6% of GDP. The budget for 2008-2009 proposes a fiscal balance virtually in equilibrium.

Monetary policy measures were insufficient to keep inflation in check in 2008, owing to a combination of external factors, associated mainly with still rising global food prices, and domestic pressures generated by fiscal liquidity injections. In this context, in 2008 the central bank raised the benchmark "repo" interest rate three times, to reach 8.75% in September (8% in December 2007).

TRINIDAD AND TOBAGO: GDP, INFLATION AND UNEMPLOYMENT

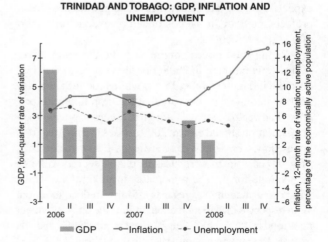

Source: Economic Commission for Latin America and the Caribbean (ECLAC), on the basis of official figures.

---

[1]   The fiscal year runs from 1 October to 30 September.

With a two-digit inflation rate, however, real interest rates remained highly negative, thus increasing domestic demand. Moreover, as fiscal injections expanded by 3.8% in fiscal year 2007-2008 relative to 2006-2007, the central bank raised the commercial bank reserve requirement from 11% to 15% and then, in October, to 17%. The central bank also stepped up its open market liquidity absorption operations by a huge 135%, from TT$ 3.458 billion in 2006-2007 to TT$ 8.16 billion in 2007-2008. In 2009 monetary policy will continue to focus on absorbing fiscal injections through open market operations, within the exchange-rate regime that seeks to maintain a fixed nominal exchange rate with the United States dollar. Given the inflation rate differential, this implies a permanent real appreciation of the local currency, with its pernicious effects on tradable sectors, especially non-energy exports. The maintenance of the dirty peg has been possible largely thanks to the central bank's strong reserve position, sustained by large foreign exchange inflows from the hydrocarbons industry.

Contagion from the global turmoil mainly took the form of a steep dip in oil prices, which were more than halved between July and November. The immediate impact on the local financial sector was negligible, given its small balance sheet holdings of United States assets. In addition, the sector's solid international reserve position and the level of resources in the Heritage and Stabilisation Fund (10.2% of GDP at the end of fiscal year 2007-2008) reduces the country's vulnerability. Nevertheless, the recession in the United States will continue to act as a brake on growth in 2009, since that country is the destination market for almost 60% of Trinidad and Tobago's exports and its main source of external financing. The central bank projects growth of around 2% in 2009. In the context of falling international oil prices, the non-energy sector will continue to grow faster than the energy sector. The construction sector is expected to lose momentum, as some public investment projects are likely to be postponed if revenue falls short of budget projections.

Rising food prices continued to be the main driver of domestic inflation in 2008. For the year up to October, headline inflation stood at 15.4% while food inflation was 33.4% year-on-year, showing that the drop in world food prices had yet to be passed through to domestic prices. Food price inflation should ease in 2009 as rises in imported food prices slow. Conversely, there are signs that wage demands may increase in the private and public sectors alike to compensate for the sharp increases in food prices, which will pose a challenge as regards efforts to reduce inflation. With respect to the labour market, in June the unemployment rate stood at 4.6%, below the 2007 average of 5.6%, and it is expected to remain at similar levels throughout 2009.

In recent years, the boom in energy prices has translated into massive trade and current account surpluses, which

TRINIDAD AND TOBAGO: MAIN ECONOMIC INDICATORS

	2006	2007	2008 [a]
	Annual growth rates		
Gross domestic product	12.0	5.5	3.5
Per capita gross domestic product	11.6	5.1	3.1
Consumer prices	9.1	7.6	15.4 [b]
Money (M1)	9.7	12.0	16.1 [c]
Real effective exchange rate [d]	-2.2	-1.9	-3.1 [e]
	Annual average percentages		
Unemployment rate [f]	6.2	5.6	5.0 [g]
Central government overall balance / GDP	6.9	2.6	6.5 [h]
Nominal deposit rate [i]	2.4	2.4	2.3 [j]
Nominal lending rate [k]	10.2	10.5	12.1 [j]
	Millions of dollars		
Exports of goods and services	12 100	13 391	16 731
Imports of goods and services	6 843	7 670	11 033
Current account	4 809	5 381	4 902
Capital and financial account	-3 690	-3 840	-3 102
Overall balance	1 119	1 541	1 800

Source: Economic Commission for Latin America and the Caribbean (ECLAC), on the basis of official figures.
[a] Preliminary estimates.
[b] Twelve-month variation to October 2008.
[c] Twelve-month variation to August 2008.
[d] A negative rate indicates an appreciation of the currency in real terms.
[e] Year-on-year average variation, January to October.
[f] Includes hidden unemployment.
[g] Average of the March and June figures.
[h] Fiscal year 2007-2008.
[i] Average of savings rates.
[j] Average from January to August, annualized.
[k] Prime rate.

stood at 29% and 27% of GDP, respectively, in 2007. In 2008 the combination of slackening world demand and lower international prices reduced both surpluses by some five GDP percentage points. In addition, the deterioration in international conditions is likely to widen the financial account deficit, which stood at US$ 3.5 billion in 2007. Conversely, the large current account surplus will translate into a significant build-up of international reserves, from US$ 6.7 billion in 2007 to US$ 8.5 billion (equivalent to 11 months of import cover) in 2008. With world economic perspectives gloomy for 2009, the current account surplus is likely to contract further while the financial account deficit widens again. This will not necessarily preclude another year of significant foreign exchange reserves accumulation, however.

As regards regional integration, in August Trinidad and Tobago signed a Memorandum of Understanding with Grenada, Saint Lucia and Saint Vincent and the Grenadines, agreeing in principle to economic union by 2011 and political union by 2013. In addition, the Economic Partnership Agreement (EPA) between the European Union and the Caribbean Forum of African, Caribbean and Pacific States (CARIFORUM), which comprises the Caribbean Community (CARICOM) countries and the Dominican Republic, is due to enter the implementation phase in 2009. These agreements represent both challenges and opportunities for Trinidad and Tobago.

Member countries of the Eastern Caribbean Currency Union (ECCU)

The economic outlook for the Eastern Caribbean Currency Union (ECCU)[1] for 2008 continues to be fairly positive with economic growth projected at 3.1% for 2008 (5.3% in 2007). In 2009, however, the slowdown in the global economy will have an adverse impact on these economies, especially the tourism and tourism-related construction sectors, which have been the main engines of growth over the past several years. Increases in oil and food prices until the first half of 2008 led to a worsening of the external current account and a balance-of-payments deficit, compared to a surplus in 2007. The economies of the ECCU continue to be prone to natural disasters and burdened with high levels of public debt.

The overall fiscal deficit, 3.9% of GDP in 2007, is expected to further improve in 2008-2009. This is mainly due to a decline in capital expenditure (9% as of the third quarter of 2008 compared with the same period in 2007) resulting from the completion of several public-sector projects. Current fiscal operations caused a fall in the surplus, owing to an increase of over 16% in current expenditure driven by large fiscal spending commitments and salary increases, far surpassing the 9% increase in current revenue.

As at June 2008, the debt-to-GDP ratio for the ECCU countries was recorded at 94%. Public debt exceeded 100% of GDP in Dominica, Grenada and Saint Kitts and Nevis and was above 70% of GDP in Antigua and Barbuda, Saint Lucia and Saint Vincent and the Grenadines. There were marginal declines in the debt levels of Anguilla and Antigua and Barbuda. The Canadian International Development Agency (CIDA) assisted in a reclassification of government debt for Antigua and Barbuda with its Education Board, successfully reducing its debt stock. Saint Lucia issued lower-interest debt instruments through the Regional Government Securities Market (RGSM), replacing existing high-interest debt. There should be no significant increase in the debt level of Grenada despite the change of government in July 2008, as the current tight liquidity will hold back government-funded projects in the near future.

The monetary policy stance of ECCU has remained unchanged in 2008, with the discount rate and interbank market rate remaining at 6.5% and 4.5%, respectively. The Eastern Caribbean dollar (EC$) is pegged to the United States dollar at EC$ 2.70 to US$ 1.00, backed by 100% foreign reserves, so the currency is expected to remain stable in future despite fluctuations on international currency markets.

Broad money (M3) was up 3% in September 2008 (compared with December 2007), reflecting increases in private-sector savings and time deposits. The net foreign assets of the ECCU countries declined further in 2008 as commercial banks continued to draw down on foreign assets to meet increased demand for domestic credit, which grew by 7%. Private-sector credit was up 8%, well below the 20% increase in 2007, while net credit to the government declined by 16%. There was some tightening of credit, indicated by the increase in the ECCU weighted average lending rate from 9.3% in June 2008 to 9.4% in September 2008, mainly reflecting the increased lending rate in Saint Lucia.

In August 2008 the governments of Grenada, Saint Lucia, Saint Vincent and the Grenadines and Trinidad and Tobago signed a Memorandum of Understanding for the establishment of an economic union by 2011 and a political union by 2013. However, the implementation of the union may be complex and is not expected to make significant progress in the near future.

---

[1]   ECCU member countries are Anguilla, Antigua and Barbuda, Dominica, Grenada, Montserrat, Saint Kitts and Nevis, Saint Lucia and Saint Vincent and the Grenadines.

The ECCU economies are expected to grow by 3.1% in 2008 and then to slow to 1.5% in 2009. Value added in the tourism and construction sectors is expected to exceed 5% while marginal increases are expected in agriculture and manufacturing. The tourism sector is under threat in the ECCU countries as conditions worsen in the economies of its major source markets. While cumulative data for January to September still showed an increase in stay-over visitors and cruise-ship passengers, the number of stay-over visitors from the United States declined in the third quarter (July-September). Contributing to a worsening scenario in the fourth quarter of 2008 and in 2009 is the decision by American Airlines and American Eagle to cut the number of flights serving the Caribbean. The suspension of operations in September 2008 by XL Airways, a United Kingdom carrier which had been serving several destinations in the subregion, and the murder of a British couple on honeymoon in Antigua in July 2008 were additional blows to Caribbean tourism.

Banana production is not expected to recover fully to pre-hurricane Dean (2007) levels in 2008, because of moko disease and leaf spot disease. It remains to be seen what impact the Economic Partnership Agreement negotiated with the European Union will have on Caribbean trade.

The rise in consumer prices continued up to the third quarter of 2008 in Anguilla, Montserrat, Saint Kitts and Nevis and Saint Vincent and the Grenadines, with inflation rates ranging from nearly 5% to as high as 9.5% compared to the 2%-8.3% range recorded at the end of 2007. To keep up with the price increases, public-sector wages were raised in Anguilla, Saint Kitts and Nevis and Saint Vincent and the Grenadines. The removal of VAT on a number of items and the suspension of the common external tariff on selected goods seem to have eased the level of inflation in Antigua, Dominica, Grenada and Saint

EASTERN CARIBBEAN CURRENCY UNION: MAIN ECONOMIC INDICATORS

	2006	2007	2008 [a]
Annual growth rates			
Gross domestic product	6.3	5.3	3.1
Consumer prices	1.3	6.1	...
Annual average percentages			
Central government overall balance / GDP	-4.9	-3.9	...
Nominal deposit rate	3.3	3.3	...
Nominal lending rate	9.9	9.5	...
Millions of dollars			
Exports of goods and services	1 887	2 010	2 045
Imports of goods and services	-3 054	-3 401	-3 550
Current account	-1 218	-1 486	-1 580
Capital and financial account	1 310	1 533	1 575
Overall balance	92	47	-5

Source: Economic Commission for Latin America and the Caribbean (ECLAC), on the basis of official figures.
[a] Preliminary estimates.

Lucia, with rates declining to a range of 3-5% compared to 5-7.5% in 2007. The labour market is expected to loosen owing to a decline in construction activity, especially in the public sector, and employment would suffer badly from any slowdown in tourism.

It is expected that in 2008 the balance of payment surplus will turn into a deficit owing to a decline in tourism-related foreign direct investment, capital grants and remittances. The current account deficit will widen by an estimated 6.3% to stand at approximately 40% of GDP, primarily because of a 4% increase in the import bill. Two member countries of ECCU, Dominica and Saint Kitts and Nevis, have begun geothermal energy exploration, which could have positive implications for the external accounts as these countries might significantly reduce their energy imports.

Statistical Annex

Table A-1
LATIN AMERICA AND THE CARIBBEAN: MAIN ECONOMIC INDICATORS

	2000	2001	2002	2003	2004	2005	2006	2007	2008 [a]
	Annual growth rates								
Gross domestic product [b]	4.0	0.4	-0.4	2.2	6.1	4.9	5.8	5.7	4.6
Per capita gross domestic product [b]	2.5	-1.0	-1.7	0.9	4.7	3.6	4.4	4.4	3.3
Consumer prices [c]	8.0	5.6	11.2	8.0	7.1	5.9	4.9	6.4	8.8
	Percentages								
Urban open unemployment [d]	10.4	10.2	11.0	11.0	10.3	9.1	8.6	7.9	7.5
Total gross external debt/GDP [e]	35.2	36.4	40.0	40.0	34.5	25.1	21.0	20.1	18.6
Total gross external debt/ exports of goods and services	172.6	181.5	177.8	169.2	137.9	100.8	84.1	82.4	73.6
Balance of payments	**Millions of dollars**								
Current account balance	-48 622	-54 153	-16 144	7 201	19 727	33 362	45 569	14 191	-31 133
Merchandise trade balance	-679	-7 554	20 456	40 837	56 293	76 344	90 911	64 262	43 882
Exports of goods f.o.b.	363 732	348 782	352 713	384 039	473 216	568 968	677 131	762 781	901 386
Imports of goods f.o.b.	364 411	356 336	332 257	343 202	416 923	492 624	586 220	698 519	857 504
Services trade balance	-14 979	-17 550	-12 634	-11 234	-11 535	-15 501	-17 093	-22 314	-29 433
Income balance	-54 520	-55 369	-53 740	-58 861	-68 558	-79 186	-90 108	-91 775	-111 131
Net current transfers	21 555	26 320	29 773	36 458	43 524	51 704	61 859	64 017	65 659
Capital and financial balance [f]	64 167	37 755	-9 784	3 278	-6 766	24 196	14 945	108 620	84 227
Net foreign direct investment	72 172	66 546	50 374	38 356	48 942	53 657	30 461	84 601	81 816
Financial capital [g]	-7 432	-28 077	-60 108	-34 095	-54 743	-28 757	-15 069	24 754	3 281
Overall balance	15 545	-16 398	-25 928	10 479	12 962	57 558	60 514	122 810	53 094
Variation in reserve assets [h]	-7 332	168	3 507	-29 084	-21 831	-35 480	-47 255	-124 589	-53 344
Other financing [i]	-8 213	16 230	22 421	18 606	8 869	-22 078	-13 259	1 778	249
Net transfer of resources	1 056	-1 392	-41 425	-37 974	-67 594	-79 275	-92 728	14 383	-30 756
International reserve assets [j]	169 818	163 049	165 143	200 926	227 465	263 313	321 056	459 729	510 663
Fiscal sector [k]	**Percentage of GDP**								
Overall balance	-2.6	-3.2	-2.9	-2.9	-1.9	-1.1	0.1	0.4	-0.3
Primary balance	-0.2	-0.8	-0.5	-0.2	0.6	1.4	2.3	2.4	1.6
Total revenue	16.7	16.7	16.8	17.0	17.3	18.3	19.4	20.0	19.2
Tax revenue	12.4	12.4	12.5	12.7	13.1	13.9	14.2	14.7	13.4
Total expenditure	19.2	19.8	19.7	19.8	19.1	19.4	19.3	19.5	19.7
Central-government public debt	43.3	45.6	58.6	57.7	51.1	43.0	36.0	30.3	26.1
Public debt of the non-financial public sector	47.4	49.6	64.5	62.2	55.3	47.6	39.9	33.0	28.6

Source: Economic Commission for Latin America and the Caribbean (ECLAC), on the basis of official figures.
[a] Preliminary figures.
[b] Based on official figures expressed in constant 2000 dollars.
[c] December - December variation.
[d] The data for Argentina and Brazil have been adjusted to allow for changes in methodology in 2003 and 2002, respectively.
[e] Estimates based on figures expressed in dollars at current prices.
[f] Includes errors and omissions.
[g] Refers to the capital and financial balances (including errors and omissions) minus net foreign direct investment.
[h] A minus sign (-) indicates an increase in reserve assets.
[i] Includes the use of IMF credit and loans and exceptional financing.
[j] Including gold.
[k] Central government, except for Bolivia and Mexico whose coverage correspond to general government and public sector, respectively. Simple averages.

Table A-2
LATIN AMERICA AND THE CARIBBEAN: GROSS DOMESTIC PRODUCT
(Annual growth rates)

	2000	2001	2002	2003	2004	2005	2006	2007	2008 [a]
Latin America and the Caribbean	**4.0**	**0.4**	**-0.4**	**2.2**	**6.1**	**4.9**	**5.8**	**5.7**	**4.6**
Antigua and Barbuda	1.5	2.2	2.5	5.2	7.2	4.7	12.6	10.0	2.5
Argentina	-0.8	-4.4	-10.9	8.8	9.0	9.2	8.5	8.7	6.8
Bahamas	4.3	-0.3	2.0	-2.4	-0.2	3.3	4.6	2.8	1.5
Barbados	2.3	-4.6	0.7	2.0	4.8	4.3	3.3	3.2	1.5
Belize	12.3	5.0	5.1	9.3	4.6	3.0	4.7	1.2	6.0
Bolivia	2.5	1.7	2.5	2.7	4.2	4.4	4.8	4.6	5.8
Brazil	4.3	1.3	2.7	1.1	5.7	3.2	4.0	5.7	5.9
Chile	4.5	3.4	2.2	3.9	6.0	5.6	4.3	5.1	3.8
Colombia	2.9	2.2	2.5	4.6	4.7	5.7	6.8	7.7	3.0
Costa Rica	1.8	1.1	2.9	6.4	4.3	5.9	8.8	7.3	3.3
Cuba	5.9	3.2	1.4	3.8	5.8	11.2	12.1	7.3	4.3
Dominica	0.6	-3.6	-4.2	2.2	6.3	3.4	5.2	3.4	3.4
Ecuador	2.8	5.3	4.2	3.6	8.0	6.0	3.9	2.5	6.5
El Salvador	2.2	1.7	2.3	2.3	1.9	3.1	4.2	4.7	3.0
Grenada	17.5	-3.9	2.1	8.4	-6.5	12.0	-1.9	3.6	2.1
Guatemala	3.6	2.3	3.9	2.5	3.2	3.3	5.3	5.7	3.3
Guyana	-1.4	2.3	1.1	-0.7	1.6	-2.0	5.1	5.4	4.8
Haiti	0.9	-1.0	-0.3	0.4	-3.5	1.8	2.3	3.2	1.5
Honduras	5.7	2.7	3.8	4.5	6.2	6.1	6.3	6.3	3.8
Jamaica	0.7	1.5	1.1	2.3	1.0	1.4	2.5	1.2	0.0
Mexico	6.6	-0.0	0.8	1.4	4.0	3.2	4.8	3.2	1.8
Nicaragua	4.1	3.0	0.8	2.5	5.3	4.3	3.9	3.8	3.0
Panama	2.7	0.6	2.2	4.2	7.5	7.2	8.5	11.5	9.2
Paraguay	-3.3	2.1	-0.0	3.8	4.1	2.9	4.3	6.8	5.0
Peru	3.0	0.2	5.0	4.0	5.1	6.7	7.6	8.9	9.4
Dominican Republic	5.7	1.8	5.8	-0.3	1.3	9.3	10.7	8.5	4.5
Saint Kitts and Nevis	4.3	2.0	1.0	0.5	7.6	5.6	5.3	4.0	9.7
Saint Vincent and the Grenadines	1.8	1.0	3.7	3.2	6.2	3.6	9.6	7.7	1.0
Saint Lucia	-0.2	-5.1	3.1	4.3	5.2	6.0	4.0	1.1	2.3
Suriname	4.0	5.9	1.9	6.1	7.7	5.6	5.8	5.3	5.0
Trinidad and Tobago	6.9	4.2	7.9	14.4	8.8	8.0	12.0	5.5	3.5
Uruguay	-1.4	-3.4	-11.0	2.2	11.8	6.6	7.0	7.4	11.5
Venezuela (Bolivarian Republic of)	3.7	3.4	-8.9	-7.8	18.3	10.3	10.3	8.4	4.8

Source: Economic Commission for Latin America and the Caribbean (ECLAC), on the basis of official figures expressed in constant 2000 dollars.
[a] Preliminary figures.

Table A-3
LATIN AMERICA AND THE CARIBBEAN: PER CAPITA GROSS DOMESTIC PRODUCT
(Annual growth rates)

	2000	2001	2002	2003	2004	2005	2006	2007	2008 [a]
Latin America and the Caribbean	**2.5**	**-1.0**	**-1.7**	**0.9**	**4.7**	**3.6**	**4.4**	**4.4**	**3.3**
Antigua and Barbuda	-0.7	0.3	0.8	3.7	5.7	3.3	11.2	8.7	1.3
Argentina	-1.8	-5.4	-11.7	7.8	8.0	8.1	7.4	7.6	5.8
Bahamas	2.8	-1.6	0.7	-3.6	-1.4	2.1	3.4	1.5	0.3
Barbados	1.8	-5.0	0.3	1.6	4.4	3.9	3.0	2.9	1.2
Belize	9.5	2.4	2.6	6.8	2.2	0.7	2.4	-0.9	3.8
Bolivia	0.1	-0.6	0.2	0.4	1.9	2.2	2.6	2.4	3.7
Brazil	2.8	-0.2	1.2	-0.3	4.2	1.8	2.6	4.3	4.5
Chile	3.2	2.2	1.0	2.8	4.9	4.5	3.3	4.0	2.8
Colombia	1.3	0.6	0.9	3.0	3.1	4.2	5.3	6.3	1.7
Costa Rica	-0.5	-1.0	0.9	4.4	2.4	4.0	6.9	5.5	1.6
Cuba	5.6	2.9	1.2	3.6	5.6	11.1	12.0	7.3	4.3
Dominica	0.8	-3.5	-4.0	2.4	6.5	3.6	5.5	3.8	3.8
Ecuador	1.3	3.8	2.8	2.1	6.5	4.5	2.4	1.0	5.0
El Salvador	0.2	-0.2	0.4	0.5	0.1	1.3	2.4	2.9	1.3
Grenada	16.8	-4.8	1.1	7.2	-7.4	11.3	-2.3	3.6	2.2
Guatemala	1.2	-0.1	1.3	0.0	0.6	0.7	2.7	3.2	0.8
Guyana	-1.3	2.2	1.0	-0.9	1.4	-2.0	5.2	5.5	5.1
Haiti	-0.8	-2.7	-1.8	-1.2	-5.0	0.2	0.7	1.5	-0.2
Honduras	3.6	0.6	1.7	2.5	4.1	3.9	4.2	4.2	1.7
Jamaica	-0.1	0.8	0.4	1.5	0.3	0.8	1.9	0.6	-0.5
Mexico	5.1	-1.1	-0.1	0.6	3.2	2.3	3.7	2.0	0.6
Nicaragua	2.4	1.5	-0.6	1.2	4.0	2.9	2.5	2.4	1.7
Panama	0.8	-1.3	0.4	2.3	5.6	5.4	6.7	9.7	7.5
Paraguay	-5.3	0.0	-2.0	1.8	2.1	0.9	2.4	4.9	3.0
Peru	1.6	-1.1	3.7	2.8	3.9	5.5	6.3	7.6	8.2
Dominican Republic	3.9	0.1	4.1	-1.8	-0.3	7.6	9.0	6.9	3.0
Saint Kitts and Nevis	3.0	0.7	-0.3	-0.8	6.3	4.3	3.9	2.6	8.3
Saint Vincent and the Grenadines	1.3	0.4	3.2	2.6	5.6	3.1	9.0	7.1	0.5
Saint Lucia	-1.1	-6.1	2.0	3.1	4.0	4.8	2.9	-0.0	1.2
Suriname	3.0	5.0	1.1	5.3	7.0	4.9	5.1	4.7	4.4
Trinidad and Tobago	6.5	3.8	7.6	14.0	8.4	7.6	11.6	5.1	3.1
Uruguay	-1.8	-3.6	-11.0	2.2	11.9	6.6	6.8	7.2	11.2
Venezuela (Bolivarian Republic of)	1.8	1.5	-10.5	-9.4	16.2	8.4	8.5	6.6	3.1

Source: Economic Commission for Latin America and the Caribbean (ECLAC), on the basis of official figures expressed in constant 2000 dollars.
[a] Preliminary figures.

Table A-4
LATIN AMERICA AND THE CARIBBEAN: GROSS FIXED CAPITAL FORMATION
(Percentages of GDP)

	2000	2001	2002	2003	2004	2005	2006	2007	2008 [a]
Latin America and the Caribbean	**18.5**	**18.0**	**16.8**	**16.4**	**17.4**	**18.5**	**19.6**	**20.8**	**21.9**
Argentina	16.2	14.3	10.2	12.9	15.9	17.9	19.5	20.4	21.2
Bahamas	33.8	31.2	29.8	31.1	29.0	36.0	41.2	41.8	41.6
Belize	28.7	25.6	23.1	18.1	16.4	17.2	16.7	17.4	16.2
Bolivia	17.9	13.8	16.0	13.9	13.2	13.4	14.0	15.1	15.1
Brazil	16.8	16.6	15.4	14.5	15.0	15.0	15.7	16.9	18.6
Chile	19.8	19.9	19.8	20.2	20.9	24.5	24.2	25.8	30.0
Colombia	13.0	14.0	14.7	16.0	17.4	19.9	22.4	25.4	27.3
Costa Rica	17.8	18.0	18.7	18.8	18.0	17.7	18.1	19.6	21.9
Cuba	11.9	12.6	6.8	6.1	6.2	6.7	8.6	8.2	8.2
Ecuador	20.5	24.0	27.4	26.4	25.7	26.8	26.8	26.8	28.1
El Salvador	16.9	16.9	17.1	17.1	15.9	15.8	16.9	17.1	16.9
Guatemala	19.1	19.0	20.0	18.9	18.1	18.3	20.1	20.5	20.3
Haiti	27.3	27.3	28.0	28.8	28.9	28.8	28.8	28.7	28.9
Honduras	25.8	24.3	21.7	22.1	25.7	23.8	25.3	27.4	28.5
Mexico	21.4	20.2	19.9	19.7	20.5	21.1	22.1	22.6	23.1
Nicaragua	29.9	27.4	25.5	25.0	25.4	26.8	26.6	27.1	27.6
Panama	21.2	15.7	14.4	17.1	17.4	17.3	18.6	22.4	25.1
Paraguay	17.5	16.1	15.0	15.5	15.6	17.3	17.2	18.3	20.8
Peru	20.2	18.5	17.5	17.8	18.3	19.2	21.2	24.0	27.1
Dominican Republic	20.5	19.3	19.1	15.3	14.8	15.4	16.9	17.5	17.9
Uruguay	13.2	12.4	9.4	8.1	9.5	10.4	12.3	12.1	14.4
Venezuela (Bolivarian Republic of)	21.0	23.1	20.7	14.1	17.9	22.4	25.7	29.8	28.0

Source: Economic Commission for Latin America and the Caribbean (ECLAC), on the basis of official figures expressed in constant 2000 dollars.
[a] Preliminary figures.

Table A-5a
LATIN AMERICA AND THE CARIBBEAN: FINANCING OF GROSS DOMESTIC INVESTMENT
(Percentages of GDP) [a]

	2000	2001	2002	2003	2004	2005	2006	2007	2008 [b]
1. Domestic saving	20.7	18.6	19.7	20.6	22.7	22.6	23.8	23.3	22.9
2. Net factor income	-2.6	-2.7	-2.9	-3.1	-3.1	-3.0	-2.9	-2.5	-2.7
3. Net transfers	1.0	1.3	1.6	1.9	2.0	1.9	1.9	1.7	1.6
4. Gross national saving	19.1	17.1	18.4	19.4	21.5	21.5	22.9	22.5	21.7
5. External saving	2.3	2.6	0.8	-0.5	-1.0	-1.4	-1.6	-0.5	0.6
6. Gross domestic investment	21.4	19.8	19.2	18.9	20.5	20.2	21.3	22.0	22.4

Source: Economic Commission for Latin America and the Caribbean (ECLAC), on the basis of official figures.
[a] Based on values calculated in national currency and expressed in current dollars.
[b] Preliminary figures.

Table A-5b
LATIN AMERICA AND THE CARIBBEAN: GROSS DOMESTIC INVESTMENT, NATIONAL INCOME AND SAVING
(Annual growth rates)

	2000	2001	2002	2003	2004	2005	2006	2007	2008 [a]
Gross domestic investment	7.5	-2.0	-7.6	-1.8	11.7	6.0	12.9	11.1	12.0
Gross national disposable income	4.9	-0.3	-0.3	2.5	7.1	6.1	7.2	6.5	5.5
National saving	13.7	-0.7	-0.8	6.6	17.7	13.9	15.3	12.8	10.2

Source: Economic Commission for Latin America and the Caribbean (ECLAC), on the basis of official figures expressed in constant 2000 dollars.
[a] Preliminary figures.

Table A-6
LATIN AMERICA AND THE CARIBBEAN: BALANCE OF PAYMENTS
(Millions of dollars)

	Exports of goods f.o.b			Exports of services			Imports of goods f.o.b			Imports of services		
	2006	2007	2008 [d]	2006	2007	2008 [d]	2006	2007	2008 [d]	2006	2007	2008 [d]
Latin America and the Caribbean [e]	**691 456**	**778 696**	**919 609**	**87 151**	**100 367**	**115 403**	**596 429**	**709 973**	**871 716**	**103 561**	**121 962**	**144 946**
Latin America and the Caribbean [f]	**677 131**	**762 781**	**901 386**	**85 241**	**98 285**	**115 403**	**586 220**	**698 519**	**857 504**	**102 334**	**120 599**	**144 946**
Antigua and Barbuda	74	76	78	477	517	542	560	649	684	259	283	296
Argentina	46 546	55 780	73 071	8 001	10 320	12 384	32 588	42 525	55 282	8 532	10 846	13 558
Bahamas	665	802	914	2 436	2 599	2 729	2 763	2 956	2 808	1 611	1 580	1 453
Barbados	465	484	661	1 529	1 665	...	1 468	1 536	1 808	718	774	...
Belize	427	426	498	374	398	402	612	642	770	163	168	161
Bolivia	3 875	4 458	6 019	477	468	501	2 632	3 455	4 837	827	628	659
Brazil	137 807	160 649	199 205	19 476	23 808	30 713	91 351	120 622	173 696	29 116	36 861	49 025
Chile	58 485	67 644	68 320	7 824	8 786	10 543	35 899	43 991	58 068	8 452	9 947	12 434
Colombia	25 181	30 577	37 689	3 377	3 636	4 142	24 859	31 173	36 251	5 496	6 243	6 661
Costa Rica	8 102	9 308	9 618	2 972	3 551	4 265	10 829	12 285	14 108	1 621	1 818	1 991
Cuba	3 167	3 830	...	6 667	8 192	...	9 498	10 083	...	211	292	...
Dominica	44	40	36	100	96	98	147	172	195	52	66	70
Ecuador	13 176	14 870	19 331	1 037	1 200	1 392	11 408	13 047	17 483	2 341	2 572	2 880
El Salvador	3 760	4 035	4 732	1 426	1 492	1 589	7 300	8 108	9 346	1 505	1 734	1 855
Grenada	31	45	29	130	148	147	263	309	287	99	107	113
Guatemala	6 082	7 012	8 049	1 519	1 709	1 865	10 934	12 482	13 915	1 785	2 029	2 252
Guyana	585	681	831	148	173	...	885	1 063	1 372	245	273	...
Haiti	492	522	475	203	260	343	1 548	1 618	1 958	588	701	729
Honduras	5 195	5 594	5 793	686	750	845	7 317	8 556	9 661	984	1 037	1 127
Jamaica	2 134	2 344	2 661	2 649	2 595	2 636	5 077	5 771	7 719	2 021	2 132	2 306
Mexico	249 925	271 875	304 500	16 221	17 617	19 202	256 058	281 949	320 012	21 957	23 556	25 677
Nicaragua	2 034	2 313	2 742	341	372	425	3 451	4 117	5 122	478	556	676
Panama	8 478	9 338	10 311	3 938	4 924	5 882	10 190	12 521	14 374	1 728	2 107	2 634
Paraguay	4 401	5 471	7 903	753	853	927	5 022	6 027	8 850	384	459	571
Peru	23 800	27 956	31 590	2 647	3 343	4 279	14 866	19 599	29 007	3 428	4 270	5 765
Dominican Republic	6 610	7 237	7 237	4 543	4 690	4 925	12 174	13 817	17 548	1 558	1 722	1 895
Saint Kitts and Nevis	59	58	58	173	174	180	220	244	257	102	102	110
Saint Vincent and the Grenadines	41	51	51	171	162	160	240	288	302	88	114	119
Saint Lucia	97	112	123	334	372	390	521	542	558	169	188	197
Suriname	1 174	1 359	...	234	245	...	1 013	1 185	...	264	317	...
Trinidad and Tobago	12 100	13 391	16 731	...	...	...	6 843	7 670	11 033	...	...	...
Uruguay	4 400	5 025	6 287	1 385	1 771	2 023	4 895	5 591	7 581	987	1 249	1 457
Venezuela (Bolivarian Rep. of)	65 210	69 165	94 064	1 572	1 673	1 874	32 498	45 463	46 827	6 005	7 524	8 276

Table A-6 (continued)

	Trade balance			Income balance			Current transfers balance			Current account balance		
	2006	2007	2008 [d]	2006	2007	2008 [d]	2006	2007	2008 [d]	2006	2007	2008 [d]
Latin America and the Caribbean [e]	**79 068**	**47 694**	**18 644**	**-91 335**	**-92 958**	**-112 665**	**62 233**	**64 545**	**66 136**	**49 965**	**19 281**	**-26 933**
Latin America and the Caribbean [f]	**73 819**	**41 948**	**14 340**	**-90 108**	**-91 775**	**-111 131**	**61 859**	**64 017**	**65 659**	**45 569**	**14 191**	**-31 133**
Antigua and Barbuda	-267	-340	-359	-64	-67	-43	22	24	24	-309	-382	-379
Argentina	13 427	12 729	16 616	-6 161	-5 931	-6 524	446	315	315	7 712	7 113	10 406
Bahamas	-1 273	-1 135	-618	-218	-232	-127	52	52	53	-1 439	-1 314	-692
Barbados	-192	-161	-1 147	-171	-191	-203	86	107	109	-277	-245	-286
Belize	26	13	-30	-125	-158	-182	74	93	108	-25	-51	-105
Bolivia	892	844	1 024	-397	-173	-150	822	1 091	1 179	1 317	1 763	2 053
Brazil	36 816	26 975	7 197	-27 480	-29 291	-39 300	4 306	4 029	4 351	13 643	1 712	-27 752
Chile	21 959	22 491	8 361	-18 418	-18 265	-17 000	3 297	2 974	3 000	6 838	7 200	-5 639
Colombia	-1 797	-3 203	-1 081	-5 929	-7 886	-10 784	4 743	5 231	5 422	-2 982	-5 859	-6 442
Costa Rica	-1 376	-1 244	-2 216	4	-865	-765	349	469	539	-1 023	-1 639	-2 442
Cuba	125	1 647	...	-618	-960	...	278	-199	...	-215	488	...
Dominica	-54	-102	-131	-17	-16	-17	20	21	21	-52	-98	-127
Ecuador	464	452	360	-1 950	-2 047	-2 200	3 104	3 246	3 408	1 618	1 650	1 568
El Salvador	-3 619	-4 315	-4 880	-528	-579	-527	3 472	3 776	4 066	-675	-1 119	-1 342
Grenada	-200	-224	-224	-29	-34	-36	36	24	25	-193	-233	-235
Guatemala	-5 118	-5 790	-6 252	-662	-770	-932	4 268	4 863	5 361	-1 512	-1 697	-1 823
Guyana	-398	-481	-692	-69	-37	-41	216	287	318	-250	-232	-416
Haiti	-1 441	-1 537	-1 868	7	3	13	1 361	1 505	1 686	-73	-29	-168
Honduras	-2 420	-3 249	-4 150	-539	-598	-462	2 450	2 622	2 930	-509	-1 225	-1 683
Jamaica	-2 316	-2 963	-4 728	-616	-806	-821	1 749	1 969	2 128	-1 183	-1 800	-3 422
Mexico	-11 869	-16 013	-21 986	-14 486	-14 122	-16 500	24 124	24 322	23 350	-2 231	-5 813	-15 136
Nicaragua	-1 553	-1 988	-2 630	-129	-135	-163	1 003	1 075	1 043	-679	-1 048	-1 750
Panama	498	-365	-814	-1 278	-1 311	-1 567	253	253	261	-527	-1 422	-2 121
Paraguay	-252	-162	-591	-54	-166	-113	426	373	369	120	45	-335
Peru	8 153	7 429	1 097	-7 581	-8 418	-9 600	2 185	2 495	2 869	2 757	1 505	-5 635
Dominican Republic	-2 579	-3 612	-7 281	-1 827	-2 028	-2 089	3 144	3 410	3 546	-1 262	-2 231	-5 824
Saint Kitts and Nevis	-89	-115	-129	-32	-31	-33	32	33	33	-90	-112	-130
Saint Vincent and the Grenadines	-116	-189	-211	-24	-23	-25	20	20	19	-120	-192	-217
Saint Lucia	-259	-246	-242	-56	-68	-74	12	14	13	-303	-300	-303
Suriname	130	102	...	-52	9	...	36	76	...	115	187	...
Trinidad and Tobago	5 708	6 287	6 143	-936	-964	-1 290	36	58	50	4 809	5 381	4 902
Uruguay	-98	-45	-727	-428	-325	-510	126	134	141	-400	-235	-1 096
Venezuela (Bolivarian Rep. of)	28 279	17 851	40 835	-1 092	2 565	-600	-38	-415	-600	27 149	20 001	39 635

Table A-6 (concluded)

	Capital and financial balance [a]			Overall balance			Reserve assets (variation) [b]			Other financing [c]		
	2006	2007	2008 [d]	2006	2007	2008 [d]	2006	2007	2008 [d]	2006	2007	2008 [d]
Latin America and the Caribbean [e]	11 848	105 523	81 524	61 812	124 805	54 591	-48 570	-126 622	-58 841	-13 241	1 817	249
Latin America and the Caribbean [f]	14 945	108 620	84 227	60 514	122 810	53 094	-47 255	-124 589	-53 344	-13 259	1 778	249
Antigua and Barbuda	324	383	379	15	1	1	-15	-1	-1	0	0	0
Argentina	6 800	4 660	-10 766	14 513	11 772	-360	-3 530	-13 098	360	-10 982	1 326	0
Bahamas	1 360	1 269	912	-79	-46	220	79	46	-220	0	0	0
Barbados	320	523	325	43	278	39	-41	-278	-39	0	0	0
Belize	75	74	158	50	23	53	-50	-23	-53	0	0	0
Bolivia	121	117	247	1 439	1 880	2 300	-1 286	-1 952	-2 300	-152	73	0
Brazil	16 927	85 772	54 752	30 569	87 484	27 000	-30 569	-87 484	-27 000	0	0	0
Chile	-4 841	-10 414	10 839	1 997	-3 214	5 200	-1 997	3 214	-5 200	0	0	0
Colombia	3 005	10 572	9 053	23	4 714	2 611	-23	-4 714	-2 611	0	0	0
Costa Rica	2 053	3 096	1 992	1 031	1 457	-450	-1 031	-1 457	450	0	0	0
Cuba	...	...	...	...	...	...	...	...	...	...	...	...
Dominica	65	97	126	13	-1	-1	-13	1	1	0	0	0
Ecuador	-1 748	-263	1 132	-131	1 387	2 700	124	-1 497	-2 700	7	111	0
El Salvador	747	1 399	1 639	72	280	297	-72	-280	-297	0	0	0
Grenada	198	244	226	6	11	-8	-6	-11	8	0	0	0
Guatemala	1 765	1 913	2 123	252	216	300	-252	-216	-300	0	0	0
Guyana	293	231	74	43	-1	-342	-61	-37	342	18	39	0
Haiti	166	188	239	93	159	70	-109	-208	-142	15	49	71
Honduras	820	1 063	1 457	311	-162	-225	-310	109	160	-1	53	65
Jamaica	1 413	1 390	4 486	230	-410	1 065	-230	410	-1 065	0	0	0
Mexico	1 228	16 099	17 636	-1 003	10 286	2 500	1 003	-10 286	-2 500	0	0	0
Nicaragua	740	1 140	1 802	62	92	52	-186	-173	-120	124	80	67
Panama	699	2 044	2 775	172	622	654	-162	-611	-650	-10	-10	-4
Paraguay	263	678	527	383	723	192	-387	-723	-195	4	0	4
Peru	-30	8 082	9 095	2 726	9 588	3 460	-2 753	-9 654	-3 500	27	67	40
Dominican Republic	1 452	2 888	5 508	190	657	-316	-314	-692	310	124	35	6
Saint Kitts and Nevis	107	119	124	17	7	-5	-17	-7	5	0	0	0
Saint Vincent and the Grenadines	132	190	213	12	-2	-3	-12	2	3	0	0	0
Saint Lucia	317	319	299	14	19	-3	-14	-19	3	0	0	0
Suriname	-21	-10	...	94	177	...	-94	-177	...	0	0	...
Trinidad and Tobago	-3 690	-3 840	-3 102	1 119	1 541	1 800	-1 119	-1 541	-1 800	0	0	0
Uruguay	2 798	1 245	3 388	2 399	1 010	2 291	15	-1 005	-2 291	-2 414	-5	-0
Venezuela (Bolivarian Rep. of)	-22 011	-25 743	-36 135	5 138	-5 742	3 500	-5 138	5 742	-3 500	0	0	0

Source: Economic Commission for Latin America and the Caribbean (ECLAC), on the basis of official figures from the International Monetary Fund (IMF) and national sources.

[a] Includes errors and omissions.
[b] A minus sign (-) indicates an increase in reserve assets.
[c] Includes the use of IMF credit and loans and exceptional financing.
[d] Preliminary figures.
[e] Excluding Cuba.
[f] Includes only the countries with complete balance-of-payments data.

Table A-7
LATIN AMERICA AND THE CARIBBEAN: EXPORTS OF GOODS, f.o.b.
(Indices 2000=100)

	Value			Volume			Unit value		
	2006	2007	2008 [a]	2006	2007	2008 [a]	2006	2007	2008 [a]
Latin America and the Caribbean	**186.6**	**210.3**	**247.7**	**137.1**	**141.6**	**144.3**	**136.1**	**148.6**	**172.5**
Argentina	176.7	211.8	277.4	145.2	155.3	162.8	121.7	136.3	170.4
Bolivia	310.9	357.8	483.0	183.4	183.5	221.2	169.5	195.0	218.4
Brazil	250.2	291.6	361.6	185.7	195.0	195.0	134.7	149.6	185.4
Chile	304.4	352.1	355.6	144.9	155.2	152.2	210.1	226.9	233.7
Colombia	183.0	222.2	273.9	135.7	143.3	146.0	134.8	155.1	187.6
Costa Rica	139.4	160.1	165.4	147.2	167.4	169.6	94.7	95.6	97.5
Cuba	189.0	228.6	...	96.7	98.1	...	195.5	232.9	...
Ecuador	256.5	289.5	376.3	184.8	189.6	195.6	138.8	152.7	192.4
El Salvador	126.9	136.2	159.7	118.4	121.0	137.8	107.2	112.5	115.9
Guatemala	153.5	177.0	203.2	136.6	148.6	157.9	112.4	119.1	128.7
Haiti	148.3	157.4	143.2	132.6	136.7	115.2	111.8	115.2	124.4
Honduras	155.4	167.3	173.3	164.4	168.6	161.7	94.5	99.2	107.2
Mexico	150.4	163.7	183.3	124.4	126.5	127.6	120.9	129.4	143.6
Nicaragua	231.0	262.7	311.4	225.8	246.9	276.1	102.3	106.4	112.8
Panama	145.2	159.9	176.6	137.2	145.3	152.8	105.9	110.1	115.6
Paraguay	189.0	234.9	339.4	173.4	195.9	252.7	109.0	119.9	134.3
Peru	342.2	402.0	462.2	176.4	181.8	195.4	194.0	221.1	236.6
Dominican Republic	115.2	126.2	126.2	103.4	104.4	102.3	111.4	120.9	123.3
Uruguay	184.6	210.8	263.7	163.1	174.0	201.6	113.2	121.1	130.8
Venezuela (Bolivarian Republic of)	194.5	206.3	280.5	91.0	84.7	85.9	213.7	243.6	326.5

Source: Economic Commission for Latin America and the Caribbean (ECLAC), on the basis of official figures from the International Monetary Fund (IMF) and national sources.
[a] Preliminary figures.

Table A-8
LATIN AMERICA AND THE CARIBBEAN: IMPORTS OF GOODS, f.o.b.
(Indices 2000=100)

	Value			Volume			Unit value		
	2006	2007	2008 [a]	2006	2007	2008 [a]	2006	2007	2008 [a]
Latin America and the Caribbean	**161.5**	**192.3**	**233.0**	**136.6**	**152.7**	**168.9**	**118.2**	**125.9**	**139.8**
Argentina	136.4	178.0	231.4	126.6	152.9	177.5	107.8	116.4	130.4
Bolivia	163.5	214.6	300.4	129.8	153.5	202.7	125.9	139.8	148.2
Brazil	163.8	216.2	311.4	126.2	154.3	185.1	129.8	140.2	168.2
Chile	210.0	257.4	339.7	183.7	216.4	257.4	114.4	118.9	132.0
Colombia	224.2	281.1	326.9	191.5	225.5	245.1	117.0	124.6	133.4
Costa Rica	179.8	203.9	234.2	162.8	181.1	196.2	110.4	112.6	119.4
Cuba	198.1	210.3	...	166.1	155.8	...	119.2	135.0	...
Ecuador	304.8	348.6	467.1	241.4	258.0	317.2	126.3	135.1	147.3
El Salvador	155.2	172.4	198.7	138.3	144.9	154.6	112.3	119.0	128.5
Guatemala	196.7	224.5	250.3	156.7	165.7	169.4	125.5	135.5	147.7
Haiti	142.5	148.9	180.2	113.3	111.7	96.6	125.7	133.2	186.5
Honduras	183.5	214.6	242.3	161.5	176.5	179.5	113.6	121.6	135.0
Mexico	146.8	161.6	183.4	126.3	131.2	137.9	116.2	123.2	133.0
Nicaragua	191.5	228.5	284.3	148.6	168.9	191.0	128.9	135.3	148.8
Panama	146.0	179.3	205.9	125.3	146.6	158.4	116.5	122.3	129.9
Paraguay	175.2	210.3	308.8	153.6	175.5	240.9	114.1	119.8	128.2
Peru	201.8	266.1	393.8	157.2	188.4	242.5	128.4	141.2	162.4
Dominican Republic	128.4	145.8	185.1	109.4	118.2	139.0	117.4	123.3	133.2
Uruguay	147.8	168.9	228.9	115.9	126.1	151.3	127.6	133.9	151.3
Venezuela (Bolivarian Republic of)	192.7	269.6	277.7	166.3	223.6	221.5	115.9	120.5	125.4

Source: Economic Commission for Latin America and the Caribbean (ECLAC), on the basis of official figures from the International Monetary Fund (IMF) and national sources.
[a] Preliminary figures.

Table A-9
LATIN AMERICA AND THE CARIBBEAN: TERMS OF TRADE FOR GOODS f.o.b./f.o.b.
(Indices 2000=100)

	2000	2001	2002	2003	2004	2005	2006	2007	2008 [a]
Latin America and the Caribbean	**100.0**	**96.3**	**96.6**	**98.6**	**103.6**	**108.7**	**115.1**	**118.0**	**123.4**
Argentina	100.0	99.3	98.7	107.2	109.2	106.9	113.0	117.1	130.7
Bolivia	100.0	95.8	96.2	98.5	104.1	111.8	134.6	139.5	147.4
Brazil	100.0	99.6	98.4	97.0	97.9	99.2	103.8	106.7	110.3
Chile	100.0	93.3	97.2	102.8	124.9	139.8	183.7	190.7	177.0
Colombia	100.0	94.2	92.5	95.2	102.3	111.0	115.2	124.4	140.7
Costa Rica	100.0	98.4	96.9	95.5	91.9	88.3	85.8	84.9	81.7
Cuba	100.0	114.0	105.1	121.0	133.3	129.8	164.0	172.6	...
Ecuador	100.0	84.6	86.8	89.8	91.5	102.4	109.9	113.0	130.6
El Salvador	100.0	102.5	101.6	97.7	96.8	96.8	95.5	94.6	90.2
Guatemala	100.0	96.7	95.8	93.0	92.1	91.3	89.6	87.9	87.1
Haiti	100.0	101.2	100.2	98.7	96.0	92.4	88.9	86.4	66.7
Honduras	100.0	94.8	92.0	88.0	87.2	87.2	83.2	81.6	79.4
Mexico	100.0	97.4	97.9	98.8	101.6	103.6	104.1	105.1	108.0
Nicaragua	100.0	88.4	87.0	84.1	82.5	81.4	79.4	78.6	75.8
Panama	100.0	102.7	101.6	97.2	95.3	93.5	90.8	90.0	89.0
Paraguay	100.0	100.2	96.7	101.4	104.3	97.4	95.5	100.1	104.7
Peru	100.0	95.6	98.4	102.2	111.3	119.4	151.1	156.6	145.7
Dominican Republic	100.0	100.9	101.5	97.9	96.7	95.8	94.9	98.0	92.6
Uruguay	100.0	104.0	102.6	103.5	99.9	90.7	88.7	90.4	86.4
Venezuela (Bolivarian Republic of)	100.0	82.2	87.6	98.7	118.1	154.4	184.4	202.1	260.4

Source: Economic Commission for Latin America and the Caribbean (ECLAC), on the basis of official figures from the International Monetary Fund (IMF) and national sources.

[a] Preliminary figures.

Table A-10
LATIN AMERICA AND THE CARIBBEAN: NET RESOURCE TRANSFER [a]
(Millions of dollars)

	2000	2001	2002	2003	2004	2005	2006	2007	2008 [b]
Latin America and the Caribbean	**1 056**	**-1 392**	**-41 425**	**-37 974**	**-67 594**	**-79 275**	**-92 728**	**14 383**	**-30 756**
Antigua and Barbuda	16	48	49	85	56	136	260	316	336
Argentina	993	-16 030	-20 773	-12 535	-7 175	-3 712	-10 343	54	-17 290
Bahamas	240	366	174	279	213	358	1 142	1 037	777
Barbados	241	241	42	131	58	-16	149	332	122
Belize	161	121	92	64	7	25	-50	-84	-22
Bolivia	182	30	-156	-226	-565	-535	-428	17	97
Brazil	4 077	6 778	-10 252	-14 234	-29 955	-35 633	-10 553	56 481	15 452
Chile	-1 621	-2 022	-2 068	-4 076	-10 102	-10 220	-23 259	-28 679	-6 161
Colombia	-2 214	-323	-1 439	-2 609	-848	-1 846	-2 924	2 686	-1 730
Costa Rica	-714	-63	580	443	432	1 160	2 058	2 231	1 227
Dominica	31	39	36	32	23	64	49	81	110
Ecuador	-2 020	-817	-100	-953	-1 084	-1 580	-3 691	-2 200	-1 068
El Salvador	132	-293	-42	595	117	-69	219	819	1 111
Grenada	61	67	109	83	30	131	170	211	190
Guatemala	1 494	1 618	993	1 251	1 359	995	1 102	1 144	1 191
Guyana	81	81	58	39	-1	143	242	232	174
Haiti	45	129	26	5	94	-18	188	240	323
Honduras	348	322	86	94	743	177	280	519	1 060
Jamaica	517	1 168	208	-246	612	561	797	584	3 665
Mexico	6 491	11 161	8 502	5 706	315	-1 269	-13 258	1 977	1 136
Nicaragua	624	455	607	520	616	590	736	1 085	1 707
Panama	3	202	-39	-508	-413	418	-589	723	1 203
Paraguay	-30	237	-134	168	-98	72	213	512	417
Peru	-293	391	512	-670	-1 262	-4 596	-7 584	-269	-465
Dominican Republic	-85	168	-881	-2 787	-2 324	-321	-251	894	3 425
Saint Kitts and Nevis	32	84	95	71	40	23	75	88	91
Saint Vincent and the Grenadines	19	30	18	55	99	70	108	167	189
Saint Lucia	64	73	75	115	45	62	261	251	226
Suriname	31	123	18	91	112	127	-72	-1	...
Trinidad and Tobago	-732	-453	-440	-1 257	-1 309	-2 461	-4 626	-4 804	-4 392
Uruguay	672	707	-2 602	979	-137	84	-44	916	2 877
Venezuela (Bolivarian Republic of)	-7 792	-6 030	-14 783	-8 679	-17 292	-22 195	-23 103	-23 178	-36 735

Source: Economic Commission for Latin America and the Caribbean (ECLAC), on the basis of official figures from the International Monetary Fund (IMF) and national sources.

[a] The net resource transfer is calculated as total capital income minus the income balance (net payments of profits and interest). Total net capital income is the balance on the capital and financial accounts plus errors and omissions, plus loans and the use of IMF credit plus exceptional financing. Negative figures indicate resources transferred outside the country.

[b] Preliminary figures.

Table A-11
LATIN AMERICA AND THE CARIBBEAN: NET FOREIGN DIRECT INVESTMENT [a]
(Millions of dollars)

	2000	2001	2002	2003	2004	2005	2006	2007	2008 [b]
Latin America and the Caribbean	**72 190**	**66 564**	**50 996**	**38 414**	**48 926**	**53 710**	**30 461**	**84 601**	**81 816**
Antigua and Barbuda	43	98	66	166	80	214	374	356	301
Argentina	9 517	2 005	2 776	878	3 449	3 954	3 100	4 997	4 900
Bahamas	250	192	209	247	443	563	706	713	800
Barbados	18	17	17	58	-16	53	...	...	...
Belize	23	61	25	-11	111	126	103	126	134
Bolivia	734	703	674	195	63	-242	278	200	280
Brazil	30 498	24 715	14 108	9 894	8 339	12 550	-9 380	27 518	20 000
Chile	873	2 590	2 207	2 701	5 610	4 801	4 482	10 627	11 170
Colombia	2 111	2 526	1 277	783	2 873	5 590	5 558	8 127	8 645
Costa Rica	400	451	625	548	733	904	1 371	1 634	2 048
Dominica	18	17	20	31	26	33	27	53	52
Ecuador	720	1 330	1 275	872	837	493	271	193	700
El Salvador	178	289	496	123	366	398	151	1 390	438
Grenada	37	59	54	89	65	70	85	171	140
Guatemala	230	138	183	218	255	470	531	658	769
Guyana	67	56	44	26	30	77	102	152	...
Haiti	13	4	6	14	6	26	160	75	30
Honduras	375	301	269	391	553	599	674	815	899
Jamaica	394	525	407	604	542	582	797	...	...
Mexico	17 789	23 045	22 158	15 341	18 451	14 471	13 573	16 763	20 100
Nicaragua	267	150	204	201	250	241	287	382	400
Panama	624	467	99	818	1 019	918	2 498	1 907	1 800
Paraguay	98	78	12	22	32	47	156	194	209
Peru	810	1 070	2 156	1 275	1 599	2 579	3 467	5 343	6 500
Dominican Republic	953	1 079	917	613	909	1 123	1 459	1 698	2 500
Saint Kitts and Nevis	96	88	80	76	46	93	110	158	88
Saint Vincent and the Grenadines	38	21	34	55	66	40	109	117	96
Saint Lucia	54	59	52	106	77	78	234	242	180
Suriname	-148	-27	-74	-76	-37	28	-163	-247	-140
Trinidad and Tobago	654	685	684	1 034	972	599	513	830	...
Uruguay	274	291	180	401	315	811	1 495	1 000	1 509
Venezuela (Bolivarian Republic of)	4 180	3 479	-244	722	864	1 422	-2 666	-1 591	-3 700

Source: Economic Commission for Latin America and the Caribbean (ECLAC), on the basis of official figures from the International Monetary Fund (IMF) and national sources.
[a] Corresponds to direct investment in the reporting country after deduction of direct investment outside the country by residents of that country. Includes reinvestment of profits.
[b] Preliminary figures.

Table A-12
LATIN AMERICA AND THE CARIBBEAN: TOTAL GROSS EXTERNAL DEBT [a]
(Millions of dollars)

	2000	2001	2002	2003	2004	2005	2006	2007	2008 [b]
Latin America and the Caribbean	**743 509**	**750 001**	**738 804**	**767 425**	**763 678**	**673 517**	**662 958**	**733 904**	**761 590**
Antigua and Barbuda	465	493	539	607	706	470	491	501	524
Argentina	155 014	166 272	156 748	164 645	171 205	113 799	108 873	123 989	128 685
Bahamas [c]	350	328	309	363	345	338	334	326	...
Barbados	928	1 117	1 130	1 188	1 207	1 334	1 473	1 415	...
Belize [c]	431	495	652	822	913	970	985	972	962
Bolivia	6 740	6 861	6 945	7 709	7 562	7 666	6 278	5 415	2 313
Brazil	216 921	209 935	210 711	214 929	201 373	169 451	172 589	193 219	205 536
Chile	37 177	38 527	40 504	43 067	43 517	44 934	47 590	55 822	63 314
Colombia	36 130	39 163	37 382	38 065	39 497	38 507	40 157	44 721	45 613
Costa Rica	5 307	5 265	5 310	5 575	5 710	6 485	6 996	8 384	8 848
Cuba [c d]	10 961	10 893	10 900	11 300	5 806	5 898	7 794	8 908	9 906
Dominica	154	182	209	230	224	242	249	247	248
Ecuador	13 216	14 376	16 236	16 756	17 211	17 237	17 099	17 445	16 799
El Salvador [e]	2 831	3 148	3 987	7 917	8 211	8 761	9 584	9 060	9 196
Grenada	132	176	316	352	420	447	473	491	494
Guatemala [c]	2 644	2 925	3 119	3 467	3 844	3 723	3 958	4 226	4 374
Guyana [c]	1 193	1 197	1 247	1 085	1 071	1 215	1 043	718	...
Haiti [c]	1 170	1 189	1 229	1 316	1 376	1 335	1 484	1 628	1 852
Honduras	4 711	4 757	4 922	5 242	5 912	5 093	3 879	3 029	3 203
Jamaica [c]	3 375	4 146	4 348	4 192	5 115	5 372	5 794	6 122	6 456
Mexico	148 652	144 526	134 980	132 273	130 925	128 248	116 668	124 583	126 196
Nicaragua [c]	6 660	6 374	6 363	6 596	5 391	5 348	4 527	3 385	3 466
Panama [c]	5 604	6 263	6 349	6 504	7 219	7 580	7 788	8 276	8 456
Paraguay	3 275	3 074	3 336	3 371	3 330	3 056	3 031	3 087	...
Peru	27 981	27 195	27 872	29 587	31 244	28 657	28 395	32 566	35 961
Dominican Republic [c]	3 679	4 176	4 536	5 987	6 380	6 813	7 266	7 566	7 929
Saint Kitts and Nevis	162	214	265	317	317	311	306	285	296
Saint Vincent and the Grenadines	163	172	172	207	243	250	255	220	240
Saint Lucia	178	213	260	338	369	388	404	415	415
Suriname [c]	291	350	371	382	382	388	389	296	...
Trinidad and Tobago [c]	1 680	1 666	1 549	1 568	1 382	1 361	1 295	1 421	1 429
Uruguay	8 895	8 937	10 548	11 013	11 593	11 418	10 560	12 218	12 682
Venezuela (Bolivarian Republic of)	36 437	35 398	35 460	40 456	43 679	46 427	44 952	52 949	56 198

Source: Economic Commission for Latin America and the Caribbean (ECLAC), on the basis of official figures from the International Monetary Fund (IMF) and national sources.
[a] Total gross external debt includes debt owed to IMF.
[b] Figures for the first semester.
[c] Refers to external public debt.
[d] From 2004 refers only to active external debt; excludes other external debt, 60.2% of which is official debt with the Paris Club.
[e] Until 2002, corresponds to public external debt. From 2003, corresponds to total external debt.

Table A-13
LATIN AMERICA AND THE CARIBBEAN: INTERNATIONAL RESERVE ASSETS [a]
(Millions of dollars)

	2000	2001	2002	2003	2004	2005	2006	2007	2008 I	2008 II	2008 III	2008 IV [b]
Latin America and the Caribbean	169 818	163 049	165 143	200 926	227 465	263 313	321 056	459 729	489 389	508 482	528 786	500 087
Antigua and Barbuda	65	80	88	114	120	127	143	144	167	...	...	...
Argentina	34 234	15 232	10 476	14 119	19 646	28 077	32 037	46 176	50 464	47 516	47 121	46 072
Bahamas	343	312	373	484	668	579	500	464	540	675	650	626
Barbados	473	690	669	738	580	603	636	839	912	889	827	...
Belize	123	112	115	85	48	71	114	109	111	138	170	172
Bolivia	1 160	1 139	897	1 096	1 272	1 798	3 193	5 319	6 232	7 118	7 809	7 615
Brazil	33 011	35 866	37 823	49 296	52 935	53 799	85 839	180 334	195 232	200 827	207 494	207 346
Chile	15 110	14 400	15 351	15 851	16 016	16 963	19 429	16 910	17 898	20 251	24 204	22 028
Colombia	9 006	10 245	10 844	10 921	13 540	14 957	15 440	20 955	22 138	22 855	24 094	23 169
Costa Rica	1 318	1 334	1 500	1 839	1 922	2 313	3 115	4 114	4 891	4 334	3 814	3 744
Dominica	29	31	45	48	42	49	63	61	61	65	59	...
Ecuador	1 180	1 074	1 008	1 160	1 437	2 147	2 023	3 521	4 144	6 103	6 511	4 826
El Salvador	1 894	1 712	1 591	1 910	1 893	1 833	1 908	2 198	2 275	2 305	2 263	2 413
Grenada	58	64	88	83	122	94	100	111	102	114	102	...
Guatemala	1 874	2 348	2 370	2 919	3 528	3 782	4 061	4 320	4 338	4 771	4 745	4 726
Guyana	305	287	284	276	232	252	280	313	353	381	352	...
Haiti	181	186	137	112	162	184	293	501	...	...	...	643
Honduras	1 312	1 414	1 523	1 430	1 971	2 330	2 633	2 733	2 737	2 505	2 505	2 505
Jamaica	1 054	1 903	1 643	1 196	1 882	2 169	2 399	1 906	2 106	2 477	2 281	1 817
Mexico	35 585	44 814	50 674	59 028	64 198	74 110	76 330	87 211	91 134	94 045	98 863	89 666
Nicaragua	497	383	454	504	670	730	924	1 103	1 073	1 123	1 165	1 115
Panama	707	1 075	1 166	992	611	1 192	1 335	1 935	1 801	1 757	1 757	1 757
Paraguay	772	723	641	983	1 168	1 297	1 703	2 462	2 638	3 197	2 999	2 657
Peru	8 563	8 838	9 690	10 206	12 649	14 120	17 329	27 720	33 608	35 550	34 732	31 282
Dominican Republic	552	1 071	544	186	728	1 837	2 151	2 843	...	...	...	2 533
Saint Kitts and Nevis	45	56	66	65	78	72	89	99	116	91	105	...
Saint Vincent and the Grenadines	55	61	53	51	75	70	79	88	81	90	84	...
Saint Lucia	79	89	94	107	133	116	135	155	163	154	150	...
Suriname	127	188	112	113	137	140	237	434	459	445	475	453
Trinidad and Tobago	1 403	1 924	2 049	2 258	2 993	4 787	6 777	7 053	7 494	9 092	8 729	...
Uruguay	2 823	3 100	772	2 087	2 512	3 078	3 091	4 121	4 993	6 101	6 344	5 952
Venezuela (Bolivarian Republic of)	15 883	12 296	12 003	20 666	23 498	29 636	36 672	33 477	31 130	33 514	38 380	36 971

Source: Economic Commission for Latin America and the Caribbean (ECLAC), on the basis of official figures from the International Monetary Fund (IMF) and national sources.

[a] Including gold.
[b] Includes the latest data available.

Table A-14
LATIN AMERICA AND THE CARIBBEAN: STOCK EXCHANGE INDICES
(National indices to end of period, 31 December 2000=100)

	2000	2001	2002	2003	2004	2005	2006	2007	2008 I	2008 II	2008 II	2008 IV [a]
Argentina	100	71	126	257	330	370	502	516	505	506	383	238
Brazil	100	89	74	146	172	219	291	419	400	426	325	240
Chile	100	109	92	137	166	181	248	281	268	277	254	222
Colombia	100	134	206	291	542	1 187	1 393	1 335	1 120	1 146	1 154	913
Costa Rica	100	113	117	104	88	96	169	193	235	232	209	159
Ecuador	100	130	195	178	216	272	353	329	353	347	341	347
Jamaica	100	117	157	234	390	362	348	374	372	380	353	301
Mexico	100	113	108	156	229	315	468	523	547	520	440	363
Peru	100	97	115	202	307	397	1 066	1 450	1 439	1 348	931	613
Trinidad and Tobago	100	98	124	157	243	242	220	222	225	261	241	198
Venezuela (Bolivarian Republic of)	100	96	117	325	439	299	765	555	514	546	556	505

Source: Economic Commission for Latin America and the Caribbean (ECLAC) on the basis of information from Bloomberg.
[a] Figures at 30 November.

Table A-15
LATIN AMERICA AND THE CARIBBEAN: OVERALL REAL EFFECTIVE EXCHANGE RATES [a]
(Índices 2000=100, deflated by CPI)

	2000	2001	2002	2003	2004	2005	2006	2007 [b]	2008 [b c]
Latin America and the Caribbean [d]	**100.0**	**99.2**	**111.0**	**120.5**	**119.6**	**111.5**	**108.5**	**105.3**	**99.1**
Argentina	100.0	95.9	225.8	205.1	212.8	213.3	218.1	222.8	232.3
Bolivia	100.0	101.1	95.5	104.2	109.3	116.7	119.2	118.0	109.7
Brazil	100.0	120.4	132.6	131.2	123.8	100.4	88.9	82.1	75.7
Chile	100.0	111.7	109.4	114.7	108.5	103.1	100.8	102.2	98.4
Colombia	100.0	104.2	105.7	119.6	107.1	96.7	95.5	85.3	80.4
Costa Rica	100.0	97.5	98.7	104.5	106.1	107.2	106.1	103.8	101.1
Cuba [e]	100.0	90.6	94.2	99.8	106.1	105.3	106.2	110.8	123.8
Ecuador	100.0	70.7	61.8	60.3	61.6	64.5	65.3	68.6	69.8
El Salvador	100.0	99.8	99.7	100.2	98.9	100.9	101.3	102.6	104.7
Guatemala	100.0	95.9	88.4	88.7	85.7	79.8	77.5	77.5	74.0
Honduras	100.0	97.2	96.9	98.5	100.9	100.5	98.0	96.3	93.7
Jamaica	100.0	101.7	101.2	116.9	113.6	104.4	104.6	107.8	101.7
Mexico	100.0	94.4	94.0	104.5	108.3	104.6	104.6	105.3	104.9
Nicaragua	100.0	101.1	103.2	106.9	107.8	108.5	107.2	109.4	104.8
Panama	100.0	103.1	101.2	103.2	108.4	110.9	112.4	114.1	113.4
Paraguay	100.0	102.8	106.5	112.6	106.4	118.7	106.4	95.3	83.2
Peru	100.0	98.1	95.8	99.8	99.9	101.1	103.9	104.9	101.7
Dominican Republic [f]	100.0	96.5	98.5	131.3	125.5	87.4	95.7	95.8	98.3
Trinidad and Tobago	100.0	94.5	91.1	91.9	93.6	91.0	89.0	87.3	84.6
Uruguay	100.0	101.4	118.4	150.5	152.5	134.1	128.2	126.9	115.0
Venezuela (Bolivarian Republic of)	100.0	95.3	125.1	141.1	139.5	141.0	132.3	117.8	98.3

Source: Economic Commission for Latin America and the Caribbean (ECLAC), on the basis of official figures from the International Monetary Fund (IMF) and national sources.
[a] Annual averages. A country's overall real effective exchange rate index is calculated by weighting its real bilateral exchange rate indices with each of its trading partners by each partner's share in the country's total trade flows in terms of exports and imports. The extraregional real effective exchange rate index excludes trade with other Latin American and Caribbean countries. A currency depreciates in real effective terms when this index rises and appreciates when it falls.
[b] Preliminary figures, weighted by trade in 2006.
[c] January-October average.
[d] Simple average of the extraregional real effective exchange rate for 20 countries (does not include Cuba).
[e] Preliminary figures. Yearly calculation by ECLAC, based on consumer price data and nominal exchange rates provided by the National Statistical Office of Cuba.
[f] Owing to lack of data, the period 2002-2008 has been weighted using trade figures for 2001.

Table A-16
LATIN AMERICA AND THE CARIBBEAN: PARTICIPATION RATE
(Average annual rates)

		2000	2001	2002	2003	2004	2005	2006	2007	2007	2008 [a]
										January to September average	
Argentina [b]	Urban areas	57.7	57.3	57.2	60.1	60.3	59.9	60.3	59.5	59.7	58.6
Brazil [b]	Six metropolitan areas	58.0	56.4	55.1	57.1	57.2	56.6	56.9	56.9	56.9	56.9 [c]
Chile	National total	54.4	53.9	53.7	54.4	55.0	55.6	54.8	54.9	54.7	56.0
Colombia	13 metropolitan areas	63.5	64.4	64.8	65.0	63.6	63.3	62.0	61.8	61.8	62.7 [c]
Costa Rica	National total	53.6	55.8	55.4	55.5	54.4	56.8	56.6	57.0	57.0	56.7 [d]
Cuba [e]	National total	70.1	70.9	71.0	70.9	71.0	72.1	72.1	73.7	73.7	74.8
Ecuador	Urban total	57.3	63.1	58.3	58.2	59.1	59.5	59.1	61.2	62.2	60.7
Honduras	National total	...	52.5	51.7	50.0	50.6	50.9	50.7	50.8	...	...
Jamaica [f]	National total	63.3	63.0	63.6	64.4	64.3	63.9	64.7	64.8	64.8	65.0 [g]
Mexico	Urban areas	58.7	58.1	57.8	58.3	58.9	59.5	60.7	60.7	60.7	60.6 [c]
Panama	National total	59.9	60.5	62.6	62.8	63.5	63.5	62.6	62.7	62.7	63.9 [h]
Peru	Metropolitan Lima	64.4	66.7	68.4	67.4	68.1	67.1	67.4	68.9	69.2	68.5
Dominican Republic	National total	55.2	54.3	55.1	54.7	56.3	55.9	56.0	56.0	56.0	55.7 [i]
Trinidad and Tobago	National total	61.2	60.7	60.9	61.6	63.0	63.7	63.9	63.5	62.9	63.0 [j]
Uruguay	Urban total	59.6	60.6	59.1	58.1	58.5	58.5	60.9	62.7	62.7	62.3 [c]
Venezuela (Bolivarian Republic of)	National total	64.6	66.5	68.7	69.2	68.5	66.3	65.4	64.9	65.1	64.9 [c]

Source: Economic Commission for Latin America and the Caribbean (ECLAC), on the basis of official figures.
[a] Preliminary figures.
[b] New measurements have been used since 2003; the data are not comparable with the previous series.
[c] The figures in the last two columns refer to the period from January to October.
[d] The figures in the last two columns refer to data for July.
[e] In Cuba, the working-age population is measured as follows: for males, 17 to 59 years and for females, 15 to 54 years.
[f] New measurements have been used since 2002; the data are not comparable with the previous series.
[g] The figures in the last two columns refer to the average of the January and April data.
[h] The figures in the last two columns refer to data for August.
[i] The figures in the last two columns refer to data for April.
[j] The figures in the last two columns refer to the average of the March and June data.

Table A-17
LATIN AMERICA AND THE CARIBBEAN: OPEN URBAN UNEMPLOYMENT
(Average annual rates)

		2000	2001	2002	2003	2004	2005	2006	2007	2008 [a]
Latin America and the Caribbean [b]		**10.4**	**10.2**	**11.0**	**11.0**	**10.3**	**9.1**	**8.6**	**7.9**	**7.5**
Argentina [c]	Urban areas	15.1	17.4	19.7	17.3	13.6	11.6	10.2	8.5	8.0 [d]
Bahamas [e]	National total	...	6.9	9.1	10.8	10.2	10.2	7.6	7.9	8.7
Barbados [e]	National total	9.2	9.9	10.3	11.0	9.8	9.1	8.7	7.4	8.3 [f]
Belize [e]	National total	11.1	9.1	10.0	12.9	11.6	11.0	9.4	8.5	...
Bolivia	Urban total [f]	7.5	8.5	8.7	9.2	6.2	8.1	8.0	7.7	...
Brazil [g]	Six metropolitan areas	7.1	6.2	11.7	12.3	11.5	9.8	10.0	9.3	7.9 [h]
Chile	National total	9.7	9.9	9.8	9.5	10.0	9.2	7.7	7.1	7.7 [h]
Colombia [e]	Thirteen metropolitan areas	17.3	18.2	17.6	16.6	15.3	13.9	12.9	11.4	11.5 [d]
Costa Rica	Urban total	5.3	5.8	6.8	6.7	6.7	6.9	6.0	4.8	4.8
Cuba	National total	5.4	4.1	3.3	2.3	1.9	1.9	1.9	1.8	1.6
Ecuador [e]	Urban total [i]	14.1	10.4	8.6	9.8	9.7	8.5	8.1	7.4	6.9 [d]
El Salvador	Urban total	6.5	7.0	6.2	6.2	6.5	7.3	5.7	5.8	...
Guatemala	Urban total	...	...	3.1	3.4	3.1	...	...	...	...
Honduras	Urban total	...	5.9	6.1	7.6	8.0	6.5	4.9	4.0	...
Jamaica [e]	National total	15.5	15.0	14.2	11.4	11.7	11.3	10.3	9.9	11.1 [j]
Mexico	Urban areas	3.4	3.6	3.9	4.6	5.3	4.7	4.6	4.8	4.9 [h]
Nicaragua	Urban total [m]	7.8	11.3	11.6	10.2	9.3	7.0	7.0	6.9	...
Panama [e]	Urban total [n]	15.2	17.0	16.5	15.9	14.1	12.1	10.4	7.8	6.5
Paraguay	Urban total	10.0	10.8	14.7	11.2	10.0	7.6	8.9	7.2	...
Peru	Metropolitan Lima	8.5	9.3	9.4	9.4	9.4	9.6	8.5	8.4	8.3 [h]
Dominican Republic [e]	National total	13.9	15.6	16.1	16.7	18.4	18.0	16.2	15.6	14.0 [k]
Trinidad and Tobago [e]	National total	12.2	10.8	10.4	10.5	8.4	8.0	6.2	5.6	5.0 [l]
Uruguay	Urban total	13.6	15.3	17.0	16.9	13.1	12.2	11.4	9.6	7.9 [h]
Venezuela (Bolivarian Rep. of)	National total	13.9	13.3	15.8	18.0	15.3	12.4	10.0	8.4	7.4 [h]

Source: Economic Commission for Latin America and the Caribbean (ECLAC), on the basis of official figures.
[a] Preliminary figures.
[b] The data for Argentina and Brazil have been adjusted to reflect changes in methodology in 2003 and 2002, respectively.
[c] New measurements have been used since 2003; the data are not comparable with the previous series.
[d] Estimate based on data from January to September.
[e] Includes hidden unemployment.
[f] January-June average.
[g] New measurements have been used since 2002; the data are not comparable with the previous series.
[h] Estimate based on data from January to October.
[i] Up to 2003, the figures relate to Cuenca, Guayaquil and Quito
[j] Average of the January and April data.
[k] Figure for April.
[l] Average of the March and June data.

Table A-18
LATIN AMERICA AND THE CARIBBEAN: EMPLOYMENT RATE
(Employed population as a percentage of working-age population, average annual rates)

		2000	2001	2002	2003	2004	2005	2006	2007	2007	2008 [a]
										January to September average	
Argentina [b]	Urban areas	49.0	47.4	45.9	49.8	52.0	52.9	54.1	54.5	54.4	53.9
Brazil [b]	Six metropolitan areas	53.8	52.9	48.7	50.1	50.6	51.0	51.2	51.6	51.4	52.4 [c]
Chile	National total	49.1	48.6	48.4	49.3	49.5	50.4	50.5	51.0	50.8	51.5
Colombia	Thirteen metropolitan areas	52.6	52.7	53.4	54.2	53.8	54.5	54.0	54.8	54.5	55.4 [c]
Costa Rica	National total	50.8	52.4	51.8	51.8	50.9	53.0	53.3	54.4	54.4	53.9 [d]
Cuba [e]	National total	66.3	68.0	68.6	69.2	69.7	70.7	70.7	72.4	72.4	73.6
Ecuador	Urban total	52.1	56.2	52.9	51.5	53.5	54.4	54.3	56.8	57.4	56.6
Honduras	National total	...	50.3	49.7	47.4	48.6	48.6	49.0	49.2	...	...
Jamaica [f]	National total	53.4	53.5	54.0	57.1	56.8	56.7	58.0	58.4	58.2	57.8 [g]
Mexico	Urban areas	56.8	56.0	55.5	55.6	55.8	56.7	57.9	57.8	57.7	57.7 [c]
Panama	National total	51.8	52.0	54.1	54.6	55.9	57.3	57.2	58.7	58.7	60.3 [h]
Peru	Metropolitan Lima	59.7	60.5	62.0	61.1	61.6	60.7	61.8	63.0	63.1	62.7
Dominican Republic	National total	47.6	45.8	46.2	45.4	46.0	45.9	46.8	47.3	47.2	47.8 [i]
Trinidad and Tobago	National total	53.8	53.8	54.6	55.2	57.8	58.6	59.9	59.9	58.9	59.9 [j]
Uruguay	Urban total	51.6	51.4	49.1	48.3	50.9	51.4	53.9	56.7	56.5	57.3 [c]
Venezuela (Bolivarian Rep. of)	National total	55.5	57.6	57.8	56.8	58.1	58.1	58.9	59.5	59.2	59.9 [c]

Source: Economic Commission for Latin America and the Caribbean (ECLAC), on the basis of official figures.
[a] Preliminary figures.
[b] New measurements have been used since 2003; the data are not comparable with the previous series.
[c] The figures in the last two columns refer to the period January-October.
[d] The figures in the last two columns refer to data for July.
[e] In Cuba, the working-age population is measured as follows: for males, 17 to 59 years and for females, 15 to 54 years.
[f] New measurements have been used since 2002; the data are not comparable with the previous series.
[g] The figures in the last two columns refer to the average of the January and April data.
[h] The figures in the last two columns refer to the data for August.
[i] The figures in the last two columns refer to the data for April.
[j] The figures in the last two columns refer to the average of the March and June data.

Economic Commission for Latin America and the Caribbean (ECLAC)

Table A-19
LATIN AMERICA AND THE CARIBBEAN: REAL AVERAGE WAGES
(Average annual Index, 2000=100)

	2000	2001	2002	2003	2004	2005	2006	2007	2008 [a]
Argentina [b]	100.0	99.2	85.4	83.9	92.2	99.0	107.8	117.6	127.8 [c]
Bolivia	100.0	105.8	109.3	111.1	114.1	110.0	101.2	98.4 [d]	...
Brazil [e]	100.0	95.1	93.1	84.9	85.5	85.2	88.2	89.5	91.0 [c]
Chile [f]	100.0	101.7	103.7	104.6	106.5	108.5	110.6	113.7	113.4 [g]
Colombia [b]	100.0	99.7	102.7	102.0	103.8	105.3	109.3	108.7	106.8 [h]
Costa Rica [i]	100.0	101.0	105.1	105.5	102.8	100.8	102.4	103.8	102.2 [h]
Cuba	100.0	96.2	105.1	107.8	114.6	129.5	144.5	143.1	140.5
Guatemala	100.0	100.5	99.6	100.0	97.8	93.9	92.9	88.6	...
Mexico [j]	100.0	106.7	108.7	110.2	110.5	110.2	110.6	111.7	112.5 [c]
Nicaragua [i]	100.0	101.0	104.5	106.5	104.2	104.5	105.9	104.0	98.7 [c]
Panama [k]	100.0	98.8	95.8	95.3	94.5	93.4	95.3	96.2	95.4 [l]
Paraguay	100.0	101.4	96.3	95.6	97.2	98.2	98.8	101.1	100.3 [d]
Peru [m]	100.0	99.1	103.7	105.3	106.5	104.4	105.7	103.8	106.5 [d]
Uruguay	100.0	99.7	89.0	77.9	77.9	81.5	85.0	89.0	91.9 [g]
Venezuela (Bolivarian Republic of) [n]	100.0	106.9	95.1	78.4	78.6	80.7	84.8	85.8	82.2 [c]

Source: Economic Commission for Latin America and the Caribbean (ECLAC), on the basis of official figures.
[a] Preliminary figures.
[b] Manufacturing. From 2005, registered private-sector workers.
[c] Estimate based on data from January to September.
[d] Figure for June.
[e] Workers covered by social and labour legislation. Since 2003, only the private sector.
[f] General index of hourly wages.
[g] Estimate based on data from January to October.
[h] Estimate based on data from January to August.
[i] Average wages declared by workers covered by social security.
[j] Manufacturing.
[k] Average wages declared by workers covered by social security. Figures from 2007 take into account average wages in manufacturing, commerce and services in the Panamá and San Miguelito districts.
[l] Average of the data from January to June.
[m] Private sector workers in the Lima metropolitan area.
[n] General index of wages.

Table A-20
LATIN AMERICA AND THE CARIBBEAN: MONETARY INDICATORS
(Percentages of GDP, end-of-year balances)

	Monetary base				Money Supply (M3) [a]				Foreign-currency deposits			
	2005	2006	2007	2008 [b]	2005	2006	2007	2008 [b]	2005	2006	2007	2008 [b]
Antigua and Barbuda	14.2	12.7	11.9	...	92.6	91.1	90.0	...	5.8	7.5	9.2	...
Argentina	8.7	8.0	6.7	8.5	25.8	25.8	26.2	22.7	2.0	2.3	2.6	2.6
Bahamas	4.0	5.0	4.5	4.5	72.5	73.6	77.5	77.7	2.2	2.3	2.8	2.0
Barbados	18.0	12.1	11.3	11.5	108.1	110.8	119.2	117.9	16.4	11.3	19.9	13.4
Belize	9.1	9.5	10.0	11.3	59.6	62.0	68.0	...	...	...	...	...
Bolivia	6.8	6.3	7.7	9.0	43.0	42.4	47.8	42.2	30.9	26.7	23.9	17.7
Brazil	3.4	3.8	4.0	4.3 [c]	27.1	28.5	30.8	36.1 [d]	...	...	...	...
Chile	3.1	3.1	3.4	3.6	53.3	53.4	58.2	60.8	4.7	4.7	4.8	7.3
Colombia	4.9	5.1	5.4	5.8 [e]	31.0	32.3	34.0	32.6 [d]	...	...	...	...
Costa Rica	4.0	3.9	4.3	4.6	44.1	44.3	43.9	44.1	21.8	20.8	18.2	18.9
Cuba	23.4	23.0	22.7	21.8	46.2	38.2	37.3	... [d]	...	...	...	...
Dominica	15.6	13.6	13.6	15.4	77.6	80.2	83.5	83.4	1.3	1.3	1.1	1.4
Ecuador	0.9	0.9	1.3	1.1	23.0	24.2	26.6	27.3 [d]	...	...	...	...
El Salvador	10.2	8.8	8.3	7.7	37.2	38.0	40.9	44.3 [d]	...	...	...	...
Grenada	15.7	21.6	15.7	15.2	98.2	97.8	102.3	98.8	6.8	5.1	7.5	5.2
Guatemala	8.2	8.3	8.2	8.6	35.7	37.9	37.8	33.0	3.9	4.2	4.7	4.6
Guyana	24.1	23.6	22.3	20.9	75.2	78.5	75.1	73.7	...	...	...	...
Haiti	17.1	15.9	15.4	14.9	42.1	37.8	35.6	34.5	18.0	15.6	15.1	15.8
Honduras	6.5	7.2	7.1	7.3	50.8	55.5	56.9	50.4	13.5	13.9	14.1	13.9
Jamaica	6.7	6.6	6.4	6.1	38.1	37.6	38.9	31.0	12.1	11.0	12.7	9.9
Mexico	3.3	3.3	3.4	3.8	48.6	49.5	50.2	50.7	1.5	1.4	1.3	1.3
Nicaragua	5.5	5.7	6.0	6.2	41.3	39.4	41.0	35.5	27.8	25.8	26.8	24.5
Panama	...	...	...	...	78.0	86.1	88.1	80.6	...	...	...	...
Paraguay	7.5	7.8	7.0	6.7	27.5	26.8	30.6	29.1	11.7	10.6	11.0	10.0
Peru	2.8	3.1	3.5	3.6	25.8	24.3	27.0	29.1	14.1	12.4	12.4	13.7
Dominican Republic	7.6	6.6	6.8	6.7	27.7	25.2	25.7	...	0.0	0.0	0.0	...
Saint Kitts and Nevis	13.8	15.8	13.6	15.1	97.3	97.1	101.3	91.6	28.4	30.4	31.1	24.7
Saint Vincent and the Grenadines	13.3	12.5	11.4	12.0	72.7	69.4	66.3	61.2	1.2	2.3	2.6	2.2
Saint Lucia	12.3	13.7	12.7	13.1	74.6	83.4	92.7	91.1	2.7	8.4	4.7	5.3
Suriname	10.5	10.5	10.5	11.0	53.9	56.6	67.5	58.5	25.7	27.1	32.3	27.3
Trinidad and Tobago	4.9	4.1	5.4	5.5	37.2	37.9	37.3	...	7.7	9.2	9.0	...
Uruguay	3.4	3.3	3.8	3.3	60.6	58.6	51.3	43.7	49.7	47.0	38.3	31.8
Venezuela (Bolivarian Republic of)	3.7	4.2	4.7	6.6	23.3	30.3	31.3	26.4	...	...	...	...

Source: Economic Commission for Latin America and the Caribbean (ECLAC), on the basis of official figures.
[a] According to the ECLAC definition, this corresponds to M1 plus savings and time deposits in national currency plus foreign currency deposits.
[b] Figures up to the latest date available.
[c] According to the country's definition, this corresponds to M1 plus special interest-bearing deposits, savings deposits and securities issued by deposit institutions.
[d] Refers to M2.
[e] According to the country's definition, this also includes deposits of entities in liquidation, term deposit certificates of special entities and demand deposits of non-bank entities.

Table A-21
LATIN AMERICA AND THE CARIBBEAN: REPRESENTATIVE LENDING RATES
(Annual average of monthly annualized rates)

	2000	2001	2002	2003	2004	2005	2006	2007	2008 [a]
Antigua and Barbuda [b]	...	...	...	...	...	11.2	10.7	10.3	10.1 Sep
Argentina [c]	11.1	26.5	53.0	19.1	6.8	6.2	8.6	11.1	17.3 Oct
Bahamas [d]	...	...	...	12.0	11.2	10.3	10.0	10.6	11.2 Jun
Barbados [c]	...	...	...	7.6	7.4	8.5	10.0	10.4	10.1 Aug
Belize [e]	16.0	15.5	14.8	14.4	13.9	14.2	14.2	14.3	...
Bolivia [f]	...	13.7	10.9	9.1	8.2	8.2	7.8	8.2	8.8 Nov
Brazil [g]	41.9	41.1	44.4	49.8	41.1	43.7	40.0	34.5	36.7 Oct
Chile [h]	18.7	16.7	14.4	13.0	11.0	13.5	14.4	13.6	15.2 Nov
Colombia [i]	18.8	20.7	16.3	15.2	15.1	14.6	12.9	15.4	17.1 Oct
Costa Rica [j]	28.1	26.7	26.8	26.2	23.4	24.0	22.7	17.3	16.3 Nov
Cuba [k]	...	...	...	9.6	9.7	9.8	9.4	9.1	...
Dominica [b]	...	...	...	...	...	9.9	9.5	9.2	9.1 Sep
Ecuador [l]	15.2	15.5	14.1	12.6	10.2	8.7	8.9	10.1	...
El Salvador [m]	10.7	9.6	7.1	6.6	6.3	6.9	7.5	7.8	7.6 Oct
Granada [b]	...	...	...	...	...	10.0	9.8	9.7	9.5 Sep
Guatemala [b]	20.9	19.0	16.9	15.0	13.8	13.0	12.8	12.8	13.3 Oct
Guyana [c]	17.2	17.3	17.3	16.6	16.6	15.1	14.9	14.1	13.9 Sep
Haiti [n]	25.1	28.6	25.5	30.7	34.1	27.1	29.5	31.2	23.3 Oct
Honduras [b]	26.8	23.8	22.7	20.8	19.9	18.8	17.4	16.6	17.4 Sep
Jamaica [o]	32.9	29.4	26.1	25.1	25.1	23.2	22.0	22.0	22.1 Sep
Mexico [p]	16.9	12.8	8.2	6.9	7.2	9.9	7.5	7.6	8.3 Oct
Nicaragua [q]	18.1	18.6	18.3	15.5	13.5	12.1	11.6	13.0	13.1 Oct
Panama [r]	10.3	10.6	9.2	8.9	8.2	8.2	8.1	8.3	8.2 Oct
Paraguay [s]	26.8	28.3	34.3	30.5	21.2	15.3	16.6	14.6	13.6 Oct
Peru [t]	...	...	22.3	20.2	18.7	17.9	17.1	16.5	16.7 Nov
Dominican Republic [c]	23.6	20.0	21.3	27.8	30.3	21.4	15.7	11.7	15.5 Nov
Saint Kitts and Nevis [b]	...	...	...	...	...	9.9	9.2	9.3	8.6 Sep
Saint Vincent and the Grenadines [b]	...	...	...	...	...	9.6	9.7	9.6	9.5 Sep
Saint Lucia [b]	...	...	...	...	...	10.4	10.5	9.9	9.2 Sep
Suriname [p]	29.0	25.7	22.2	21.0	20.4	18.1	15.7	13.8	12.5 May
Trinidad and Tobago [c]	16.5	15.6	13.4	11.0	9.4	9.1	10.2	10.5	12.1 Aug
Uruguay [u]	32.1	38.1	116.4	56.6	26.0	15.3	10.7	10.0	12.0 Oct
Venezuela (Bolivarian Republic of) [v]	24.5	24.8	38.4	25.7	17.3	15.6	14.6	16.7	23.0 Nov

Source: Economic Commission for Latin America and the Caribbean (ECLAC), on the basis of official figures.
[a] Average from January to the month indicated, annualized monthly rates.
[b] Weighted average lending rates.
[c] Prime lending rate.
[d] Interest rate on loans and overdrafts, weighted average.
[e] Rate for personal and business loans, residential and other construction loans; weighted average.
[f] Nominal dollar rate for 60-91-day banking operations.
[g] Preset lending rates for legal persons.
[h] Lending rates for periods of 90-360 days, non-adjustable operations.
[i] Total lending rate of the system. Weighted average of all lending rates.
[j] Average rate of the financial system for loans in national currency.
[k] Average of loans to enterprices.
[l] Benchmark dollar lending rate.
[m] Basic lending rate for up to 1 year.
[n] Average of minimum and maximum lending rates.
[o] Average interest rate on loans.
[p] Lending rate published by the International Monetary Fund.
[q] Weighted average of the weekly lending rate for loans in national currency in the system.
[r] Interest rate on 1-year trade credit.
[s] Weighted average of effective lending rates in national currency, not including overdrafts or credit cards.
[t] Average lending rate, constant structure.
[u] Business credit, 30-367 days.
[v] Average rate for loan operations for the six major commercial banks.

Table A-22
LATIN AMERICA AND THE CARIBBEAN: CONSUMER PRICES
(Percentage variation December-December)

	2000	2001	2002	2003	2004	2005	2006	2007	2008 [a]
Latin America and the Caribbean [b]	**8.0**	**5.6**	**11.2**	**8.0**	**7.1**	**5.9**	**4.9**	**6.4**	**8.8**
Antigua and Barbuda	...	...	2.5	1.8	2.8	2.5	0.0	5.1	...
Argentina	-0.7	-1.5	41.0	3.7	6.1	12.3	9.8	8.5	7.9
Bahamas	0.6	3.4	1.9	2.3	1.0	2.1	2.3	2.7	5.1 [c]
Barbados	3.8	-0.6	0.9	0.3	4.3	7.4	5.6	3.9	8.9 [c]
Belize	1.0	0.9	3.2	2.3	3.1	4.2	2.9	4.1	9.5 [d]
Bolivia	3.4	0.9	2.4	3.9	4.6	4.9	4.9	11.7	12.1
Brazil	6.0	7.7	12.5	9.3	7.6	5.7	3.0	4.5	6.4
Chile	4.5	2.6	2.8	1.1	2.4	3.7	2.6	7.8	8.9
Colombia	8.8	7.6	7.0	6.5	5.5	4.9	4.5	5.7	7.7
Costa Rica	10.2	11.0	9.7	9.9	13.1	14.1	9.4	10.8	16.3
Cuba e/	...	-1.4	7.3	-3.8	2.9	3.7	5.7	2.8	0.4 [f]
Dominica	1.1	1.1	0.5	2.8	...	...	...	4.8	5.2 [d]
Ecuador	91.0	22.4	9.3	6.1	1.9	3.1	2.9	3.3	9.1
El Salvador	4.3	1.4	2.8	2.5	5.4	4.3	4.9	4.9	5.3
Grenada	3.4	-0.7	2.3	...	...	...	...	7.4	8.9 [c]
Guatemala	5.1	8.9	6.3	5.9	9.2	8.6	5.8	8.7	10.9
Guyana	5.8	1.5	6.0	...	...	8.2	4.2	14.1	7.4 [c]
Haiti	19.0	8.1	14.8	40.4	20.2	14.8	10.3	10.3	18.0 [f]
Honduras	10.1	8.8	8.1	6.8	9.2	7.7	5.3	8.9	10.9
Jamaica	5.9	8.6	7.3	13.8	13.6	12.6	5.8	14.3	19.6
Mexico	9.0	4.4	5.7	4.0	5.2	3.3	4.1	3.8	6.2
Nicaragua	9.9	4.7	4.0	6.6	8.9	9.6	10.2	16.2	15.2
Panama	0.7	0.0	1.5	1.5	3.5	3.4	2.2	6.4	7.7
Paraguay	8.6	8.4	14.6	9.3	2.8	9.9	12.5	6.0	8.3
Peru	3.7	-0.1	1.5	2.5	3.5	1.5	1.1	3.9	6.7
Dominican Republic	9.0	4.4	10.5	42.7	28.7	7.4	5.0	8.9	7.2
Saint Kitts and Nevis	...	...	1.7	3.1	1.7	6.0	5.9	4.0	...
Saint Vincent and the Grenadines	1.4	-0.2	0.4	2.7	1.7	3.9	4.8	8.3	11.0 [c]
Saint Lucia	0.2	5.5	-0.7	0.5	3.5	5.2	-0.6	8.2	8.9 [c]
Suriname	...	...	...	...	...	...	...	5.6	17.8 [f]
Trinidad and Tobago	...	...	...	...	5.6	7.2	9.1	7.6	15.4 [f]
Uruguay	5.1	3.6	25.9	10.2	7.6	4.9	6.4	8.5	8.5
Venezuela (Bolivarian Republic of)	13.4	12.3	31.2	27.1	19.2	14.4	17.0	22.5	32.7

Source: Economic Commission for Latin America and the Caribbean (ECLAC), on the basis of official figures.
[a] Twelve-month variation to November 2008.
[b] The only English-speaking Caribbean countries included are Barbados, Jamaica and Trinidad and Tobago.
[c] Twelve-month variation to June 2008.
[d] Twelve-month variation to August 2008.
[e] Refers to national-currency markets.
[f] Twelve-month variation to October 2008.

Table A-23
LATIN AMERICA AND THE CARIBBEAN: CENTRAL GOVERNMENT BALANCE
(Percentages of GDP)

	Primary balance					Overall balance				
	2004	2005	2006	2007	2008[a]	2004	2005	2006	2007	2008[a]
Latin America and the Caribbean (exc. Cuba)	**0.6**	**1.4**	**2.3**	**2.4**	**1.6**	**-1.9**	**-1.1**	**0.1**	**0.4**	**-0.3**
Latin America and the Caribbean (inc. Cuba)	**0.4**	**1.2**	**2.1**	**2.2**	**1.4**	**-2.0**	**-1.2**	**-0.1**	**0.2**	**-0.5**
Argentina[b]	3.2	2.3	2.7	2.7	3.2	2.0	0.4	1.0	0.6	1.0
Bolivia[c]	-3.1	0.3	5.2	3.5	4.3	-5.7	-2.3	3.4	2.3	3.0
Brazil[d]	2.6	2.5	2.1	2.3	2.2	-1.9	-3.6	-2.9	-2.0	-2.6
Chile	3.1	5.4	8.4	9.4	7.1	2.1	4.6	7.7	8.8	6.9
Colombia[e]	-1.6	-1.5	-0.1	0.8	0.4	-5.0	-4.5	-3.8	-3.0	-2.7
Costa Rica	1.4	2.0	2.7	3.7	1.8	-2.7	-2.1	-1.1	0.6	-0.5
Cuba	-3.0	-3.3	-2.0	-1.8	-2.8	-3.7	-4.6	-3.2	-3.2	-4.2
Ecuador[f]	1.5	1.8	2.1	1.9	1.9	-1.0	-0.5	-0.2	-0.1	-0.1
El Salvador	0.9	1.1	2.0	2.2	1.8	-1.1	-1.0	-0.4	-0.2	-0.6
Guatemala[g]	0.3	-0.3	-0.6	0.0	0.3	-1.1	-1.7	-1.9	-1.5	-1.2
Haiti	-2.4	0.4	1.1	-1.2	-1.8	-3.1	-0.6	0.3	-1.6	-2.1
Honduras	-1.5	-1.1	-0.1	-2.2	-1.2	-2.6	-2.2	-1.1	-2.9	-1.9
Mexico[h]	1.7	1.9	2.1	1.9	2.0	-0.2	-0.1	0.1	0.0	0.0
Nicaragua	-0.1	0.1	1.8	2.1	0.3	-2.2	-1.8	0.0	0.6	-0.8
Panama[i]	-1.2	0.5	4.4	4.7	2.5	-5.4	-3.9	0.2	1.2	-1.0
Paraguay[g]	2.7	2.0	1.5	1.8	1.2	1.6	0.8	0.5	1.0	0.5
Peru	0.6	1.1	3.2	3.4	3.9	-1.3	-0.7	1.5	1.8	2.3
Dominican Republic[j]	-1.6	0.7	0.3	1.8	-2.0	-3.4	-0.6	-1.1	0.6	-3.2
Uruguay	2.4	2.8	3.3	2.2	2.8	-2.5	-1.6	-1.0	-1.7	-1.0
Venezuela (Bolivarian Republic of)	1.8	4.6	2.1	4.5	-0.5	-1.9	1.6	0.0	3.0	-1.8

Source: Economic Commission for Latin America and the Caribbean (ECLAC), on the basis of official figures.
[a] Preliminary figures.
[b] National public administration, on an accrual basis.
[c] General government.
[d] Federal government. The figures are derived from the primary balance based on the below-the-line criterion and nominal interest.
[e] Central national government. Does not include the cost of financial restructuring.
[f] Accrual basis.
[g] Central administration.
[h] Public sector. Balances include non-recurrent income from the sale of companies and the non-budgetary balance.
[i] The overall balance for 2005 includes an adjustment for compensation to bondholders amounting to 111.6 million balboas.
[j] Accrual basis. The overall balance includes the residue and other transfer payments.

Table A-24
LATIN AMERICA AND THE CARIBBEAN: CENTRAL GOVERNMENT REVENUE AND EXPENDITURE
(Percentages of GDP)

	Total revenue			Tax revenue			Total expenditure		
	2006	2007	2008 [a]	2006	2007	2008 [a]	2006	2007	2008 [a]
Latin America and the Caribbean (exc. Cuba)	**19.4**	**20.0**	**...**	**14.2**	**14.7**	**...**	**19.3**	**19.5**	**...**
Latin America and the Caribbean (inc. Cuba)	**20.6**	**21.3**	**...**	**15.0**	**15.4**	**...**	**20.6**	**21.0**	**...**
Argentina	17.2	18.2	22.5	16.0	17.2	21.1	16.2	17.5	21.5
Bolivia	32.8	32.7	...	18.0	18.3	...	29.3	30.5	...
Brazil	23.3	24.8	24.8	...	...	...	26.3	26.8	27.4
Chile	25.9 [b]	27.5 [b]	27.0 [b]	18.4	20.2	18.5	18.2 [c]	18.7 [c]	20.1 [c]
Colombia	14.9 [d]	15.1 [d]	15.8 [d]	13.6	13.5	16.9	18.4	17.8	18.5
Costa Rica	14.2 [e]	15.5 [e]	15.6 [e]	14.0	15.3	15.0	15.3 [f]	15.0 [f]	16.1 [f]
Cuba	43.2	46.0	44.4	30.0	27.7	25.5	46.4	49.2	48.6
Ecuador	16.7	18.5	...	10.3	10.4	...	16.9	18.7	...
El Salvador	14.4 [e]	14.6 [e]	14.6 [e]	13.3	13.4	13.4	14.8 [f]	14.8 [f]	15.2 [f]
Guatemala	12.7	13.0	12.6	12.1	12.5	11.9	14.7	14.5	13.8
Haiti	10.8 [e]	10.8 [e]	11.5 [e]	10.2	10.3	...	10.6	12.4	13.6
Honduras	18.2 [e]	19.2 [e]	19.1 [e]	15.4	16.3	...	19.3 [f]	22.1 [f]	21.0 [f]
Mexico	22.0	22.3	22.1	8.6	9.0	7.8	21.9 [g]	22.2 [g]	22.1 [g]
Nicaragua	22.8 [e]	23.2 [e]	22.1 [e]	17.5	18.0	16.6	22.7	22.6	22.9
Panama	18.6 [e]	19.5 [e]	18.0 [e]	10.3	10.7	...	18.4	18.3	19.0
Paraguay	18.3	18.0	17.5	13.1	12.9	12.1	17.8 [f]	17.0 [f]	17.0 [f]
Peru	17.5	18.3	17.6	15.0	15.6	14.8	16.1	16.5	15.3
Dominican Republic	16.1 [e]	17.7 [e]	17.1 [e]	14.9	16.0	...	17.1	17.2	20.3
Uruguay	21.9	21.3	23.7	19.3	18.7	...	22.9	22.9	24.7
Venezuela (Bolivarian Republic of)	29.6	28.9	25.0	15.6	16.1	12.9	29.6 [h]	25.8 [h]	26.8 [h]

Source: Economic Commission for Latin America and the Caribbean (ECLAC), on the basis of official figures.
[a] Preliminary figures.
[b] Total income includes income and sale of financial assets.
[c] Total expenditure refers to expenditure plus investment, capital transfers and fixed capital consumption.
[d] Total revenue includes special funds and does not include accrued revenue.
[e] Total revenue includes grants.
[f] Total expenditure includes net lending.
[g] Total expenditure includes not-programable expenditure.
[h] Total expenditure includes extrabudgetary expenditure and net lending.

Table A-25
LATIN AMERICA AND THE CARIBBEAN: PUBLIC DEBT
(Percentages of GDP)

	Central government debt					Non-financial public sector debt				
	2004	2005	2006	2007	2008 [a]	2004	2005	2006	2007	2008 [a]
Latin America and the Caribbean	**51.1**	**43.0**	**36.0**	**30.3**	**26.1**	**55.3**	**47.6**	**39.9**	**33.0**	**28.6**
Argentina	126.4 [b]	72.8 [b]	63.6 [b]	55.7 [b]	48.0 [b]	143.3	87.6	76.3	66.6	58.9
Bolivia	81.1 [c]	75.6 [c]	49.8 [c]	37.1 [c]	30.7 [c]	83.9 [d]	78.3 [d]	52.6 [d]	40.0 [d]	33.0 [d]
Brazil	31.0 [e]	30.9 [e]	31.7 [e]	32.7 [e]	30.1 [e]	49.3 [f]	46.7 [f]	46.0 [f]	46.1 [f]	42.6 [f]
Chile	10.7 [g]	7.3 [g]	5.3 [g]	4.1 [g]	3.5 [g]	16.8 [g]	13.0 [g]	10.6 [g]	9.1 [g]	7.4 [g]
Colombia	40.0 [h]	39.6 [h]	38.1 [h]	35.2 [h]	33.2 [h]	42.4 [i]	38.9 [i]	36.5 [i]	32.6 [i]	28.9 [i]
Costa Rica	41.0	37.6	33.3	27.7	23.5	46.9	43.0	38.4	32.0	27.3
Ecuador	40.8	35.9	29.7	27.5	22.6	43.7 [d]	38.6 [d]	32.3 [d]	30.0 [d]	24.7 [d]
El Salvador	38.1 [c]	37.6 [c]	37.5 [c]	34.5 [c]	31.2 [c]	40.8 [d]	40.6 [d]	39.6 [d]	36.5 [d]	33.1 [d]
Guatemala	21.4 [c]	20.8 [c]	21.7 [c]	21.7 [c]	19.3 [c]	22.4 [d]	21.5 [d]	21.9 [d]	21.9 [d]	19.5 [d]
Haiti	46.7 [j]	44.1 [j]	35.6 [j]	32.2 [j]	29.4 [j]	51.1 [j]	47.5 [j]	38.1 [j]	34.4 [j]	35.0 [j]
Honduras	59.6	44.7	28.9	17.4	17.4	59.4	44.8	30.2	18.3	17.3
Mexico	20.8 [k]	20.3 [k]	20.7 [k]	21.1 [k]	20.4 [k]	24.2 [l]	23.0 [l]	22.7 [l]	23.0 [l]	22.6 [l]
Nicaragua	100.6	92.6	68.7	42.2	34.6	100.7	92.8	69.1	43.0	35.4
Panama	69.6 [m]	65.1 [m]	60.3 [m]	53.2 [m]	46.6 [m]	70.4	66.2	61.0	53.7	47.1
Paraguay	38.0	31.4	23.8	17.3	12.1	41.7	32.8	24.8	20.3	14.2
Peru	41.7 [n]	38.2 [n]	31.2 [n]	27.2 [n]	22.8 [n]	41.7	38.2	31.2	27.2	22.8
Dominican Republic	...	22.0	20.4	18.4	16.7	...	...	...	19.0 [o]	17.4 [o]
Uruguay	74.6	67.1	59.3	50.7	39.9	78.9	70.4	62.7	54.0	42.8
Venezuela (Bolivarian Republic of)	38.1	32.8	23.9	19.3	14.0	38.1	32.8	23.9	19.3	14.0

Source: Economic Commission for Latin America and the Caribbean (ECLAC), on the basis of official figures.
[a] Preliminary figures to June 2008.
[b] National public administration. As from 2005, does not include debt not presented for swap.
[c] Does not include publicly guaranteed private debt.
[d] Includes external debt of the non-financial public sector and domestic debt of the central government.
[e] Net public debt. Federal government and central bank.
[f] Net public debt. Public sector.
[g] Consolidated gross public debt.
[h] Central national government.
[i] Consolidated non-financial public sector.
[j] Does not include public sector commitments to commercial banks.
[k] Federal government.
[l] Includes external debt of the public sector and domestic debt of the federal government.
[m] Does not include domestic floating debt.
[n] Includes local and regional government debt with the Banco de la Nación.
[o] Public sector.

Naciones Unidas
United Nations

Publicaciones de la CEPAL / *ECLAC publications*

Comisión Económica para América Latina y el Caribe / *Economic Commission for Latin America and the Caribbean*
Casilla 179-D, Santiago de Chile. E-mail: publications@cepal.org
Véalas en: www.cepal.org/publicaciones
Publications may be accessed at: www.eclac.org

Revista CEPAL / *CEPAL Review*

La *Revista* se inició en 1976 como parte del Programa de Publicaciones de la Comisión Económica para América Latina y el Caribe, con el propósito de contribuir al examen de los problemas del desarrollo socioeconómico de la región. Las opiniones expresadas en los artículos firmados, incluidas las colaboraciones de los funcionarios de la Secretaría, son las de los autores y, por lo tanto, no reflejan necesariamente los puntos de vista de la Organización.

La *Revista CEPAL* se publica en español e inglés tres veces por año.

Los precios de suscripción anual vigentes para 2008 son de US$ 30 para la versión en español y de US$ 35 para la versión en inglés. El precio por ejemplar suelto es de US$ 15 para ambas versiones. Los precios de suscripción por dos años (2008-2009) son de US$ 50 para la versión en español y de US$ 60 para la versión en inglés.

CEPAL Review first appeared in 1976 as part of the Publications Programme of the Economic Commission for Latin America and the Caribbean, its aim being to make a contribution to the study of the economic and social development problems of the region. The views expressed in signed articles, including those by Secretariat staff members, are those of the authors and therefore do not necessarily reflect the point of view of the Organization.

CEPAL Review is published in Spanish and English versions three times a year.

Annual subscription costs for 2008 are US$ 30 for the Spanish version and US$ 35 for the English version. The price of single issues is US$ 15 in both cases. The cost of a two-year subscription (2008-2009) is US$ 50 for Spanish-language version and US$ 60 for English.

Informes periódicos institucionales / *Annual reports*

Todos disponibles para años anteriores / *Issues for previous years also available*

- *Anuario estadístico de América Latina y el Caribe /* **Statistical Yearbook for Latin America and the Caribbean** (bilingüe/*bilingual*), 2008, 430 p.
- *Balance preliminar de las economías de América Latina y el Caribe, 2008, 184 p.*
  Preliminary Overview of the Economies of Latin America and the Caribbean, 2008, *184 p.*
- *Estudio económico de América Latina y el Caribe 2007-2008, 152 p.*
  Economic Survey of Latin America and the Caribbean 2007-2008, *146 p.*
- *Panorama de la inserción internacional de América Latina y el Caribe, 2007. Tendencias 2008, 160 p.*
  Latin America and the Caribbean in the World Economy, 2007. 2008 Trends, *148 p.*
- *Panorama social de América Latina, 2007, 294 p.*
  Social Panorama of Latin America, 2007, *290 p.*
- *La inversión extranjera en América Latina y el Caribe, 2007, 228 p.*
  Foreign Investment of Latin America and the Caribbean, 2007, *206 p.*

Libros de la CEPAL

96 *Familias y políticas públicas en América Latina: una historia de desencuentros*, Irma Arriagada (coord.), 2007, 424 p.
95 *Centroamérica y México: políticas de competencia a principios del siglo XXI*, Eugenio Rivera y Claudia Schatan (coords.), 2008, 304 p.
94 *América Latina y el Caribe: La propiedad intelectual después de los tratados de libre comercio*, Álvaro Díaz, 2008, 248 p.
93 *Tributación en América Latina. En busca de una nueva agenda de reformas*, Oscar Cetrángolo y Juan Carlos Gómez-Sabaini (comps.), 2007, 166 p.
92 *Fernando Fajnzylber. Una visión renovadora del desarrollo en América Latina*, Miguel Torres Olivos (comp.), 2006, 422 p.
91 *Cooperación financiera regional*, José Antonio Ocampo (comp.), 2006, 274 p.

90 *Financiamiento para el desarrollo. América Latina desde una perspectiva comparada*, Barbara Stallings con la colaboración de Rogério Studart, 2006, 396 p.

89 *Políticas municipales de microcrédito. Un instrumento para la dinamización de los sistemas productivos locales. Estudios de caso en América Latina*, Paola Foschiatto y Giovanni Stumpo (comps.), 2006, 244 p.

88 *Aglomeraciones en torno a los recursos naturales en América Latina y el Caribe: Políticas de articulación y articulación de políticas*, 2006, 266 p.

87 *Pobreza, desertificación y degradación de los recursos naturales*, César Morales y Soledad Parada (eds.), 2006, 274 p.

86 *Aprender de la experiencia. El capital social en la superación de la pobreza*, Irma Arriagada (ed.), 2005, 250 p.

85 *Política fiscal y medio ambiente. Bases para una agenda común*, Jean Acquatella y Alicia Bárcena (eds.), 2005, 272 p.

84 *Globalización y desarrollo: desafíos de Puerto Rico frente al siglo XXI*, Jorge Mario Martínez, Jorge Máttar y Pedro Rivera (coords.), 2005, 342 p.

83 *El medio ambiente y la maquila en México: un problema ineludible*, Jorge Carrillo y Claudia Schatan (comps.), 2005, 304 p.

82 *Fomentar la coordinación de las políticas económicas en América Latina. El método REDIMA para salir del dilema del prisionero*, Christian Ghymers, 2005, 190 p.

82 **Fostering economic policy coordination in Latin America. The REDIMA approach to escaping the prisoner's dilemma**, Christian Ghymers, 2005, 170 p.

Copublicaciones recientes / *Recent co-publications*

Fortalecer los sistemas de pensiones latinoamericanos. Cuentas individuales por reparto, Robert Holzmann, Edward Palmer y Andras Uthoff (eds.), CEPAL/Mayol, Colombia, 2008.

Competition Policies in Emerging Economies. Lessons and Challenges from Central America and Mexico, Claudia Schatan and Eugenio Rivera Urrutia (eds.), ECLAC/Springer, USA, 2008.

Estratificación y movilidad social en América Latina. Transformaciones estructurales en un cuarto de siglo, Rolando Franco, Arturo León y Raúl Atria (coords.), CEPAL/Lom, Chile, 2007.

Economic growth with equity. Challenges for Latin America, Ricardo Ffrench-Davis and José Luis Machinea (eds.), ECLAC/Palgrave Macmillan, United Kingdom, 2007.

Mujer y empleo. La reforma de la salud y la salud de la reforma en Argentina, María Nieves Rico y Flavia Marco (coords.), CEPAL/Siglo XXI, Argentina, 2006.

El estructuralismo latinoamericano, Octavio Rodríguez, CEPAL/Siglo XXI, México, 2006.

Gobernabilidad corporativa, responsabilidad social y estrategias empresariales en América Latina, Germano M. de Paula, João Carlos Ferraz y Georgina Núñez (comps.), CEPAL/Mayol, Colombia, 2006.

Desempeño económico y política social en América Latina y el Caribe. Los retos de la equidad, el desarrollo y la ciudadanía, Ana Sojo y Andras Uthoff (comps.), CEPAL/Flacso-México/ Fontamara, México, 2006.

Política y políticas públicas en los procesos de reforma de América Latina, Rolando Franco y Jorge Lanzaro (coords.), CEPAL/Flacso-México/Miño y Dávila, México, 2006.

Finance for Development. Latin America in Comparative Perspective, Barbara Stallings with Rogério Studart, ECLAC/Brookings Institution Press, USA, 2006.

Los jóvenes y el empleo en América Latina. Desafíos y perspectivas ante el nuevo escenario laboral, Jürgen Weller (ed.), CEPAL/Mayol Ediciones, Colombia, 2006.

Condiciones y políticas de competencia en economías pequeñas de Centroamérica y el Caribe, Claudia Schatan y Marcos Ávalos (coords.), CEPAL/Fondo de Cultura Económica, México, 2006.

Aglomeraciones pesqueras en América Latina. Ventajas asociadas al enfoque de cluster, Massiel Guerra (comp.) CEPAL/Alfaomega, Colombia, 2006.

Reformas para América Latina después del fundamentalismo neoliberal, Ricardo Ffrench-Davis, CEPAL/Siglo XXI, Argentina, 2006.

Seeking growth under financial volatility, Ricardo Ffrench-Davis (ed.), ECLAC/Palgrave Macmillan, United Kingdom, 2005.

Macroeconomía, comercio y finanzas para reformar las reformas en América Latina, Ricardo Ffrench-Davis (ed.), CEPAL/Mayol Ediciones, Colombia, 2005.

Beyond Reforms. Structural Dynamics and Macroeconomic Theory. José Antonio Ocampo (ed.), ECLAC/Inter-American Development Bank/The World Bank/Stanford University Press, USA, 2003.

Más allá de las reformas. Dinámica estructural y vulnerabilidad macroeconómica, José Antonio Ocampo (ed.), CEPAL/Alfaomega, Colombia, 2005.

Gestión social. Cómo lograr eficiencia e impacto en las políticas sociales, Ernesto Cohen y Rolando Franco, CEPAL/Siglo XXI, México, 2005.

Crecimiento esquivo y volatilidad financiera, Ricardo Ffrench-Davis (ed.), Mayol Ediciones, Colombia, 2005.

Pequeñas y medianas empresas y eficiencia colectiva. Estudios de caso en América Latina, Marco Dini y Giovanni Stumpo (coords.), CEPAL/Siglo XXI, México, 2005.

Coediciones recientes / *Recent co-editions*

Espacio iberoamericanos: la economía del conocimiento, CEPAL/SEGIB, Chile, 2008.

Hacia la revisión de los paradigmas del desarrollo en América Latina, Oscar Altimir, Enrique V. Iglesias, José Luis Machinea (eds.), CEPAL/SEGIB, Chile, 2008.

Por uma revisão dos paradigmas do desenvolvimento na América Latina, Oscar Altimir, Enrique V. Iglesias, José Luis Machinea (eds.), CEPAL/SEGIB, Chile, 2008.

Hacia un nuevo pacto social. Políticas económicas para un desarrollo integral en América Latina, José Luis Machinea y Narcís Serra (eds.)
   CEPAL/CIDOB, España, 2008.
Espacios iberoamericanos: comercio e inversión, CEPAL/SEGIB, Chile, 2007.
Espaços Ibero-Americanos: comércio e investimento, CEPAL/SEGIB, Chile, 2007.
Visiones del desarrollo en América Latina, José Luis Machinea y Narcís Serra (eds.), CEPAL/CIDOB, España, 2007.
Cohesión social: inclusión y sentido de pertenencia en América Latina y el Caribe, CEPAL/SEGIB, Chile, 2007.
Social Cohesion. Inclusion and a sense of belonging in Latin America and the Caribbean, ECLAC/SEGIB, Chile, 2007.
Espacios Iberoamericanos, CEPAL/SEGIB, Chile, 2006.
Espaços Ibero-Americanos, CEPAL/SEGIB, Chile, 2006.

Cuadernos de la CEPAL

92 *Estadísticas para la equidad de género: magnitudes y tendencias en América Latina,* Vivian Milosavljevic, 2007, 186 pp.
91 *Elementos conceptuales para la prevención y reducción de daños originados por amenazas naturales,* Eduardo Chaparro y Matías Renard (eds.), 2005, 144 p.
90 *Los sistemas de pensiones en América Latina: un análisis de género,* Flavia Marco (coord.), 2004, 270 p.
89 *Energía y desarrollo sustentable en América Latina y el Caribe. Guía para la formulación de políticas energéticas,* 2003, 240 p.
88 *La ciudad inclusiva,* Marcello Balbo, Ricardo Jordán y Daniela Simioni (comps.), CEPAL/Cooperazione Italiana, 2003, 322 p.

Cuadernos estadísticos de la CEPAL

35 *Resultados del Programa de Comparación Internacional para América del Sur. Solo disponible en CD,* 2007.
34 *Indicadores económicos del turismo. Solo disponible en CD,* 2006.
33 *América Latina y el Caribe. Balanza de pagos 1980-2005. Solo disponible en CD,* 2006.
32 *América Latina y el Caribe. Series regionales y oficiales de cuentas nacionales, 1950-2002. Solo disponible en CD,* 2005.
31 *Comercio exterior. Exportaciones e importaciones según destino y origen por principales zonas económicas. 1980, 1985, 1990, 1995-2002. Solo disponible en CD,* 2005.
30 *Clasificaciones estadísticas internacionales incorporadas en el banco de datos del comercio exterior de América Latina y el Caribe de la CEPAL,* 2004, 308 p.

Observatorio demográfico *ex Boletín demográfico* / *Demographic Observatory* formerly *Demographic Bulletin* (bilingüe/*bilingual*)

Edición bilingüe (español e inglés) que proporciona información estadística actualizada, referente a estimaciones y proyecciones de población de los países de América Latina y el Caribe. Incluye también indicadores demográficos de interés, tales como tasas de natalidad, mortalidad, esperanza de vida al nacer, distribución de la población, etc.

El Observatorio aparece dos veces al año, en los meses de enero y julio. Suscripción anual: US$ 20.00. Valor por cada ejemplar: US$ 15.00.
Bilingual publication (Spanish and English) proving up-to-date estimates and projections of the populations of the Latin American and Caribbean countries. Also includes various demographic indicators of interest such as fertility and mortality rates, life expectancy, measures of population distribution, etc.
The Observatory appears twice a year in January and July. Annual subscription: US$ 20.00. Per issue: US$ 15.00.

Notas de población

Revista especializada que publica artículos e informes acerca de las investigaciones más recientes sobre la dinámica demográfica en la región, en español, con resúmenes en español e inglés. También incluye información sobre actividades científicas y profesionales en el campo de población.
La revista se publica desde 1973 y aparece dos veces al año, en junio y diciembre.
Suscripción anual: US$ 20.00. Valor por cada ejemplar: US$ 12.00.
Specialized journal which publishes articles and reports on recent studies of demographic dynamics in the region, in Spanish with abstracts in Spanish and English. Also includes information on scientific and professional activities in the field of population.
Published since 1973, the journal appears twice a year in June and December.
Annual subscription: US$ 20.00. Per issue: US$ 12.00.

Series de la CEPAL

Comercio internacional / *Desarrollo productivo* / *Desarrollo territorial* / *Estudios estadísticos y prospectivos* / *Estudios y perspectivas* (Bogotá, Brasilia, Buenos Aires, México, Montevideo) / **Studies and Perspectives** (The Caribbean, Washington) / *Financiamiento del desarrollo* / *Gestión pública* / *Informes y estudios especiales* / *Macroeconomía del desarrollo* / *Manuales* / *Medio ambiente y desarrollo* / *Mujer y desarrollo* / *Población y desarrollo* / *Políticas sociales* / *Recursos naturales e infraestructura* / *Seminarios y conferencias.*
Véase el listado completo en: www.cepal.org/publicaciones / *A complete listing is available at*: www.cepal.org/publicaciones

**Las publicaciones de la Comisión Económica para América Latina y el Caribe (CEPAL) y las del Instituto
Latinoamericano y del Caribe de Planificación Económica y Social (ILPES) se pueden adquirir a los
distribuidores locales o directamente a través de:**

Publicaciones de las Naciones Unidas
2 United Nations Plaza, Room DC2-853
Nueva York, NY, 10017
Estados Unidos
Tel. (1 800)253-9646   Fax (1 212)963-3489
E-mail: publications@un.org

Publicaciones de las Naciones Unidas
Sección de Ventas
Palais des Nations
1211 Ginebra 10
Suiza
Tel. (41 22)917-2613   Fax (41 22)917-0027

Unidad de Distribución
Comisión Económica para América Latina y el Caribe (CEPAL)
Av. Dag Hammarskjöld 3477, Vitacura
7630412 Santiago
Chile
Tel. (56 2)210-2056   Fax (56 2)210-2069
E-mail: publications@cepal.org

*Publications of the Economic Commission for Latin America and the Caribbean (ECLAC) and those of the
Latin American and the Caribbean Institute for Economic and Social Planning (ILPES) can be ordered from
your local distributor or directly through:*

*United Nations Publications
2 United Nations Plaza, Room DC2-853
New York, NY, 10017
USA
Tel. (1 800)253-9646   Fax (1 212)963-3489
E-mail: publications@un.org*

*United Nations Publications
Sales Sections
Palais des Nations
1211 Geneva 10
Switzerland
Tel. (41 22)917-2613   Fax (41 22)917-0027*

*Distribution Unit
Economic Commission for Latin America and the Caribbean (ECLAC)
Av. Dag Hammarskjöld 3477, Vitacura
7630412 Santiago
Chile
Tel. (56 2)210-2056   Fax (56 2)210-2069
E-mail: publications@eclac.org*